To the teachers, teacher assistants, children, and families
who made this book possible

Contents

About the Forms

Purchasers of this book may download, print, and/or photocopy the handouts and forms for educational use. These materials are included with the print book and are also available at **www.brookespublishing.com/kidd/materials** for both print and e-book buyers.

About the Authors

Julie K. Kidd, Ed.D., George Mason University, 4400 University Dr., Fairfax, VA

Julie K. Kidd, Ed.D., is Professor of Education in the College of Education and Human Development at George Mason University. She is currently the Director of the Division of Child, Family, and Community Engagement and is affiliated with the Early Childhood Education Program. Dr. Kidd earned her Ed.D. in Curriculum and Instruction from Virginia Tech. Prior to joining the Mason faculty, she was an elementary teacher and reading specialist. Dr. Kidd's research is focused on developing the cognitive, literacy, and mathematical abilities of children from diverse cultural, linguistic, and socioeconomic backgrounds as well as on the professional development of preservice and inservice teachers. She has served as principal investigator on one federally funded research grant and co-principal investigator on seven federally funded grants. She has numerous publications, including book chapters and journal articles. She served as 2015–2016 President of the Association of Literacy Educators and Researchers.

M. Susan Burns, Ph.D., George Mason University, 4400 University Dr., Fairfax, VA

M. Susan Burns, Ph.D., is Professor Emerita at George Mason University. She currently serves as the Academic Program Coordinator for the Human Development and Family Science program. She is educated in the disciplines of education and psychology and received her Ph.D. from George Peabody College, Vanderbilt University. Her entire career has focused on literacy/cognition and early childhood education (birth through grade 3) of children and families, especially those from culturally diverse backgrounds and low-income backgrounds, and professional development for teachers and others serving these children and families. Her expertise in promoting mental health for young children and their families and the role of play-based education as a foundation for intellectual and literacy development is integrated throughout her professional activities. Major publications include *Preventing Reading Difficulties in Young Children* and *Eager to Learn: Educating Our Preschoolers*, reports of the National Academy of Sciences, and *Knowledge to Support the Teaching of Reading*, report of the National Academy of Education. Dr. Burns' publication listings (more than 75) include books, chapters, and journal articles.

Ilham Nasser, Ph.D., Senior Researcher and Education Specialist, Salam Institute, Washington, DC

Ilham Nasser, Ph.D., is an educator who spent more than 25 years in the research of child development and teacher education in different formal and informal education settings in the United States, Central Africa, and the Middle East. She completed a Ph.D. in Human Development and Child Study at the University of Maryland-College Park and worked for several years as a classroom teacher and a school counselor. In addition, she was a faculty of early childhood education for 12 years at George Mason University. Her research agenda includes studies and publications on the topic of global teachers' professional development and, more specifically, teacher preparation and professional development in social and political contexts and ways these influence children's outcomes. Recently, she led the modernization of the curriculum for kindergarten in Iraq and the design and development of the first national curriculum for kindergarten in Palestine.

About the Contributors

Leslie La Croix, Ph.D., George Mason University, 4400 University Dr., Fairfax, VA

Leslie La Croix, Ph.D., is Assistant Professor in the Early Childhood Education Program at George Mason University. Prior to joining the faculty, Dr. La Croix was a primary grade teacher with a passion for enhancing young children's literacy development through cross-curricular reading and writing experiences. Dr. La Croix's research explores instructional practices for promoting preservice and inservice teachers' understandings of diverse young learners. She is particularly interested in expanding educators' understandings of assessment practices that enhance learning opportunities for all children.

Leah Schoenberg Muccio, Ph.D.,
University of Hawai'i at Mānoa, 1776 University Ave., Honolulu, HI

Leah Schoenberg Muccio, Ph.D., is Associate Professor of Early Childhood Education at the University of Hawai'i at Mānoa. A former classroom teacher, she teaches early childhood teacher education courses and supervises teacher candidates in the field. Her research focuses on equity pedagogy, early childhood curriculum, and teacher education and professional development. The aim of Dr. Muccio's scholarship is to positively influence the early school experiences of culturally, linguistically, and ability diverse young children, their families, and their teachers.

Sehyun Yun, M.A., George Mason University, 4400 University Dr., Fairfax, VA

Sehyun Yun is a doctoral candidate in the Ph.D. in Education program at George Mason University. Her specialization is Early Childhood Education with a secondary emphasis in Multilingual/Multicultural Education. She earned an M.A. in Teaching English to Speakers of Other Languages from the University at Buffalo and taught English to young children in Korea. Her research interests are focused on the bilingual and biliteracy development of children as well as the professional development of early childhood preservice teachers. Particularly, she is interested in how teacher education programs prepare preservice teachers to assess children from diverse cultural, linguistic, and socioeconomic backgrounds.

Acknowledgments

As with any project of this size and complexity, we could not have completed our work without the support and participation of a variety of people. First and foremost, this book would not have been possible without the Head Start teachers and teacher assistants who participated in the LEARN professional development and provided consent for us to study their growth as intentional teachers and their perceptions of the LEARN professional development model. We also appreciate the Head Start directors and parent advisory boards who provided support and permission for us to work with their educators. In addition, we want to acknowledge all of the children who welcomed us into their classrooms and reminded us of the real reason we chose to pursue this work.

Second, this book would not have been possible without those who contributed to our work throughout the process. We want to acknowledge Catherine Snow and Peg Griffin, who provided expert feedback and advice throughout the project, and Research Associates Deepa Aier, Debra Fulcher, and Robert Stechuk, whose contributions helped us to shape and implement the LEARN professional development. We also appreciate our former doctoral students who contributed to the project in a variety of ways over the years. We give our thanks to Mona Assaf, Trina Campbell, Sarah Daily, Leslie La Croix, Arlene Mascarenhas, T. Kevin McGowan, Leah Muccio, Raymond Shorter, and Stacia Stribling. In addition, we would like to acknowledge the support and guidance of our Program Officers, Laura Hoard and Wendy DeCourcey.

Finally, we want to acknowledge the support of John Kidd, Sara Huether, and Mohammed Abunimer. Their belief in us and our work helped us to persevere through the challenges and enjoy the successes of the project. We would also like to acknowledge our children, Christopher Kidd, Nina Huether-Burns, Ella Huether-Burns, Ayman Abunimer, and Luma Abunimer. They provided insights and inspiration throughout our work.

Introduction

Ten years ago, we sat around Julie's kitchen table with the Head Start University Partnership Teacher Effectiveness Research Call for Proposals in hand and brainstormed a new approach to professional development. We envisioned a dynamic, effective model of professional development that would contribute to Head Start teachers' teaching effectiveness across content areas. At the time, the three of us—Julie, Susan, and Ilham—worked together in an inclusive early childhood education, preservice teacher preparation program that was designed to prepare teachers to work with young children with diverse abilities and their linguistically, culturally, and socioeconomically diverse families. We believed that the combination of our work together preparing preservice teachers, our separate experiences working with practicing teachers, and our knowledge of the literature provided us with the insights needed to develop a professional development model designed to sustain teachers' effective pedagogy. Our goal was to develop a model that increased teachers' and assistant teachers' effectiveness and enhanced children's learning outcomes.

Drawing upon Susan's work on *The Knowledge to Support the Teaching of Reading: Preparing Teachers for a Changing World* (Snow, Griffin, & Burns, 2015), we adopted a framework for our professional development model titled LEARN. Snow et al. (2015) described the four steps in the process: *learning* (L) new information, *enacting* (E) the information learned, *assessing* (A) the effectiveness of the enactment, and *reflecting* (R) on what was effective and what could be changed to increase the effectiveness of the enactment. Based on our experiences and additional review of the literature, we added *networking* (N) with mentors and peers to this process. This process of learning, enacting, assessing, reflecting, and networking became the LEARN framework that is the foundation of our LEARN professional development model (discussed later in this chapter). In this book, the LEARN model will focus on developing early educators' intentional teaching strategies. It is important to note that the LEARN framework can also be used for literacy, mathematics, or any other academic, pedagogical, or developmental content area in which teachers need professional development.

We started with the notion of intentional teaching as an approach to enhance and adjust instruction to provide quality educational experiences for young children (Burns, Kidd, Nasser, Aier, & Stechuk, 2012; Copple & Bredekamp, 2009). We recognized that intentional early educators adapt their teaching to meet the prior knowledge, interests, abilities, and needs of individual children (Burns et al.; Copple & Bredekamp). We also were aware that intentional teaching involves educators intentionally planning and implementing strategies to promote positive learning outcomes (Burns et al.; Epstein, 2007). Yet, as we delved further into the literature, we found few studies that examined and defined intentional teaching. Building on the literature and our own research in Head Start classes, we developed the following definition of intentional teaching:

> Intentional teaching means that teachers provide learning opportunities designed to meet the individual needs, interests, and prior knowledge of all children in their instructional settings. This takes place through reciprocal, codirected conversation between teachers and children in learning centers/small groups. Conversation happens with all children, rather than a selected few, and takes place on a consistent basis (high quantity as well as high quality). Children's ideas are developed, and thinking is demanded using rich curriculum content (e.g., in science, creative arts, and social studies). Planned instructional strategies/activities take place within a positive classroom climate. (Burns et al., 2012, p. 284)

This definition became our foundation for building the professional development model. The model uses the LEARN framework to develop educators' knowledge of intentional teaching and their ability to implement intentional teaching strategies in their classrooms; we called this professional development model LEARN Intentional Teaching, or LEARN IT.

With a framework in place, we knew we also needed to identify effective formats for providing our LEARN IT professional development. Once again, we decided to take a yearlong approach that included LEARN institutes with educators across sites, in-class mentoring that took place one on one with a LEARN mentor, and site-based supportive learning communities facilitated by LEARN mentors (Nasser et al., 2015). We also included an online component that enabled LEARN mentors and educators to communicate and learn from each other between face-to-face interactions (Nasser et al.).

Once our project was funded, we spent the first year developing the content for the LEARN IT professional development program. This involved extensive reviews of the literature; on-site observations to gather baseline data of current teacher practices; gathering information on the interests, strengths, and needs of the teachers and assistant teachers; and developing professional development activities focused on identified intentional teaching strategies. During the second year of the project, we implemented LEARN IT professional development at a Head Start community-based program, housed in elementary schools across a small city in the mid-Atlantic region. We used data collected in this first year of implementation, including feedback from participants, to revise the content and activities. We implemented it again in the third year of the project with teachers and teacher assistants from one public school and two community Head Start programs across a wider geographic region. We used the data collected during the second year of implementation to further revise the LEARN IT professional development model. This book draws upon what we developed and learned as we implemented and studied this model, as well as upon other work in which we have engaged since the conclusion of this project. We found that, overall, the LEARN professional development program led to high teacher satisfaction. The participants valued the support they received from the mentor (Nasser et al., 2015). They appreciated the activities, resources, and involvement provided by the mentor. The model engaged educators, enhancing their teaching and, ultimately, children's learning.

ABOUT THIS BOOK

This book provides a comprehensive professional development model designed to enhance intentional teaching practices. Many professionals can engage with and benefit from the model, including preservice teachers, practicing teachers, and assistant teachers, as well as administrators, coaches, trainers, supervisors, teacher educators, and professional developers. In this book, we use the term *professional development facilitators* or *facilitators* to encompass a range of professionals who play leadership roles in professional development for educators. Such professionals may include administrators, coaches, trainers, supervisors, teacher educators, professional developers, and others. Ultimately, our intent was that the LEARN IT framework could be applied to allow preservice and in-service educators to master intentional teaching, enhancing their effectiveness in the classroom.

Although the initial project focused on Head Start teachers and assistant teachers, all teachers and assistant teachers working with preschool to kindergarten children can participate in LEARN IT professional development. The guidance and examples throughout the book are applicable across this age range, as well as across an array of early childhood settings. Because we included teachers, teacher 2s (a second classroom teacher), assistant teachers, and paraprofessionals in our project, we use the term *educators* throughout the book to include all instructional professionals in the classroom who interact with children to promote positive learning outcomes. When the educators are participating in a professional development activity, we also refer to them as *participants*.

This book provides an in-depth examination of the LEARN IT professional development model as a tool to help educators develop intentional teaching strategies that enhance teaching and learning. Specifically, this book focuses on educators' use of effective instructional strategies that emphasize specific components of intentional teaching (Burns et al., 2012; Nasser, Kidd, Burns, & Campbell, 2015):

1. Learning through play

2. Including each child

3. Culturally responsive practice

4. Assessing diverse young children

5. Linking assessment with curriculum and instruction

HOW THIS BOOK IS ORGANIZED

Chapters 1 through 7 begin with a vignette that illustrates how educators engage in the LEARN IT professional development. Each vignette is designed to introduce the content of the chapter through the experiences of educators and their students. These educators and children appear throughout the chapters to more concretely illustrate key concepts and develop important points. While these vignettes are based on real observations and interactions with educators and children, they were created for illustrative purposes and may combine characteristics and experiences of several educators and students.

Following each vignette is the Foundations section, which presents a review of the literature and content knowledge that educators need to learn in order to develop intentional teaching strategies. This is the *L* or *learn* element in LEARN. Next, each chapter includes a Professional Development Activities section, which provides replicable, facilitated activities to develop educators' intentional teaching practices. These activities present effective ways for educators to master strategies for and practical applications of intentional teaching. In these activities, educators enact, assess, and reflect on specific intentional teaching strategies while networking with their peers. Just as the Foundations section supports the *learn* step, the Activities section supports the *enact, assess, reflect,* and *network* steps. Specifically, educators

Learn new information by linking their background to practical knowledge

Enact intentional teaching through implementation in their classroom

Assess the effectiveness of the intentional teaching strategies enacted

Reflect to make informed and intentional instructional decisions

Network with colleagues and mentors to share ideas for making intentional teaching work in their early childhood education classrooms

We conclude each chapter with a summary of the major content addressed in the chapter and a link to the next chapter.

Notably, the LEARN IT professional development model is flexible; the ideas should be adapted to the contexts and needs of the participants. For example, professional development facilitators and administrators can use the model to implement yearlong professional development for groups of prekindergarten and kindergarten educators. Teacher educators might integrate the information and activities into their existing courses and adapt the activities to fit their needs. Educators themselves can read the chapters and work through the pertinent activities with a small group of their fellow teachers. Furthermore, the activities prescribed can themselves be adapted. For instance, if mentors might be from a different school or district from that of the educators, mentoring sessions might be conducted via video chat. Supportive learning communities may choose to set up an online discussion board to facilitate networking when they are unable to meet in person. Whatever approach is taken, it is important to keep the LEARN framework as a central focus. Educators need opportunities to *learn* new information, *enact* new strategies, *assess* the effectiveness of their enactment of the strategies, *reflect* on next steps, and *network* with mentors and peers. This process is essential to fully integrating new knowledge and skills into practice.

In Chapter 1, we present the LEARN framework as a multifaceted, integrated approach to professional development. We explain what the LEARN IT professional development model is and how it incorporates research findings on professional development. In Chapter 2, we turn our focus to intentional teaching. We define intentional teaching and explain why it is key to effective interactions that promote young children's learning. Our research is presented along with theory and research from the field on intentional teaching. Together, Chapters 1 and 2 introduce intentional teaching and the LEARN professional development model.

Chapters 3 through 7 examine key intentional teaching strategies, as defined in our definition of intentional teaching. Chapter 3 examines how intentional teaching takes place within the context of play and how educators can develop knowledge and strategies that enable them to engage in intentional teaching as children play. Chapter 4 focuses on the topic of including each child and explains that educators must prioritize intentional interactions with each child in their classroom. Chapter 5 presents culturally responsive practice and includes a specific focus on children who are multilingual or dual language learners. Chapter 6 discusses the assessment of diverse young learners. Chapter 7 emphasizes linking assessment with curriculum and instruction. The appendix, entitled Approach and Efficacy of the Study, provides an in-depth discussion of our research that informed the development of the LEARN professional development model.

REFERENCES

Burns, M. S., Kidd, J. K., Nasser, I., Aier, D. J., & Stechuk, R. (2012). An interaction, a conversation, often in the context of play: Constructing intentional teaching in early childhood education. *NHSA Dialog, 15,* 272–285. doi:10.1080/15240754.2012.694496

Copple, C., & Bredekamp, S. (2009). *Developmentally appropriate practice in early childhood programs serving children birth through age 8* (3rd ed.). Washington, DC: National Association for the Education of Young Children.

Nasser, I., Kidd, J. K., Burns, M. S., & Campbell, T. (2015). Head Start classroom teachers' and assistant teachers' perceptions of professional development using a LEARN framework. *Professional Development in Education, 41,* 344–365.

Snow, C., Griffin, P., & Burns, M. S. (2005). *The knowledge to support the teaching of reading: Preparing teachers for a changing world.* San Francisco, CA: John Wiley & Sons.

Understanding LEARN IT

A Multifaceted, Integrated
Approach to Professional Development

With Leslie La Croix

Lillie, a Head Start teacher in a rural area, recently attended a LEARN Intentional Teaching (LEARN IT) professional development institute that was part of a yearlong multifaceted approach to professional development. Through LEARN IT, which is described in more detail in this chapter, early educators *learn* (L) new knowledge about intentional teaching, *enact* (E) or practice intentional teaching strategies, *assess* (A) the effectiveness of the strategies implemented, *reflect* (R) on their practice, and *network* (N) with their peers and mentors to develop and refine their *intentional teaching* (IT) strategies (Nasser, Kidd, Burns, & Campbell, 2015). The LEARN IT professional development program includes institutes guided by professional development facilitators; classroom implementation of new strategies with the support of a mentor; and supportive, on-site learning communities with mentors and other early educators. Intentional teaching, which will be discussed in more depth in Chapter 2, is a teaching framework in which educators provide "learning opportunities" that are "designed to meet the individual needs, interests, and prior knowledge of all children" (Burns, Kidd, Nasser, Aier, & Stechuk, 2012, p. 281). Intentional teaching occurs when educators engage in high-quality, codirected conversations with children that develop children's ideas and require them to think (Burns et al., 2012). LEARN IT prepares teachers to successfully implement intentional teaching practices.

During the recent LEARN IT institute, Lillie learned that one example of an intentional teaching strategy is dialogic reading. *Dialogic reading* is defined as "an interactive shared picture book reading practice designed to enhance young children's language and literacy skills" (What Works Clearinghouse [WWC], 2007, p. 1). Lillie learned that implementing dialogic reading with her 4-year-olds could have positive effects on their oral language development (Lonigan, Anthony, Bloomfield, Dyer, & Samwel, 1999; Wasik & Bond, 2001; WWC, 2009). In the session, she learned ways to encourage children to talk about what is happening in the pictures and in the story as she reads aloud (WWC, 2009). Before leaving the LEARN IT institute, Lillie began to conceptualize opportunities to enact dialogic reading in her classroom. She planned to purposefully engage her students in a picture book by listening actively to her students' responses, asking questions, and providing prompts that elicit more detailed descriptions (Lonigan et al.; WWC, 2009). By engaging children in interactive shared reading experiences, she hoped to expand their expressive and receptive vocabulary (National Literacy Panel, 2008; Zucker, Cabell, Justice, Pentimonti, & Kaderavek, 2013).

A few days after the LEARN IT institute, Lillie sat with Ashley and Tanesha with a copy of *Nana in the City* by Lauren Castillo (2014). Lillie had read the book to a group of children earlier in the day, and she decided to use the book to focus on vocabulary development with Ashley and Tanesha. When they got to the page where the boy and his Nana are entering the subway train, Lillie asked, "What is going on here?" Ashley responded, "There's his Nana." Tanesha went on to talk about the boy and Nana getting on the train with all the other people who also want to ride the subway to get to another part of the city. As they continued to look at the book, Lillie used anecdotal notes to briefly capture the children's responses. She noticed that Ashley's responses to questions about the pictures and story were limited to phrases or short sentences, whereas Tanesha often talked at length when she responded to questions about the pictures and story. Later that day, Lillie reflected on what she noticed as she read to Ashley and Tanesha. She paused to think about how each responded to her prompts. She wondered why Ashley's responses were so short whereas Tanesha's were full of description.

The next morning, Lillie talked with Sheri, who had also attended the LEARN IT institute on dialogic reading. Lillie shared with Sheri what she observed and asked if Sheri had any ideas that would help. Sheri pointed out possible differences in Tanesha's and Ashley's prior knowledge that Lillie might take into account. Sheri reminded Lillie that Tanesha often visits her uncle who lives in the city. Her existing vocabulary from that prior experience might make it easier for her to expand on the pictures and story. Ashley, on the other hand, may not have many opportunities to visit the city and may not possess some of the vocabulary to provide rich descriptions of the pictures and text. She suggested that Lillie ask Ashley more specific questions (e.g., "What are the boy and his Nana going to ride?" and "What are all these people doing?") to encourage Ashley to put words to the objects and actions in the story before asking more open-ended questions like the one asked earlier (Lonigan et al., 1999). Sheri also encouraged Lillie to talk with Janet, her LEARN IT mentor, about coming into her classroom to observe Lillie and provide feedback about her implementation of dialogic reading. She also suggested that Lillie ask Janet to model the strategies or co-teach with her while trying out the strategies. Sheri reminded Lillie that Janet is available to provide implementation and mentoring support to specifically address her concerns and questions. By the end of their conversation, Lillie felt more confident and was ready to give dialogic reading another try.

It was no accident that Lillie struck up a conversation with Sheri while assessing and reflecting on her attempts to enact what she learned about dialogic reading in the LEARN IT institute. This type of collaboration and problem solving among colleagues is an integral part of LEARN IT. Through the program, Lillie learned new information, enacted what she learned, assessed the effectiveness of the instruction, reflected on next steps, and networked with her colleague, and later her mentor, to further develop knowledge and skills. Throughout this book, we share vignettes of early childhood educators engaged in the LEARN IT approach to illustrate how the model can promote educators' knowledge and use of intentional teaching strategies. By sharing their experiences, we demonstrate how early educators engage in meaningful professional development and embrace intentional teaching practices to enhance children's learning.

WHAT TO EXPECT
IN THIS CHAPTER

Like Lillie, many early educators leave professional development sessions ready to try out new ideas or refine existing strategies, but they find it is not always easy to get the results promised by facilitators. Educators may then be tempted to discard the new approach and move on to some other idea or to revert back to what has always been done. Yet, with more time and development, that new strategy could have proved promising. Facilitators and mentors must provide resources to help educators adjust the strategy for their teaching style and pedagogical skill, as well as for their class' interests, past experiences, prior knowledge, strengths, and needs.

This chapter provides an overview of LEARN IT, a professional development model that supports learning, enacting, assessing, and reflecting (Snow, Griffin, & Burns, 2005) while networking with mentors and peers (Nasser et al., 2015). Educators can use and/or adapt information and strategies found in the Foundations section to enhance their own intentional teaching practices. Likewise, professional development facilitators, coaches, teacher educators, administrators, and mentors can use the knowledge from the Foundations section to improve early educators' intentional teaching abilities. They can also implement the Professional Development Activities section that follows to put the foundational knowledge into practice and create a LEARN IT professional development program at their school. This chapter

- Reviews what is known about effective professional development for early educators and draws upon adult learning theories to guide our discussion

- Discusses the importance of engaging educators in a multifaceted, integrated approach to professional development focused on intentional teaching that includes opportunities to apply the LEARN framework through institutes, implementation and mentoring, and supportive learning communities (Nasser et al., 2015)

- Suggests strategies for applying the knowledge on teacher professional development to early educators' own professional growth and development

- Provides guidance on assessing and reflecting on knowledge and strategies enacted in the classroom

- Emphasizes the important role networking plays in effective professional development

- Describes LEARN IT experiences that support early childhood educators' understanding and use of LEARN in their professional growth and development

FOUNDATIONS: EFFECTIVE PROFESSIONAL
DEVELOPMENT FOR EARLY CHILDHOOD EDUCATORS

High-quality early education develops the knowledge and skills that serve as a foundation for enhancing children's later academic and social success. Rich educational opportunities are especially important for classrooms with children living in poverty, children with diverse learning abilities, and children from varied linguistic and cultural backgrounds (Diamond, Justice, Siegler, & Snyder, 2013). A landmark report, *Eager to*

Learn: Educating Our Preschoolers (Bowman, Donovan, & Burns, 2000), presented the culmination of more than 2 years of work by an esteemed panel of social scientists to review and synthesize theory and research. The panel concluded that children who attend well-planned, high-quality programs and are in the care of well-prepared teachers are better prepared to succeed in school than children who do not attend such programs. A more recent report, *Synthesis of IES Research on Early Intervention and Early Childhood Education* (Diamond et al.), supports the assertion that quality instruction and well-prepared teachers are important to student success. In this report, Diamond et al. conclude, "Increasing teachers' use of research-based instructional practices, with fidelity, promotes more effective learning by children enrolled in their classrooms" (p. 32). Diamond et al. also determined that providing quality professional development can enhance classroom instruction. Accordingly, providing early educators with quality professional development positively influences teachers' instructional decisions that, in turn, enhance children's learning.

Because high-quality professional development influences children's learning outcomes, it is important to consider what constitutes effective professional development. Isolated workshops, common in many schools, do not provide the tools for reinforcement and implementation that result in lasting pedagogical changes and, therefore, are not the answer (Diamond et al., 2013; Tooley & Connally, 2016; Zaslow, Tout, Halle, & Starr, 2011; Zaslow, Tout, Halle, Whittaker, & Lavelle, 2010). Instead, researchers highlight the importance of providing coherent, ongoing opportunities for teachers to engage in professional development activities (Bowman et al., 2000; Diamond & Powell, 2011; Tooley & Connally, 2016; Wayne, Yoon, Zhu, Cronen, & Garet, 2008). Converging evidence from research suggests that, at a minimum, early childhood educators need specific content knowledge, pedagogical understanding, and instructional strategies to fully support and enrich children's learning experiences (Snow et al., 2005). Schools should provide multifaceted, integrated professional development "that balances teacher self-direction and input from instructional experts" in order to enhance educators' successful implementation and long-term use of effective instructional strategies (Tooley & Connally, 2016, p. 11).

In their groundbreaking report on how people learn, Bransford, Brown, and Cocking (2000) asserted that learning takes place in learner-centered, knowledge-centered, assessment-centered, and community-centered environments. Learner-centered environments build on teachers' interests and abilities and take into account their varied levels of expertise. These environments focus on developing teachers' research-based content and pedagogical knowledge, and they use assessment-centered practices that provide opportunities to enact new strategies, assess their effectiveness, and receive feedback to guide future enactments. These learning experiences take place within a community-centered environment that provides opportunities to learn with and from peers and expert mentors (Bransford et al.).

Research also suggests that effective professional development is relevant to educators' professional roles and responsibilities (Tooley & Connally, 2016; Wayne et al., 2008) and provides opportunities for learners to actively engage in learning (Darling-Hammond & Bransford, 2005; Donovan, Bransford, & Pellegrino, 1999). Tooley and Connally explain, "Adult learning theory posits that making PD [professional development] content relevant to teachers' daily practice is effective because it helps motivate professional learning" (p. 8). When educators learn information, skills, and strategies that they can apply to their own work with children, they are more likely to retain and implement their new knowledge. As Bransford et al. (2000) pointed out, learners have higher levels of motivation to learn when the usefulness and impact of the information is apparent. Adult learning theory also suggests that learning occurs when learners are actively engaged in their learning (Bransford et al.; Darling-Hammond & Bransford). Therefore, effective professional development takes an interactive approach that includes active engagement with relevant content, enactment of new information and strategies, feedback from more expert mentors and peers, and individual and collaborative problem solving (Nasser et al., 2015; Tooley & Connally).

Adult learning theory also recognizes teachers as lifelong learners whose levels of expertise progress from novice to master teachers. In their study of 263 early childhood educators, Weber-Mayrer, Piasta, and Pelatti (2015) found that participants varied in their qualifications, areas of expertise, and number of years of teaching, and suggested that effective professional development takes into account these differences among participants. Snow et al. (2005) proposed "progressive differentiation" as a framework for teacher development; when there is evidence that a teacher's capacity for a particular skill is ineffective, that capacity should not be superseded. Instead, the capacity should be "analyzed and elaborated," leading to the educator reorganizing his or her "enacted knowledge into reflective knowledge" (Snow et al., p. 6). They explain, "Preservice, apprentice, and novice teachers are most heavily involved in new learning" (Snow et al., p. 6). These preservice and early career teachers initially rely on declarative knowledge, the facts and information that they receive from instruction, as they learn about teaching and learning. Later, they put into practice what they are learning and develop procedural knowledge, the knowledge necessary to perform particular activities. On the other hand, experienced teachers have a wealth of knowledge to build upon and engage in assessment and reflection of their teaching as they develop "expert, adaptive knowledge" (Snow et al., p. 8). This knowledge enables them to identify instructional challenges, obtain evidence-based knowledge, and integrate new and existing knowledge. Master teachers develop "reflective, organized, analyzed knowledge" (Snow et al., p. 9). They use their experiences to analyze and evaluate new knowledge as they reflect on instructional decisions.

Although the development of teachers' knowledge and skills is important in teacher professional development, teachers' beliefs, dispositions, and cultural values play an essential role in their professional growth as well (Aikens, Akers, & Atkins-Burnett, 2016; Avalos, 2011; Kidd, Sánchez, & Thorp, 2008; Sheridan, Edwards, Marvin, & Knoche, 2009; Weber-Mayrer et al., 2015). Weber-Mayrer et al. note that beliefs influence changes in behavior; therefore, they encourage professional development facilitators to "be aware of educators' beliefs, including their feelings of efficacy, openness to change, and approaches and orientations to teaching and learning" (p. 55). Educators who have high levels of self-efficacy and report being open to change tend to be more likely to implement new instructional approaches than those who question their abilities and the value of the professional development content (Weber-Mayrer et al.). Research suggests that when the content of teacher professional development conflicts with their beliefs and values, teachers are less likely to continue to implement instructional strategies beyond the time of the professional development (Sanford DeRousie & Bierman, 2012; Schachter, 2015). Kidd et al. noted the influence of beliefs, dispositions, and cultural values in their work with early childhood education preservice teachers.

They share a story about one preservice teacher that illustrates the conflicts teachers may feel when what they are learning is counter to their upbringing:

> One preservice teacher, in particular, shared the conflict she felt between her own upbringing in a family from Korea and the cultural values of her focus child's White family. She described the mismatch between her upbringing that valued dependence and the focus child's family who valued independence. In her story, she acknowledged the importance of respecting and responding to the family's values and goals, but admitted that it was a challenge to truly understand and act upon those values when working with the family's child. (Kidd et al., 2008, p. 327)

In their study of Head Start teachers, Sanford DeRousie and Bierman (2012) reported similar findings. In interviews, teachers acknowledged that once they were no longer required to implement particular instructional strategies, they did not incorporate strategies that conflicted with their beliefs about how children best learn (Sanford DeRousie & Bierman). Sheridan et al. (2009) asserted that attention must be given to "uncover process variables that promote change in practitioners' knowledge, skills, and dispositions that are indicative of effective practice" (p. 396). They contended that professional development that includes targeted training, individual coaching and consulting, and communities of practice help teachers acquire new knowledge, develop their skills, and implement practices supported by research (Sheridan et al., 2009).

The LEARN Framework

LEARN IT is an approach to developing early educators' intentional teaching practices, taking into account what is known about effective professional development and adult learning theory. Underlying this approach is LEARN (i.e., learn, enact, assess, reflect, network), a framework that is integrated into educators' professional lives (Nasser et al., 2015; Snow et al., 2005). This framework is based on the premise that early educators develop professionally as they 1) learn new knowledge and skills, 2) enact what is learned, 3) assess the effectiveness of the enactment, 4) reflect on next steps and future practices, and 5) network with colleagues and mentors. When this framework is integrated into all aspects of early educators' professional development, it enables early educators to take ownership of their professional growth and use professional development opportunities to target their own individual interests, strengths, and needs. The goal is for educators to develop adaptive, reflective knowledge that enables them to implement intentional teaching strategies in the classroom, beyond their active engagement in professional development activities (Snow et al.). They do this by learning knowledge directly applicable to their teaching, transferring this knowledge into enacted classroom practice, and assessing and reflecting on the outcomes of enacted intentional teaching strategies to make instructional decisions (Snow et al.).

As seen in Figure 1.1, the LEARN framework guides early educators' learning as they participate in the program's three components:

1. *LEARN IT institutes:* Gathering of educators, across sites or across a school, that meets for long blocks of time (e.g., half day or all day) throughout the year to learn specific knowledge and intentional teaching strategies.

2. *Implementation and mentoring:* Guidance, support, and feedback provided by a mentor while educators enact, assess, and reflect on new knowledge and teaching strategies.

3. *Supportive learning communities:* Small groups of educators with common interests who meet formally and informally in person and online to provide support as educators enact, assess, and reflect on new knowledge and teaching strategies.

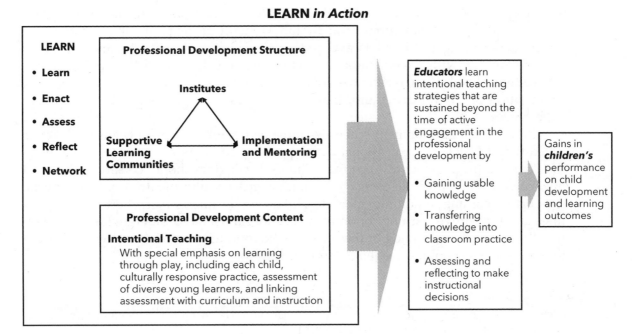

Figure 1.1. LEARN in action.

These opportunities support early educators as they learn with others across schools or sites, within their own classrooms, and with supportive colleagues in their own buildings (Nasser et al., 2015). Specifically, in the LEARN IT professional development, early educators learn and enact knowledge focused on supporting their efforts to embrace intentional teaching practices that promote learning in individual children. Intentional teaching practices, underscored throughout the LEARN IT professional development, include an emphasis on 1) play-based learning opportunities; 2) inclusive and culturally responsive practices; 3) assessment of diverse young learners; and 4) the strategic linking of assessment, curriculum, and instruction (see Figure 1.1). The subsequent section provides advice on getting started on a LEARN IT program focused on developing early educators' intentional teaching strategies. It also describes in more detail each facet of the LEARN framework and the role of institutes, implementation and mentoring, and supportive learning communities in early educators' professional development. Chapters 3 through 7 further discuss the intentional teaching practices noted in Figure 1.1.

Getting Started on LEARN IT

Successful professional development does not just happen; professional developers must plan and prepare for each aspect of the experience. Although this book contains descriptions of experiences that professional development facilitators should implement for each key concept, the specific content, activities, and schedules may need to be adapted to fit participants' interests and needs. Professional development facilitators must consider the strengths, prior experiences, interests, and abilities of the early educators who will participate and the schedules that will best align with their day-to-day routines and academic calendars. To gain an understanding of participants and their contexts, professional development facilitators and mentors should get to know who educators are and what they bring to the professional development, their everyday contexts, and their students. Facilitators can accomplish this by spending time in participants' classrooms and by talking with participants about their prior experiences, pedagogical beliefs and practices, vision, and goals. In this way, they become familiar with the educators and children as well as the school and community settings. In addition, facilitators should also be aware of any new initiatives, such as adoption of a new curriculum, that may influence the professional development experiences.

Professional development schedules must be feasible and practical as well. While scheduling LEARN IT, professional development facilitators can use the questions in the Planning the Logistics text box that follows. Facilitators should consider when and how often to hold institutes, engage in implementation and mentoring, and convene supportive learning community meetings. Likewise, the question of where to hold institutes and supportive learning community meetings must be considered. It is important that the locations and timing of these forums be conducive to adult learners and have the space and technology needed to support learning.

PLANNING THE LOGISTICS

Use the following questions to guide your thinking as you plan for LEARN IT institutes, implementation and mentoring, and supportive learning community meetings.

Institutes

- Is it feasible to hold a 2- or 3-day summer institute at the beginning of the professional development experience? Is there money to bring educators in before their contracts begin? Are there days already in the schedule before the children report to school that can be dedicated to professional development?
- Are there days in the academic calendar that will be conducive to holding full-day or half-day institutes throughout the academic year? Will additional days need to be identified and plans for class coverage be needed?
- How many days will be scheduled for institutes and how often throughout the year will they occur?
- Where will institutes be held and what will be the start and end times? What is a convenient location for all if there is cross-site participation? What location will take participants out of their everyday context and give them an opportunity to engage in learning without interruptions that might occur when their classroom is down the hall or when nonparticipating colleagues are nearby? What start and end times will work with educators' schedules?
- What types of space and technologies are available? Is the space and furniture appropriate for adult learners? Is the space conducive to activities that range from large-group forums to small-group activities? Are needed technologies available or easy to set up?

Implementation and Mentoring

- How often will implementation and mentoring take place? What would be ideal? What is feasible given current resources?
- What time of day will mentors work with educators?
- When and how will debriefing between early educators and mentors take place?

Supportive Learning Community Meetings

- When and how often will supportive learning communities meet? What scheduling opportunities and constraints must be considered? Is there a common time within the day that is available? If meeting after the children leave, what obligations might have an impact on what time the meeting needs to begin or end?
- Where will the meetings be held? Are there spaces available with adult furniture that will be more comfortable for meeting? Is there a space where technology is available or easy to set up?

Facilitators must also carefully consider and identify the content and intentional teaching strategies to address and plan activities that will promote learning. Knowing who the participants are and what they bring to the professional development experience will inform the content and strategies emphasized as well as the types of learning experiences incorporated to promote effective implementation. The space and technologies available may also influence decisions and should be taken into consideration when planning; arrangements for appropriate spaces and technologies should be made in advance. In addition, attention must be given to the structure and organization of the LEARN IT institutes, implementation and mentoring, and supportive learning communities to ensure that each experience includes opportunities to learn, enact, assess, and reflect while networking with mentors and peers. These considerations are apparent in the subsequent discussions and in the Professional Development Activities detailed later in this chapter.

Learn New Knowledge

When early educators participate in LEARN IT, they learn how to implement intentional teaching strategies as well as the theory and research that supports their use (Nasser et al., 2015). Understanding theory and research and how they link to practice allows educators not only to implement strategies in their classroom but also to modify and adapt strategies to support the learning of the diverse children in their classrooms (Allen & Kelly, 2015). This knowledge also gives them the freedom to use their professional judgment as they make decisions about how, if, when, and with whom specific instructional strategies are enacted.

One way to develop early educators' knowledge of intentional teaching strategies and the theories and research that support these practices is to offer institutes like the one Lillie attended on dialogic reading. These institutes take place over the course of the year and provide opportunities for educators to gather within or across sites or schools to strategically acquire new knowledge and skills. The nature of the institutes enables early educators to delve deeply into specific intentional teaching strategies. The purpose is to activate prior knowledge, learn new content, practice specific evidence-based instructional strategies with guidance and feedback, and assess and reflect on what is learned within the context of a network of facilitators and peers (Nasser et al., 2015). An example of a schedule for a day-long professional development institute is shown in the text box that follows, Intentionally Expanding Children's Vocabulary Using Dialogic Reading: November Institute Agenda.

INTENTIONALLY EXPANDING CHILDREN'S VOCABULARY: USING DIALOGIC READING NOVEMBER INSTITUTE AGENDA

9:00 a.m.-3:00 p.m.

Networking

- Light breakfast and networking
- Warm-up activity

Welcome and Announcements

Review of October LEARN IT

- Institute highlights
- Implementation and mentoring successes
- Supportive learning communities' reflections

(continued)

(continued)

Learn About Dialogic Reading

- Dialogic reading as an intentional teaching strategy
- The role dialogic reading plays in expanding children's vocabulary
- Planning for dialogic reading

Dialogic Reading–Guided Practice

- Enact dialogic reading with facilitator-selected book and premade guide
- Assess what worked and identify areas for growth
- Reflect on what will be needed to implement dialogic reading independently
- Network with facilitators and peers to gain the information and feedback needed to implement dialogic reading independently

Lunch

Networking

- After-lunch socializing
- Warm-up activity

Dialogic Reading–Independent Practice

- Prepare materials (i.e., guide, sticky notes) for self-selected book
- Enact dialogic reading with a partner
- Assess what worked and identify areas for growth
- Reflect on what will be needed to implement dialogic reading in your classroom
- Network by sharing copies of completed guides and sticky notes

Dialogic Reading–Classroom Enactment

- Identify an opportunity to enact dialogic reading in your classroom
- Outline what you will need to do to prepare for the classroom enactment
- Anticipate what support might be needed from your LEARN IT mentor during the next implementation and mentoring session

Wrap-Up

Educators construct new knowledge by actively engaging in learning experiences that develop understandings of when and where to use knowledge as well as insights into why this knowledge is important to their work with young children (Allen & Kelly, 2015; Bransford et al., 2000). Knowing the theory and research that supports the use of evidence-based instructional strategies increases the likelihood that educators will transfer what they have learned to their work with children in their classrooms (Bransford et al.). Furthermore, purposeful practice within the context of a network of mentors and peers allows educators to practice implementing intentional teaching strategies as they receive guidance and feedback. These opportunities to practice intentional teaching strategies enable educators to assess and monitor their learning and reflect on how these strategies might work with children in their classroom (Nasser et al., 2015). The goal for each LEARN IT institute is for educators to connect theory, research, and practice to increase the likelihood that they enact these strategies in their own classroom.

When educators have opportunities to build on their prior experiences, strengths, interests, and needs in knowledge-centered environments, learning is enhanced (Bransford et al., 2000). LEARN IT institutes provide an environment that promotes learning using a variety of formats. These formats include readings, presentations, videos, discussions, interactive activities, and hands-on practice, as described in the

Professional Development Activities sections that conclude each chapter. These learning experiences take place with the guidance of more expert facilitators and mentors and in collaboration with colleagues. As educators interact with colleagues and engage in activities that encourage them to learn together and reflect on their understandings and experiences, they gain new insights and knowledge that influence their thinking and enhance their teaching (Bransford et al.; Buchanan, Morgan, Cooney, & Gerharter, 2006). LEARN IT institute activities provide a foundation for learning knowledge and skills that educators can transfer to new situations in their own classrooms.

Enact New Knowledge

LEARN IT experiences provide opportunities to enact new knowledge and skills in the classroom and integrate them into educators' existing knowledge, skills, and instructional routines (Nasser et al., 2015). As noted earlier, Lillie and others who attended the LEARN IT institute on dialogic reading practiced specific intentional teaching strategies with their peers under the guidance of the LEARN IT mentors. This practice enabled them to become more comfortable implementing specific intentional teaching strategies before enacting them in their own classrooms. They were able to assess their enactment of the strategies and reflect on ways to implement them with their own students. Engaging in this process with their peers meant they learned together as they tried out and considered new strategies.

Drawing upon what they learn and practice in the LEARN IT institutes, educators enact their learnings in their classrooms with their own students. As they apply what they learned, the knowledge, strategies, and skills become their own and they are more likely to include them in their instructional repertoire. In addition, educators identify additional knowledge and skills they may need to more effectively enact strategies to support their students' learning. As was the case for Lillie, they may find that knowledge gained during LEARN IT institute experiences may not transfer seamlessly into enacted practice in the classroom context. Recognizing that her enactment of specific intentional teaching strategies did not have the desired outcome for one of her students, Lillie reached out to her colleague, Sheri. Sheri gave her several ideas and also suggested that she enlist the help of her mentor.

Implementation and mentoring take place with LEARN IT mentors who are more experienced educators and have knowledge of how adults learn. LEARN IT mentors provide guidance, modeling, and feedback to less experienced colleagues (National Association for the Education of Young Children [NAEYC], 2011). Their goal is to enhance educators' knowledge and implementation of child-specific instructional strategies (Sheridan et al., 2009). Their work requires sharing knowledge and skills with educators in ways that recognize educators' individual styles and goals (Sheridan et al.) as well as their prior knowledge, interests, strengths, and needs. Implementation and mentoring provide educators with opportunities to enact new knowledge and strategies and examine professional dispositions and attitudes with the support of an experienced mentor.

Research suggests that mentoring provided by experienced educators is an important component of effective professional development (Algozzine et al., 2011; Allen & Kelly, 2015; Neuman & Cunningham, 2009; Neuman & Wright, 2010; Rudd, Lambert, Satterwhite, & Smith, 2009; Varol, Farran, Bilbrey, Vorhaus, & Guess Hofer, 2012). Likewise, studies focused on the professional development of early childhood educators indicate that coaching provided by experienced mentors enhances educators' implementation of classroom instructional strategies (Neuman & Cunningham; Neuman & Wright; Rudd et al.; Varol et al.). For example, Neuman and Cunningham found that early childhood home and center child care providers who participated in coursework, coupled with coaching, implemented new language and literacy instructional strategies more effectively than those who participated in coursework only or than those in the control group who received neither coursework nor coaching. Similarly, Neuman and Wright's study of urban prekindergarten teachers who participated in either coursework or coaching revealed that coaching was more effective than coursework in improving examining classroom structural characteristics as well as the quality of teachers' language and literacy instructional practices.

Similar results were found in studies focused on developing instructional strategies in mathematics. In their study of university child development center teachers, Rudd et al. (2009) concluded that coaching can enhance teachers' implementation of math-mediated language strategies presented during professional development. Likewise, Varol et al. (2012) found that the amount of in-class mentoring positively affected Head Start teachers' mathematics instructional strategies. Based on their review of studies that involved coaching in professional development for early childhood educators, Gupta and Daniels (2012) concluded that coaching that focuses on instruction "shows potential in improving the practices of teachers with varying educational backgrounds" (p. 218).

To increase the likelihood that implementation and mentoring is effective, it is important to consider how LEARN IT mentors are selected for their roles as coaches. Based on a large-scale, national study, Lloyd and Modlin (2012) concluded that selecting highly skilled coaches is key to successful implementation of effective coaching models. They assert that coaches must 1) have experience and expertise in early childhood education and development, 2) possess effective coaching skills, and 3) be knowledgeable about the content of the professional development program (Lloyd & Modlin). Coaches also need to be familiar with principles of adult learning and know how to engage those they mentor in active learning (Artman-Meeker, Fettig, Barton, Penney, & Zeng, 2015; Knoche, Kuhn, & Eum, 2013; Lloyd & Modlin). In addition, effective coaches understand the importance of establishing and maintaining relationships and developing respectful, trusting partnerships with those they mentor (Knoche et al., 2013; Sheridan et al., 2009). This means taking a strength-based approach to their relationship with early educators; mentors should recognize and value the knowledge and skills that early educators possess. Mentors should also help educators navigate difficult situations and make sound decisions when facing challenges (Lloyd & Modlin). They listen actively, provide new perspectives, and share relevant and specific feedback (Knoche et al., 2013).

Professional development facilitators should match mentors with early educators in ways that foster effective mentoring relationships. Building a positive, trusting relationship contributes to the effectiveness of the mentors' coaching activities (Knoche et al., 2013; Sheridan et al., 2009). When mentors and early educators engage in relationships built on mutual respect and interest, they have opportunities to learn from one another. Conversely, Brown, Knoche, Edwards, and Sheridan (2009) found that when relationships between mentors and early educators were not trusting and productive, early educators' participation in the project and their commitment to learning decreased. One way to promote a productive relationship is to ensure that the mentor's expertise aligns with the early educator's goals (Sheridan et al.). For example, one of

Lillie's goals was to enhance the language and literacy development of the children in her classroom. Her mentor, Janet, is highly knowledgeable about strategies that support young children's language and literacy development. This expertise made Janet a good match to help Lillie meet her goals. However, Brown et al.'s findings also suggest that being knowledgeable is not enough. Mentors, like Janet, must also use their understanding of individual early educator's goals, interests, strengths, and needs to promote professional learning. When mentors recognize that early educators bring a wealth of knowledge and experiences to the relationship and provide opportunities for them to express and show what they know, mentors are better able to engage early educators in activities that will foster learning. In addition, early educators benefit from mentors who are willing and able to adapt their approaches to meet the learning preferences of individual educators.

Although research suggests that in-class coaching by an experienced mentor enhances educators' enactment of instructional strategies, few studies focus on what mentors specifically do to enhance early childhood educators' instructional practices (Gupta & Daniels, 2012). However, there are studies suggesting that the guidance and feedback mentors provide on how to implement instructional strategies are important aspects of the mentoring process and are key to promoting successful enactment of new strategies (Algozzine et al., 2011; Buysse, Winton, & Rous, 2009). The focus on developing new strategies is a key point to consider. In a study of early childhood educators, Landry, Anthony, Swank, and Monseque-Bailey (2009) concluded that mentoring was helpful when educators enacted new instructional strategies but not as beneficial when they implemented strategies that were already part of their teaching repertoire. For this reason, mentors must take a collaborative stance and work with educators to decide which strategies they wish to implement and the types of support that will be most beneficial.

Mentoring is an individualized approach to professional development and, as such, can take place in a variety of ways. Typically, there is communication between the mentor and the individual educator prior to the implementation and mentoring session. To begin the sessions, the mentor or professional development facilitator should develop a form that lists strategies taught in the institutes and the types of mentoring support the mentor is offering (see Figure 1.2). Space should be included for the educator to identify the child or children and context in which the focus strategy will be enacted. Mentors should encourage educators to set their own goals for learning (Trivette, Raab, & Dunst, 2012) by asking educators to select the strategy they wish to address during implementation and mentoring. This approach ensures that the mentoring is focused on a strategy that educators are not currently using and that the strategy selected meets the goals of the early educator. Educators will complete this form before each implementation and mentoring session.

To respond to early educators' learning preferences, mentors should ask educators to indicate the type of support they believe would be most beneficial. Such supports include 1) mentor modeling of strategies, 2) mentor and educator co-teaching, 3) mentor observation of and feedback about the educator's implementation of a target strategy, and/or 4) other (See Figure 1.2). Modeling occurs when the mentors enact identified strategies with a child or children in the classroom while the educator observes. Having opportunities to observe experienced mentors helps early educators gain greater understandings about ways to implement specific practices and is an important option for early educators when refining new practices (Nasser et al., 2015; Trivette et al., 2012).

Implementation and Mentoring Form

Educator's name _____   Mentor _____

Site _____   Date _____

Identify the **intentional teaching strategy** you want to **enact**. Select one child to interact with during ☐ center time ☐ small group ☐ individually. Describe the support you would like from your mentor to help you implement the **intentional teaching strategy.**

Intentional teaching strategy of focus:

Culturally Responsive Practice

☐ Choose an area and set it up to reflect children's cultures
☐ Account for child's interest—background and use child's prior knowledge
☐ Inspire child to complete the idea/activity by connecting it to his/her home culture
☐ Provide specific feedback to extend child's play in that area
☐ Question to promote higher-level thinking

Interactional Reading

From *Bringing Words to Life*
☐ Choosing vocabulary words

From Dialogic Reading
☐ Prompt
  ○ Completion prompt
  ○ Recall prompt
  ○ Open-ended prompt
  ○ Wh- question prompt
  ○ Distancing prompt
☐ Evaluate the child's response
☐ Expand the child's response
☐ Repeat—child repeats the expanded response

Expanded Vocabulary

☐ Math vocabulary (5 words)
☐ Science vocabulary (5 words)

Assessment and Instruction

☐ Follow child's interest
☐ Observe and record child learning behaviors
☐ Initiate conversations and write plans with child
☐ Provide meaningful learning opportunities informed by assessment

Extending Play

☐ Redirect play to replace violent play
☐ Plan play
☐ Act out stories
☐ Dramatic use of the constructions child makes

Inclusion

☐ Adapt environment
☐ Adapt routines
☐ Adapt materials and activities
☐ Adapt requirements
☐ Adapt instruction

Continue on back if needed

Focus child

Elaborate on how you will implement the intentional teaching strategy. _____
_____
_____

What type of in-class support do you think will help you?

☐ Modeling while you take notes
☐ Assistance with co-teaching the child
☐ Feedback after observation
☐ Other _____

_____

Use back if needed

Figure 1.2.   Implementation and Mentoring Form.

Educators value these opportunities to observe new strategies being implemented with children in their own classrooms and believe modeling contributes to their effective implementation of identified strategies (Nasser et al.; Trivette et al.). Co-teaching with an experienced mentor can also benefit early educators as they work to enact new strategies. When educators and mentors teach together, educators have an opportunity to observe while at the same time try out aspects of the new strategy. This level of support provides an opportunity for mentors to intentionally scaffold the co-teaching experience and allows mentors to gradually transfer full responsibility for enacting the new strategy to educators. In addition, co-teaching provides an opportunity for mentors to guide educators' reflection on the effectiveness of the new strategy. Likewise, educators gain knowledge and expertise when they invite mentors into their classrooms to strategically observe their enactment of new strategies. This level of support allows early educators to pinpoint instructional areas of concern and seek specific feedback from a mentor who can support their learning and ability to enact new strategies more effectively with their unique student population.

After deciding to contact her LEARN IT mentor, Janet, Lillie looked at the mentoring form and decided she wanted to request implementation and mentoring on dialogic reading. Specifically, she wanted to work on using open-ended prompts. She thought she would benefit from modeling, but also knew she would remember how to enact the strategy better if she tried using open-ended prompts after observing her mentor implement the strategy. As such, she decided she wanted to prepare for a co-teaching session. In this way, she could observe Janet and then try using open-ended prompts with Janet right there to step in if she needed additional support. After deciding she would continue to work with the same students, Ashley and Tanesha, Lillie selected a book and then e-mailed the form to Janet. Janet acknowledged receipt of the form and let her know she would be back in touch to plan.

After locating a copy of the selected book in the school library, Janet e-mailed Lillie to initiate a co-planning session. Lillie e-mailed some details about her students Ashley and Tanesha to help Janet get a sense of the interests and abilities of both children. Janet modeled how to begin planning for the dialogic reading session with a focus on open-ended prompts by sharing plans she developed for the first part of the book based on what was emphasized in the institute session on dialogic reading. She asked Lillie to review the initial plans and send her a time they could videoconference to discuss the initial part of the plan and to continue the planning process. During the videoconference, they revised Janet's initial plans based on Lillie's knowledge of Ashley and Tanesha and then collaboratively finished the plan. Lillie then created sticky notes with open-ended prompts and added them to the appropriate pages in the book.

When Janet arrived in Lillie's classroom, the materials were prepared and organized. Janet took a few minutes to review the materials and observe Ashley and Tanesha. When Lillie was ready, she invited Ashley and Tanesha to a comfortable reading corner and shared with them that Miss Janet was going to join them that day. Janet started the dialogic reading session and modeled using open-ended prompts. Lillie observed Janet and noted Ashley's and Tanesha's responses to the prompts. Once she felt ready, Lillie indicated that she would like a turn reading the book. Lillie read and used the prompts while Janet observed. At one point, Janet rephrased a planned prompt when the girls did not respond as expected. At another point in the book, Janet used an open-ended prompt that was not preplanned but seemed to be one that would enhance the children's interaction with the book. Lillie continued to read and ask open-ended prompts and, like Janet, rephrased some of the planned prompts and created new prompts in response to the children's responses to the story.

Assess and Reflect on the Effectiveness of the Enactment

Debriefing is an essential aspect of each implementation and mentoring session. After modeling, co-teaching, or observing, mentors meet with individual educators and ask them to assess the enactment of the strategy and reflect on what worked well and what could be done differently in future implementations. During the debriefing sessions, mentors provide feedback and encourage educators to consider the additional knowledge and support needed to further refine the implementation of the strategy. Mentors also prompt educators to reflect on how the strategy might need to be adapted or modified when implementing with other children.

For example, after the implementation and mentoring session in the classroom, Janet and Lillie met to discuss their enactment of using open-ended questions when implementing dialogic reading. After a quick review of the knowledge they used when asking open-ended questions during dialogic reading with the children, Janet asked Lillie to talk about what she thought went well. Lillie shared that the planning process was very helpful. She indicated that having possible questions written on sticky notes helped her to stay focused on asking open-ended questions. She stated that having these written questions made her feel more confident and also enabled her to try asking questions that had not been prepared but seemed appropriate in the moment. When Janet asked her to think about what did not go as well, Lillie said that she found rephrasing the questions when the children did not respond a little challenging. She also thought she asked too many questions and it interrupted the flow of the book. After prompting from Janet to reflect on what she needs to continue to enhance her practice, Lillie indicated that she needed more practice on her own with the rephrasing questions, but would benefit from talking with others to get ideas on how they find the right balance of number of questions to ask.

Janet also wanted to encourage Lillie to think about the impact of the lesson on the children. Therefore, she asked Lillie to assess Ashley's responses to the questions. Janet asked Lillie to note whether Ashley's responses to the questions were similar to the previous day's dialogic reading lesson or whether she heard any additional elaborations or use of rich vocabulary that had not been present the last time Lillie read to Ashley. Janet encouraged Lillie to reflect on what she would do similarly and differently with Ashley the next time she engages her in dialogic reading. She also asked her to consider what additional resources she needs to support Ashley's vocabulary development. The LEARN IT Implementation and Mentoring Debriefing Guide (Figure 1.3) contains key questions to guide the debriefing session and can be completed by the educator and mentor as they assess and reflect.

Early educators appreciate the advice or tips mentors share with them as they reflect on their shared experiences enacting new strategies (Nasser et al., 2015; Neuman & Wright, 2010). Likewise, early educators find it helpful when mentors share resources such as books, articles, and web sites with instructional plans and materials. For example, beyond each debriefing session, the early educators in our initial LEARN IT programs also appreciated the resources and materials mentors brought into the classroom to facilitate each mentoring opportunity (Nasser et al.). Similarly, in another mentoring

LEARN IT Implementation and Mentoring Debriefing Guide

Learn

- What new knowledge did you use to enact the strategy?

Enact

- What strategy did you enact?

Assess

- What went well when implementing the strategy?

- What did not go as well when implementing the strategy?

- How did the child or children respond to the implementation of the strategy?

- What did you learn about the child or children when implementing the strategy?

Reflect

- What would you do the same when implementing the strategy again?

- What would you modify or do differently when implementing the strategy again?

- What additional information, support, and/or resources do you need?

Network

- What support would you like from your mentor?

- What interactions with peers would be helpful?

Figure 1.3.   LEARN IT Implementation and Mentoring Debriefing Guide.

Promoting Intentional Teaching: The LEARN Professional Development Model for Early Childhood Educators
by Julie K. Kidd, M. Susan Burns, and Ilham Nasser.

experience, Neuman and Wright reported that early educators valued the materials mentors brought, which included journals and catalogues, to support the educators' implementation of strategies related to enhancing children's literacy and play.

When early childhood educators receive guidance, support, and feedback of the nature described in this section, they are more likely "to be reflective and intentional about their practice" (Algozzine et al., 2011, p. 258). Overall, educators appreciate having the opportunity to select a target strategy and method of support (Nasser et al., 2015). Through relationship-based processes, "mentoring is intended to increase an individual's personal or professional capacity, resulting in greater professional effectiveness" (NAEYC, 2011, p. 11). As early educators enact new knowledge and skills in their classroom, they may assess the effectiveness of the instructional strategies enacted and reflect with other colleagues, in addition to their mentors (Nasser et al.; Snow et al., 2005). With their colleagues, educators assess not only their students' successes and challenges, but also the effectiveness of their implementation of instructional strategies. They reflect on these insights to make informed instructional decisions and to determine the resources they need to more effectively support their students' learning. Lillie engaged in this type of assessment and reflection when she realized the strategies she enacted were not as effective with Ashley as they were with Tanesha. She reached out to her colleague Sheri to help her reflect on the outcome of her attempts to implement dialogic reading. After talking with Sheri, she decided to adjust her instruction with Ashley and contact her mentor for additional support.

Lillie and Sheri are part of the same supportive learning community that meets on site once or twice a month to provide additional opportunities for learning and networking. At these meetings, Lillie, Sheri, and four other educators come together with their mentor to reflect on implementation and mentoring experiences, reinforce information emphasized in the institutes, and learn new information specific to their interests and needs (Nasser et al., 2015). These meetings provide a less formal context for educators to assess and reflect on their efforts, with the guidance of a mentor and within the context of a supportive community. As educators meet within this context and take advantage of ongoing opportunities to share their expertise, experiences, and knowledge, the supportive learning community evolves and provides a valued venue for learning and problem solving (Wenger & Snyder, 2000). In these communities, educators build on their collective knowledge and goals as they pursue matters of importance to themselves (Brouwer, Brekelmans, Nieuwenhuis, & Simons, 2012).

Mentors can play a significant role in facilitating supportive learning communities that are sustainable beyond the more formal professional development opportunities. Mentors should spend time discovering initial interest, conducting a needs assessment, and assessing educators' strengths and goals in order to tailor the community to meet the specific interests and needs of its members. Knowing the prior experiences, interests, strengths, needs, and goals of each individual educator enables mentors to plan content and activities that support individual learning. This prior knowledge provides the foundation for educators to take ownership of their own professional growth and development.

One way to identify educators' strengths, needs, interests, and goals is to give them a self-assessment that lists topics or outcomes relevant to the professional development and encourages them to identify their level of interest and/or need. The self-assessment can include broad topics, as seen in Figure 1.4, but can also include specific outcomes focused on a particular topic.

LEARN Interests/Needs Self-Assessment

Name _____ Date _____

Below are the topics associated with the LEARN professional development. For each, please mark one box indicating your interests/needs in this area.

Topic	I would like professional development in this area.	I know a great deal about this area, but can still learn from professional development.	I do not need professional development in this area right now.	I know this area very well and would like to help deliver professional development in this area.
1. Intentional teaching				
2. Learning through play				
3. Including each child				
4. Culturally responsive practice				
5. Assessment of young children				
6. Linking assessment with curriculum and instruction				

Figure 1.4. LEARN Interests/Needs Self-Assessment.

One focus of the supportive learning communities is to further develop educators' understandings of effective instructional practices and to cultivate the pedagogical skills to successfully enact them in their classrooms. Mentors facilitate educators' growth by reinforcing and building upon knowledge addressed in institutes and linking discussions to the educators' enactment of specific strategies in their classrooms. Expanded knowledge and skills are introduced through readings, videos, and discussions. For example, when Lillie's supportive learning community met after her implementation and mentoring session, Janet started the meeting with a video of an early childhood educator engaged in dialogic reading with a child in his classroom. Janet used this video to encourage members of the community to identify the types of prompts the educator used and to begin a discussion of what members of the community did successfully when using prompts during dialogic reading in their own classrooms. She also asked them to consider what questions they have or what supports they need to further develop their use of prompts. Following the discussion, Janet provided information about evaluating children's responses to prompts, expanding the response, and repeating the expansion. She facilitated an activity that enabled them to practice strategies that promote children's elaborated responses to prompts. These types of activities and the nature of the supportive learning communities promote in-depth consideration of ideas and strategies and provide opportunities to address the goals of individual educators.

Assignments and activities completed by supportive learning community members also provide a vehicle for learning. For example, educators in LEARN IT might conduct an environmental analysis of their classroom, discuss their findings with their peers, and use that analysis and discussion to make changes to the physical environment in their classrooms. Later in the year, individual educators can video record themselves teaching. After viewing the video recordings and reflecting on the effectiveness of their teaching strategies, they can identify a short clip to share with their group members. The discussions of their video clips promote additional reflection and provide individual educators with valuable feedback about their enactment of specific intentional teaching strategies.

By discussing and reflecting with their supportive learning community, educators share their experiences and explore new approaches to implementing and modifying effective intentional teaching strategies (Wenger & Snyder, 2000). As a supportive learning community evolves, educators build a sustainable form of professional development that encourages them to reflect on multiple perspectives, collaborate with peers to problem-solve, and accept and use constructive feedback from others (Nasser et al., 2015). By identifying the prior experiences, interests, strengths, needs, and goals of individual educators and focusing the content and interactions on helping members meet their goals, mentors set in motion a structure that can continue to support educators' professional growth and development beyond formal professional development opportunities.

Network with Colleagues and Mentors

Although networking takes place throughout the LEARN IT institutes, implementation and mentoring, and supportive learning communities, networking also extends beyond these forums. For example, Lillie found that networking with her colleague Sheri helped her to assess and reflect on her enactment of dialogic reading. As in Lillie's conversation with Sheri, networking with colleagues takes place informally across the school day. Educators may network as they wait for buses, prepare for the day, or wrap up after school. Although informal, these networking moments are intentional dialogues informed by a shared professional development experience. Ongoing networking with other educators provides an additional support system that sustains educators outside of more formal opportunities for learning. Educators appreciate the network of support that comes from engaging in professional development with colleagues (Nasser et al., 2015; Shernoff et al., 2011). Although they also appreciate the expertise the mentors share, educators typically find that being able to talk with and rely on those who work with them on a day-to-day basis encourages them to continue to put into practice what they are learning. Through their interactions with colleagues, educators share their triumphs and challenges, seek advice, or brainstorm viable solutions. Their close colleagues know them and their students and understand their instructional context. They help them make sense of what they are learning and how the new knowledge and strategies relate to and work within their own classrooms.

In addition to face-to-face interactions with colleagues, educators may also use technology to engage in networking with mentors and peers. Although some early educators admit that technology-based supports are not as enticing to them, others value online learning experiences and take advantage of online resources (Nasser et al., 2015). Early educators can take advantage of e-mail, texting, interactive documents (e.g., Google Docs), shared folders (e.g., Dropbox), and videoconferencing (e.g., Google Hangouts and Skype) to stay in touch with their mentor and colleagues. Educators can also establish effective networking communities by leveraging platforms such as discussion boards or chat rooms. It is important that educators ensure child/family confidentiality when communicating with mentors and peers, especially in electronic communications.

In addition, some early educators appreciate online components, such as learning modules, that give educators access to learning resources when and where they want and enable them to learn at their own pace (Ayling, Owen, & Flagg, 2012). With the help of mentors and colleagues, educators can build their competence and confidence in using technology to support their professional growth.

The Learn Framework

A primary goal of professional development is for educators to take ownership of their own professional growth. Educators develop a deep understanding of the LEARN framework to embrace learning opportunities, enact what they learn in their classrooms, and assess and reflect on their implementation of new knowledge and strategies with the support of a network of peers and mentors. If educators understand and practice LEARN, they will internalize the framework and be able to apply it in the future to other aspects of their professional growth.

Before beginning the first LEARN IT Professional Development Activity that follows, educators should read the Foundations section that opens this chapter. After participants complete the reading, they engage in facilitated LEARN IT institutes, implementation and mentoring, and supportive learning communities that help them to develop concepts and put strategies into practice. The intent of this book is to provide a professional development model that can be replicated or adapted to build on the individual interests and strengths of early educators and address their specific interests, abilities, and needs.

LEARN IT Institute

As noted, LEARN IT institutes are opportunities for early educators to engage in learning new knowledge and skills. Institutes are designed to encourage participants to learn about and interact with new intentional teaching strategies. They typically take place within a school or across school sites. During the first institute, educators discover the LEARN framework and develop an understanding of the value of the institute, the implementation and mentoring session, and the supportive learning communities. To develop participants' understanding of the LEARN framework, the first institute can be modeled after the sample agenda shown in Figure 1.5. The agenda can be adapted as needed to the unique characteristics of the participants and environment.

Networking is an essential aspect of the LEARN framework, so participants frequently interact with each other throughout the LEARN IT professional development program. To promote networking across sites and teams of early educators, institutes should include informal opportunities, such as breakfast and lunch for participants to get to know each other and build relationships. Educators network in more structured ways through warm-up activities, facilitated group discussions, and varied group composition. Warm-up activities at the beginning of the day and after lunch help to break the ice and build community.

To get started, educators participate in the Circle Warm-Up Activity, described in the Circle Warm-Up Activity text box; this activity develops a positive rapport because educators and facilitators get to know each other personally and professionally. As they interact, participants can discover common connections and interesting information about others that can help them to start up conversations and develop relationships as they work together at the institutes and in their supportive learning communities.

LEARN IT Day 1 Morning Institute Agenda

9:00 a.m.–12:00 p.m.

Networking

- Light breakfast and networking

- Warm-up activity

Welcome and Announcements

LEARN Framework

- *Learn* new knowledge and strategies.

- *Enact* new knowledge and strategies with children and their families.

- *Assess* the effectiveness of the enactment of the new knowledge and strategies.

- *Reflect* on next steps and future practices.

- *Network* with mentors and colleagues.

LEARN IT Forums

- Institutes

- Implementation and mentoring

- Supportive learning communities

LEARN Tote Bags

- Use LEARN to design a tote bag that shows your understanding of the LEARN framework.

Morning Wrap-Up

- Distribute LEARN IT binders.

- Review professional development structure and processes.

Lunch

Figure 1.5. LEARN IT Day 1 Morning Institute Agenda.

Promoting Intentional Teaching: The LEARN Professional Development Model for Early Childhood Educators
by Julie K. Kidd, M. Susan Burns, and Ilham Nasser.

CIRCLE WARM-UP ACTIVITY

1. Form two circles, one inside circle and one outer circle, of equal numbers of people.
2. Instruct the inside circle to move clockwise and the outside circle to move counterclockwise.
3. Tell participants to stop and face their new partner.
4. Provide a prompt or question for the partners to discuss.
5. Repeat the process and provide a new prompt or question.
6. Use prompts and questions that range in depth and topic to meet your needs.

Some possible questions include the following:

• Where have you traveled?
• When is your ideal time to go on vacation?
• What languages do you speak? What languages do you wish you could speak?
• Who is someone who has had an influence on your life?
• Why do you enjoy teaching?

Early in the professional development program, participants discuss the LEARN framework and explore how the framework will be implemented across LEARN IT institutes, implementation and mentoring, and supportive learning communities. Facilitators can begin by presenting an overview of the LEARN framework and how the implementation of the LEARN IT program will work in practice. In a large-group setting, educators learn each aspect of the framework and provide relevant examples of how LEARN is enacted in institutes, implementation and mentoring, and supportive learning communities. Vignettes such as Lillie's, shared at the beginning of the chapter, illustrate how LEARN is enacted in the workplace and can also be beneficial to educator understanding. Then participants work with a partner to share their understanding or an example of what was discussed.

After this discussion, educators engage in an activity to enact what was learned about the LEARN framework and apply their knowledge of the process. In this activity, participants design a tote bag that reflects their understanding of the LEARN framework. Designing tote bags provides participants with a hands-on way to experience LEARN; educators network with peers to learn how to create designs on canvas bags, enact what they learned by creating their own designs, assess their design, and reflect on what they would do the same or differently if they created another tote bag. In addition, they walk away from this first session with a tote bag for their LEARN IT materials that has a logo or design that will help them to remain focused on the LEARN framework as they move through the program.

Necessary materials for this activity include a canvas tote bag, fabric markers, pencils, papers, and newspaper. To create a tote bag, participants should:

1. Place newspaper under the bag to absorb ink.
2. Draw desired images on the bag with colored fabric markers.
3. Use colored fabric markers to fill in the images.
4. Outline the design with contrasting color or black if desired.

Following those directions, participants enact what they learned as they create their own tote bag designs. Participants work on their own individual tote bags while sharing ideas and materials with others at their tables as they work. When tote bag designs are completed, participants assess and reflect on their designs as they talk with others at their table. The following questions can be used to guide their assessment and reflection:

• What worked well with the design development and implementation?
• What messages did you effectively communicate through your design?

- What would you do differently next time and why?

- How did this activity reinforce your learning about the LEARN framework?

After assessing and reflecting in small groups, the large group should reconvene and share tote bag designs and insights on the LEARN framework that emerged through this process. After the institute, participants can use the tote bags to store and carry their LEARN IT materials. The designs that participants drew will serve as a reminder that they are engaged in professional development that involves learning new knowledge, enacting the knowledge, assessing the application of the knowledge, and reflecting on future steps supported by a network of mentors and colleagues.

Implementation and Mentoring

After participants complete the first LEARN IT institute, facilitators assign participants to mentors. Mentors will provide guidance, feedback, and support as participants enact, assess, and reflect on the knowledge learned thus far. Participants and mentors set up an initial implementation and mentoring session, either in person or via videoconference.

The first implementation and mentoring session is different from the subsequent sessions, which focus on a specific strategy. The purpose of the first implementation and mentoring session is for the mentor to become more familiar with the early educators in the classroom and to come to know the children. Typically, prior to the implementation and mentoring session, educators will complete the mentoring form discussed earlier in the chapter (see Figure 1.2). In the form, participants identify a strategy learned at the institute, note how they are going to implement the strategy, and indicate what type of support they want. When the mentors receive the form, they review the plans and identify additional knowledge that might be needed. For this first implementation and mentoring session, participants instead provide information on themselves and the children in their class. This information might include, for example, the age level, number of children in the class, and children's languages and special needs. It might also include the educator's highest degree, years of experience in education, languages spoken, professional development goals, and insights on how the mentor can best support individual educator's growth. Educators complete Handout 1.1, Tell Me About Yourself and Your Class, and share it with their mentor prior to the implementation and mentoring session.

The mentor uses the information provided to plan for the first implementation and mentoring session and consider what additional information will be helpful to know. For instance, through this process, the mentor Janet discovered that Lillie held a bachelor's degree in early childhood education, had been teaching for 21 years, with most of the years being in Head Start, and spoke English only. Her class of 16 children included six who were dual language learners and two with identified disabilities. Lillie wanted Janet to know that because of her experience, she feels comfortable and competent as a preschool teacher; however, she is open to learning and trying new strategies. Her goal for LEARN IT is to learn how to be more intentional in her teaching. She is interested in learning more about strategies that will support her students' language development.

During the first implementation and mentoring session, mentors observe the early educators and children in the room. They jot down notes that will help them in their future interactions with the educators and children. They also write down questions they have as they observe. In addition, they take note of the intentional teaching strategies the educators already employ. This information gives them a starting point for working with the educators. Typically, during this time, mentors reinforce previous learning and share additional information that might be helpful in guiding the enactment of a new strategy in the classroom. As noted earlier in the chapter, educators ask their mentors to model the strategy, collaborate as a co-teacher in the implementation of the strategy, or observe and provide feedback. They can also indicate if there is another type of support they desire.

Tell Me About Yourself and Your Class

Your name: _____   Highest degree: _____

_____   _____

_____   _____

Number of years in education: _____   If post–high school diploma, major(s): _____

_____   _____

_____   _____

Age/grade level of students: _____   Number of years teaching this level: _____

_____   _____

_____   _____

Number of students in the class: _____   Number of dual or multi-language learners: _____

_____   _____

_____   _____

Languages you speak: _____   Languages your children speak: _____

_____   _____

_____   _____

Number of students identified with special needs: _____

_____

_____

Nature of identified special needs: _____

_____

_____

What do you want me to know about you? _____

_____

_____

What do you want me to know about your students? _____

_____

_____

What goals do you have for the LEARN professional development at this time? _____

_____

_____

How can I best help you reach your goals? _____

_____

_____

Although this first session involves observation, feedback is not provided. Instead, when mentors meet with participants, they use their notes to ask questions, clarify information, and engage participants in conversations that help them get to know the educators and their goals better. Mentors should also explain that in the future, after implementation, they will assess the effectiveness of the enactment of the strategy, reflect on next steps and future practices, and identify ways the supportive learning community can support the educator when trying out new knowledge and strategies.

Supportive Learning Communities

The LEARN framework is developed further through the supportive learning communities at each site. After the implementation and mentoring sessions, educators meet in supportive learning communities, which are groups of six to eight early educators who meet once or twice a month with a LEARN IT mentor or mentors. At each session, educators engage in hands-on experiences and discussions that reinforce LEARN IT experiences. These meetings reinforce and refine previously learned knowledge and introduce new information and strategies. Interactive experiences allow educators to practice strategies with their peers and receive additional guidance and feedback from their peers and mentor. This supportive environment fosters relationships among the participants that encourage efforts to seek information and support from each other outside of the scheduled professional development activities.

In the first supportive learning community session, the group should revisit the LEARN tote bag designs and discuss that LEARN provides the framework for LEARN IT. After a brief review, participants should gather in small groups. Participants use the questions in Handout 1.2, LEARN in Action Discussion Guide, to discuss their understandings of the LEARN framework, what it means to them, and the types of support they believe will support their learning.

After small-group discussion, the larger group should reconvene to discuss the LEARN framework and to reflect on what this framework means to them. Educators discuss and summarize how the LEARN framework unfolds across the institutes, implementation and mentoring, and supportive learning communities. Facilitators can highlight that in the institutes, participants will learn new knowledge through sharing information, readings, videos, discussions, and activities. They will enact strategies with their peers, assess the effectiveness of the strategies practiced, and reflect on next steps as they network with their colleagues. Likewise, facilitators should explain that during the implementation and mentoring, mentors provide individualized learning and support participants' enactment and assessment of identified strategies. Participants should reflect on their next steps and prepare for networking in their supportive learning communities. Finally, the group can explore how their particular supportive learning community serves as a network that will help participants work through the steps of LEARN. Building community among the participants in these site-based groups is especially important to the team's success.

Figure 1.6 is a checklist of this LEARN IT strand that the professional development team can use to assess whether they implemented all aspects of the LEARN framework. While planning and implementing the LEARN IT activity, facilitators use this checklist as a tool to guide the process. Likewise, educators can use the form to track each step of the LEARN IT process. If all aspects of LEARN are utilized across this strand of the professional development, participants will engage in learning knowledge and skills specific to understanding and implementing the LEARN framework. They will have multiple opportunities to enact, assess, and reflect on specific aspects of the LEARN framework within the context of their classroom and a supportive learning community.

LEARN in Action Discussion Guide

Learn new knowledge

- What does it mean to learn new knowledge?

  _____

  _____

- What are ways you learn best?

  _____

  _____

Enact new strategies

- What does it mean to enact new strategies?

  _____

  _____

- What kinds of support might help you to enact new strategies in your classroom?

  _____

  _____

Assess the effectiveness of the enactment of new strategies

- What does it mean to assess the effectiveness of the enactment of new strategies?

  _____

  _____

- What will help you assess the effectiveness of the strategies you enact?

  _____

  _____

- How does assessing your instructional strategies differ from assessing your students?

  _____

  _____

Reflect on next steps and future practice

- What does it mean to reflect on next steps and future practice?

  _____

  _____

- What will help you reflect on next steps and future practice?

  _____

  _____

Network with peers and mentors to enhance teaching

- What does it mean to network with peers and mentors to enhance your teaching?

  _____

  _____

- What will help you network with peers and mentors?

  _____

  _____

Checklist for LEARN Intentional Teaching

	LEARN IT institute	Implementation and mentoring	Supportive learning communities
Learn	❏ Facilitators presented research and best practice related to professional development and adult learning theories while explaining the LEARN framework and the three forums for engaging in LEARN IT institutes, implementation and mentoring, and supportive learning communities.	❏ Mentors helped participants identify initial goals and understand how the LEARN framework will be used to help them meet their goals.	❏ Mentors reviewed information on the LEARN framework.
Enact	❏ Facilitators encouraged participants to use information about the LEARN framework to create tote bag designs for LEARN IT.	❏ Mentors observed participants in their classrooms.	❏ Mentors engaged participants in a discussion of how each aspect of the LEARN framework is enacted.
Assess	❏ Facilitators provided participants with an opportunity to share their tote bags and discuss their understanding of the LEARN framework.	❏ Mentors guided participants to discuss the children in their classroom and their approaches to teaching.	❏ Mentors provided an opportunity for participants to share their understanding of the LEARN framework.
Reflect	❏ Facilitators encouraged participants to consider how the LEARN framework will support their professional goals.	❏ Mentors promoted reflection on participants' goals for LEARN IT.	❏ Mentors encouraged participants to consider what the LEARN framework means to participants' professional growth and how they will use this framework throughout LEARN IT.
Network	❏ Facilitators provided opportunities for participants to meet in large and small groups to learn, discuss, and reflect.	❏ Mentors provided opportunities to network with peers and follow up in supportive learning communities.	❏ Mentors provided opportunities for participants to learn together and encouraged discussion and reflection among participants.

Figure 1.6. Checklist for LEARN Intentional Teaching.

Promoting Intentional Teaching: The LEARN Professional Development Model for Early Childhood Educators
by Julie K. Kidd, M. Susan Burns, and Ilham Nasser.

SUMMARY

As demonstrated by the vignette at the beginning of this chapter, Lillie enacted what she learned about dialogic reading with Ashley and Tanesha. As she did, she observed what the children did well and made note of where their next opportunities for growth might be. However, Lillie not only assessed Ashley's and Tanesha's responses, she also assessed and reflected on her enactment of dialogic reading. Lillie's intentional reflection on her practice allowed her to determine the additional steps she needed to take to better support Ashley's and Tanesha's learning and consider how she could refine her future practice. As she reflected on this teaching event, she reached out to her colleague Sheri. This networking helped Lillie to develop a plan of action that included adjusting her instructional enactments of dialogic reading to account for Ashley's and Tanesha's unique background experiences as well as making a plan to take advantage of implementation and mentoring to further refine her enactment of the new strategy.

When early educators, like Lillie, engage in LEARN IT, they *learn* meaningful and relevant knowledge and skills, have opportunities to *enact* new intentional teaching strategies in their classroom, take time to *assess* and *reflect* on enacted instruction to make informed instructional decisions, and *network* with mentors and peers. This process can be supported when early educators 1) participate in LEARN IT institutes that develop links among theory, research, and practice; 2) take advantage of implementation and mentoring from knowledgeable LEARN IT mentors; and 3) become part of a supportive learning community that promotes learning and networking with mentors and colleagues.

The research reviewed in this chapter suggests that a multifaceted, integrated approach to professional development that provides opportunities to *learn, enact, assess,* and *reflect upon* new knowledge and strategies across time is beneficial (Allen & Kelly, 2015; Diamond et al., 2013; Markussen-Brown et al., 2017; Nasser et al., 2015; Zaslow et al., 2011; Zaslow et al., 2010). Research supporting professional development that is multifaceted and integrated indicates that this approach 1) builds on individual educators' strengths and needs, 2) develops educators' knowledge of specific content, 3) provides opportunities for educators to apply what is learned, 4) offers opportunities for feedback, and 5) takes place in collaboration with others (Diamond et al.; Snow et al., 2005; Zaslow et al., 2010). In addition, a multifaceted approach is more dynamic and provides participants with multiple ways to learn new knowledge and skills and allows for individuals to learn in different ways (Markussen-Brown et al.). The research we reviewed also suggests that preparing educators to engage in assessment focused not only on assessing child outcomes but also on their own knowledge and skills is an important part of monitoring the influence of professional development on their own professional growth (Snow et al.; Zaslow et al., 2010).

Exploring Intentional Teaching

2

Head Start educator Joan is attending the same LEARN IT professional development institute as is Lillie from Chapter 1. However, Joan's prior education and professional development experience are different from those of Lillie. Although she is quite effective as a teacher, Joan has not finished her bachelor's degree and worries that she does not have the proper background to teach her Head Start class of 16 children. Three of her young students have individualized education programs (IEPs). More than half have a home language of Spanish. Joan does not speak Spanish, but she does have an instructional assistant, Hector, who is bilingual. Hector speaks both Spanish and English but does not have a background in education; however, he is a quick learner with a keen interest in the success of all the children in their class. The classroom, overall, has a warm and relatively positive atmosphere, though much time is spent in managing behavior. Children's time is divided between large-group activities and free play at centers. Content in large groups focuses on skills development, counting, and learning alphabet sounds, colors, and shapes. Play centers include puzzles, math manipulatives, blocks, house center, drawing, and art. Ample time is allotted for play time, when children interact with each other. Teachers manage behavior and give permission for children to move from one play center to another.

Joan and Hector worry that intentional teaching is a lofty idea, given that they spend so much of their time managing behavior. They are not sure how to achieve quality teacher–child interactions. Still, they are open and committed to the LEARN IT professional development program and are eager to learn to implement intentional teaching strategies with their students. Joan, Hector, and their mentor, Marie, met and agreed to start with children learning self-regulation through planning play systematically, so that there is a possibility for high-quality conversations with children. The LEARN IT framework, discussed in Chapter 1, is used to learn new classroom strategies, enact new knowledge and skills in the classroom, and make informed decisions about future intentional interactions with children, after assessing the effectiveness of the enactment. Joan and Hector reflect on classroom practices and networking with each other and with colleagues in their school.

WHAT TO EXPECT IN THIS CHAPTER

Joan and Hector exhibit reservations held by many early childhood educators embarking on a new professional development experience. Ever optimistic, educators attend professional seminars and workshops in hopes of enriching their teaching repertoires with new and effective pedagogical practices. However, as discussed in Chapter 1, the transfer of new pedagogical knowledge and skills presented in isolated professional development workshops often goes underrealized as educators try to implement the new strategies within the context of their own classrooms. This chapter

- Provides *knowledge about intentional teaching* as a foundation for the book

- Presents guidance on how to replicate LEARN IT through professional development activities focused on *intentional teaching* through *learning* and *enacting* intentional teaching strategies, *assessing* and *reflecting* on the effectiveness of the strategies, and *networking* with peers across sites and schools and within the educator's own supportive learning communities.

FOUNDATIONS: INTENTIONAL TEACHING IS HIGH-QUALITY TEACHING

Since about 2007, there has been growing interest in intentional teaching. Epstein (2007) identified strategies to promote intentional teaching, including the balance of adult-guided experiences with child-initiated ones; best practices were identified by the National Association for the Education of Young Children (NAEYC; Copple & Bredecamp, 2009). Intentional teaching encapsulates many best practices, such as instructional planning, differentiated instruction, implementing ongoing assessment, and providing a positive learning environment that promotes child initiation (Epstein). Intentionality in teaching in early childhood is proposed as a central practice for improving the quality of instruction for young children in large- or small-group settings. Intentional teaching spans across developmental domains (i.e., cognitive, social-emotional, physical, and oral language and communication) as well as across content-specific learning domains, including mathematics (Jung & Conderman, 2013; Jung & Reifel, 2011), science (Sackes, 2014), and literacy (McIlwain, Burns, & White, 2016a, 2016b). Finally, teaching consistently with intentional teaching has been identified as being directly related to children's learning outcomes (Pianta, Belsky, Vandergrift, Houts, & Morrison, 2008).

What Is Intentional Teaching?

We established the definition of intentional teaching used in LEARN IT through literature reviews and the application of information from literature reviews to observational and reflective study (see Figure 2.1). Specifically, our work on defining intentional teaching was developed via a study of 13 prekindergarten teachers in a community-based Head Start program. The educators were observed during large-group and centers/small-group activities by four early childhood experts. Two studies using qualitative methods are presented. In two of the studies, experts together observed focus teachers with attention to coding all instances of intentional teaching.

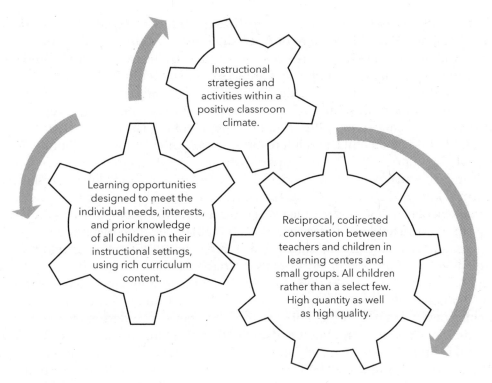

Figure 2.1.   Intentional teaching is high-quality teaching.

They then discussed their observations. Discussions were recorded and analyzed with grounded theory analyses. Features of intentional teaching were specified. Through our findings, we developed our evidence-based definition of intentional teaching, which asserts that intentional teachers do the following (Burns, Kidd, Nasser, Aier, & Stechuk, 2012):

- Design learning opportunities to meet the individual needs, interests, and prior knowledge of all children

- Use ongoing assessment practices to make informed curricular decisions and plan instructional strategies and activities

- Involve children in curricular explorations grounded in rich content (e.g., in science, creative arts, and social studies)

- Engage in high-quality, high-quantity, reciprocal, codirected conversations with each child, rather than a select few, in learning centers, small groups, and individual teaching moments

- Establish a positive classroom climate

Intentional teaching aspects inevitably interact with each other. Although we present each aspect of intentional teaching in isolation in the following subsections to provide a clear understanding of the overall construct, in practice it is necessary to pull all the aspects together. The integrated nature of the intentional teaching aspects will be underscored in the section on Professional Development Activities presented later in this chapter.

Intentional Teachers Design Learning Opportunities to Meet the Individual Needs, Interests, and Prior Knowledge of Each Child. Children's individual needs, interests, and prior knowledge are salient features in research addressing intentional teaching. Intentional teaching requires adapting curriculum and instruction for each individual child (Copple & Bredekamp, 2009). Typically, educators or schools determine how to adapt curriculum and instruction through ongoing, informal classroom assessment of children's multifaceted developmental levels. Yet curriculum must also be tailored based on children's interests and prior knowledge, often family and cultural knowledge (Epstein, 2007). In Chapter 3 on learning through play and in Chapter 5 on cultural diversity, we provide more detail on the roles of children's interests and family/cultural knowledge in intentional teaching. By using children's prior knowledge, intentional teachers tailor children's learning (Bransford, Brown, & Cocking, 2000).

Intentional teachers understand that children have different learning strengths, challenges, and developmental pathways, including variability across developmental areas, which will be addressed in more detail in Chapter 4. For example, Jung and Conderman (2013) document teachers' efforts to help students communicate what they are trying to say in mathematics (see also Jung & Reifel, 2015). Instead of considering an answer from a child incorrect when it did not match the teacher's intended response, teachers help young learners work to rephrase and clarify their thinking. Jeremy, for example, is asked, "What is 2 plus 2?" He quickly blurts out, "5," his favorite number. The teacher, Ms. Tina, then says, "Let's think about this using your counting bears." Jeremy happily takes two blue bears and two green bears and lines them up. Ms. Tina asks, "What is 2 plus 2?" Jeremy counts and says "4." Ms. Tina asks, "How did the bears help you?" Jeremy says, "They showed me the numbers." Ms. Tina says, "Numbers are so interesting and the bears help us see them." Often, educators will use visual representations or manipulatives to help children communicate their ideas more effectively. In this way, teachers are able to fully understand and see the knowledge children possess that would have been unnoticed if only one means of expressing knowledge and understanding, such as verbal response, was allowed. By considering children's thinking, teachers are able to more effectively provide instruction that addresses misconceptions and builds on children's understandings, interests, and prior experiences. In the case of Jeremy, Ms. Tina thought that Jeremy was thinking of numbers as labels rather than an issue of numeracy. She helped him to bring the task back to numeracy and will continue with similar meaning-making, including using tools such as counting bears, to bring these concepts to life.

Another example of intentional teaching that honors individual children occurs when teachers include materials and activities that focus on their students' interests. Teachers make sure that children are learning the curriculum through these interests. In intentional teaching, selection of activities, materials, and multiple aspects of the physical environment must be designed to meet the learning and developmental needs of the individual children in the learning setting. For example, in block area, teachers can incorporate materials related to curriculum content, such as figure or objects related to a new read aloud (Tepylo, Moss, & Stephenson, 2015), while simultaneously incorporating materials that support children's interests and prior knowledge.

Linked to children's interests is their prior knowledge, particularly the prior knowledge based in their cultural, ethnic, and language backgrounds. Culturally responsive practice allows teachers to effectively integrate a child's prior knowledge. Culturally responsive practice, which we review in depth in Chapter 5, is a key element of intentional teaching and is necessary for making informed instructional decisions. To be culturally responsive, teachers utilize, embrace, develop, and foster children's appreciation for and understanding of their cultural, ethnic, and language backgrounds. The awareness gained from learning about and connecting to each child's background is used to form authentic, responsive learning environments and relationships wherein the curriculum is developed through the children's home culture, prior knowledge, and lived experience.

Culturally responsive practices yield positive academic and social outcomes for children with diverse cultural or ethnic backgrounds (Banks et al., 2005). Ladson-Billings (1994), for example, observed increased academic achievement and cultural sensitivity in classrooms where teachers were using culturally responsive practices to teach African American students. Although this practice is critical, educators often hold understandings that are inaccurate or do not recognize the complexity of culturally responsive practice (Sleeter, 2011).

Research studies also document the teaching methods of intentional teachers guiding children's interactions with peers and curriculum in large and small groups, as well as with children in play, which is discussed in more detail in Chapter 3. An example is research by Wright, Diener, and Kemp (2013) that examined storytelling dramas based on Paley's (1991) work. During play centers time, children interact with teachers to write (dictate) a personal story. Teachers record and reread those stories and later, in a larger group setting, those stories are acted out by the students' peers. Children get to see their stories recorded in words, hear the words reread, and then see them acted out by other children in their class. Storytelling dramas clearly provide a curricular space for children to learn many academic skills, such as that words can be written down and reread at a future time. Moreover, content for these stories, being from children's own knowledge base and experience, emphasizes respect for children's individual needs, interests, and prior knowledge.

Intentional Teachers Use Ongoing Assessment Practices to Make Informed Curricular Decisions and Plan Instructional Strategies and Activities. To support early educators' intentional teaching efforts, mentors and professional development facilitators should guide educators to consistently assess and reflect on children's responses to new strategies, in relation to their own enactment of the instructional strategies (Nasser, Kidd, Burns, & Campbell, 2015). This aspect of intentional teaching provides functional support for addressing children's learning needs, as emphasized in the previous section. This research is consistent with authors whose writings in early childhood education also voice the importance of strategically linking curriculum with instruction and assessment. For example, Copple and Bredekamp's (2009) work on developmentally appropriate practice pointed out that intentional teachers use differentiated instruction to teach children. Accordingly, educators identify instructional goals and interact with children based on their determination of each child in relation to the instructional goals. Intentional teachers also use assessment when planning and developing experiences for children who would benefit from specialized instruction, to support continued growth across developmental domains and to ensure children make a successful transition to the next academic level (Pierce & Bruns, 2013). Epstein (2007) emphasized the direct connections among curriculum, instruction, assessment, and individual children; she explains that intentional teachers' interactions with individual children are respectful of their developmental levels and their ways of learning and exploring the world. Accordingly, teachers engage in ongoing assessment of individual children's progress and modify instruction based on their understandings of each child (Epstein).

By making ongoing assessment central to instructional strategies and activities, educators can ascertain that learning opportunities are being provided across curriculum and developmental areas, both on macro and micro levels. Early childhood research reviews, such as *Eager to Learn* (Bowman, Donovan, & Burns, 2000), and application to practice books, such as *Preschool Education in Today's World: Teaching Children With Diverse Backgrounds and Abilities* (Burns, Johnson, & Assaf, 2012), provide resources for this planning. Addressing macro levels of curriculum and developmental areas refers to major areas such as physical activity/gross motor development. Often, educators believe that providing free play provides such opportunities. However, research such as that performed by De Marco, Zeisel, and Odom (2015) indicates that intentional teaching is needed for physical activity to be included in programs for young children. *Micro-level activity* refers to inclusion of materials and questions in activities that promote understanding of particular curriculum content within traditional activities for young children. For example, the *Tools of the Mind* curriculum includes little animals or people within activities, such as sand play, that encourage sociodramatic play during these activities (Bodrova & Leong, 2007). Tepylo et al. (2015) similarly addressed rigorous block play by "selecting materials and choosing prompts to help children develop the structural and representational aspects of their building" (p. 23). Intentional teachers work to consistently monitor the interactions between children's responses to their curricular decisions and seek opportunities to enrich, extend, and monitor their instruction and environment to meet the individual needs of all children. This aspect of intentional teaching is addressed in more detail in Chapters 6 and 7.

Intentional Teachers Involve Children in Curricular Explorations Grounded in Rich Content.   To enhance teachers' efforts to provide intentional teaching for their students, LEARN professional development instructs teachers to engage children in meaningful and rich curricular experiences across all learning environments. This aspect of intentional teaching is closely associated with the preceding discussion of curriculum, instruction, and assessment. Intentional teaching strategies in early childhood education require rich curriculum, are exciting, and have depth and creativity. Espinosa (2010) discussed teachers' intent in terms of curriculum. In her discussion, intentional curriculum means "teachers have explicit instructional goals for children that guide all aspects of their interactions and classroom planning" (Espinosa, 2010, p. 53). She specified that rich content knowledge is essential. Therefore, curriculum must include all areas of learning and development necessary for young learners, such as oral language, early literacy, and early math skills. Likewise, it must include components identified by research as necessary subcomponents, such as alphabet knowledge, phonological awareness, and writing, as well as rapid naming skills for letters, numbers, and objects. Finally, Espinosa emphasized that intentional teachers know and strategically utilize instructional strategies that have shown positive influence on child outcomes, such as dialogic reading and phonological awareness activities.

Another way intentional teachers develop rich curricular experiences for children is by strategically infusing the environment with purposeful materials that extend children's exploration of particular concepts. For instance, rigorous block play may be integrated into rich curriculum and illustrates how educators can promote children's exploration of science and mathematics concepts while simultaneously enhancing children's language and social development (Tepylo et al., 2015). Jung and Conderman (2013) and Jung and Reifel (2015) offered descriptions of rich intentional mathematics teaching that included the strategic incorporation of math manipulatives to extend children's understandings of essential math concepts. Sackes, Trundle, Bell, and O'Connell (2011) echoed the necessity of materials being available for rich curriculum implementations and found a correlation between the availability of science materials and teachers' intentional teaching of science concepts in the early childhood classroom. Sackes (2014) argued that effective science curriculum requires educators to intentionally infuse early childhood classrooms with science materials that encourage children to thoughtfully "make observations, predictions, and answer questions" (p. 180). Examples can be found in "earth and space, life and physical science" in *Eager to Learn* (Bowman et al., 2000, p. 169). Examples can also be found in *Preschool Education in Today's World: Teaching Children with Diverse Backgrounds and Abilities* (Burns et al., 2012).

Finally, rich curriculum is often integrated across learning and developmental areas. When educators use a project approach to learning and instruction (Helm & Katz, 2010; Katz, Chard, & Kogan, 2014) or implement thematic-based curriculums, they exploit the natural links among content areas to help children meaningfully explore concepts from a holistic perspective. Integrated curriculums emphasize a rich theme across developmental and content areas and avoid artificially separating concepts into discrete skills or objectives to be mastered. As a result, this in-depth aspect of intentional teaching encourages children's joy in learning, as expressed through their creation of various forms and products of learning that can also be considered outcomes.

Our research team explored just such experiences when we met with teachers to discuss prekindergarten and kindergarten children's early drawing and writing (Kidd, Burns, La Croix, & Cossa, 2014). The research took place in a number of schools. Remarkable examples of early drawing and writing were produced in an urban-based, public charter school where a majority of children received free and reduced lunch. The educators in this particular school immersed children in a rich science, technology, and mathematics curriculum that provided themes across developmental and content areas. Educators intentionally integrated science into the material-rich writing center and encouraged children to represent knowledge in creative and meaningful ways.

One child created a work sample from Popsicle sticks, yarn, and yellow paper. This work sample emerged from a thematic exploration of habitats and demonstrates the child's understanding of the savannah. The prekindergarten student completed the work during a free-choice center time activity. Obviously, creative arts and literacy are integrated into the developmental and content areas addressed as part of the classroom science curriculum. In a discussion of the child's work, the teacher explained that in class they had been talking about habitats, and one of the habitats they talked about was the savannah. A few days after the class discussion, this little girl went to the art center during free play and created this work sample. The teacher explained that the child expressed that the tall Popsicle sticks were the trees in the savannah, the horizontal Popsicle sticks represented the grasses, the pieces of yellowish paper were lions, the purple yarn depicted elephants. At the bottom of the page, the child also added two drawings that were the watering holes. On the left of the paper, the child wrote that the picture was from herself (she included her first name) and that it was to the teacher (she included "M" for *Mrs.* and the teacher's last initial). The writing sample production is indicative of a rich curriculum and illustrates the wonderful opportunities and encouragement this child had to engage in symbolic expression. The intentional integration of diverse expressive materials, rich and explicit immersion in academic content, and opportunities for self-expression and exploration illustrate the powerful impact that rich curriculums have on encouraging children to joyfully engage in the meaningful creation of expressions of knowledge. As this discussion of rich curriculum reveals, good intentional teaching features all the aspects in day-to-day instruction.

Intentional Teachers Engage in High-Quality, High-Quantity, Reciprocal, Codirected Conversations With Each Child. High-quality and high-quantity reciprocal, codirected conversation between teachers and children is an essential complement to the aspects of intentional teaching highlighted in the previous sections. For example, educators' facilitation of conversation around children's explorations of math manipulatives is needed to ensure children develop essential understandings about mathematic principles. Similarly, the educator's dialogue with the child about her work representing the savannah allowed the child to purposefully use content-specific vocabulary (e.g., watering hole, grasses, elephants) and demonstrate a sophisticated understanding of characteristics of habitats. These are rich conversations. It is essential that the teachers in the LEARN professional development understand that these conversations take place with each child in the class and in all structures of activities, including learning centers, small groups, and individual teaching moments.

The scale developed by Stipek and Byler (2004) is very helpful in this regard and can be directly used as part of the professional development. The scale allows teachers to consider their conversational patterns with children by categorizing teachers' statements as 1) direct, teacher-focused instruction; 2) teacher laissez-faire instruction with little teacher direction; or 3) reciprocal, codirected conversation between teachers and children. Reciprocal, codirected conversation between teachers and children closely matches intentional teaching practices. In these conversations, both teachers and children initiate, direct, listen, and respond. In Table 2.1, excerpts of codirected teaching are presented and contrasted with didactic teaching (Stipek & Byler, 2004). These specific items from the scale clearly illustrate intentional teaching. This description is consistent with Epstein's (2007) concept of how the teacher and children both guide the learning interactions (see also Gronlund & Stewart, 2011, for concrete examples of this in preschool classrooms). Esso, Taylor, Pratt, and Roberts (2012) noted that with kindergarten and first-grade children, even in child-initiated projects, intentional teachers provide specific input relative to their activity that further connects it to the curriculum, ask for detail that encourages higher-level thinking, and help children learn alternatives to processes used.

Intentional Teachers Establish a Positive Classroom Climate. Teachers who are sensitive and who create positive environments in their classroom are more in touch with children's academic needs and their abilities (Bowman et al., 2000; Burns, Johnson et al., 2012; La Paro, Pianta, & Stuhlman, 2004). In current classroom practice, teachers often hear of this aspect of their teaching after using the Classroom Assessment Scoring System (CLASS) to measure a variety of observable aspects of their classroom environment (Pianta, La Paro, & Hamre, 2008). This instrument specifies many of the aspects

Table 2.1. Codirected teaching compared to didactic teaching

Codirected teaching (important aspect of intentional teaching)	Didactic teaching
Lessons are coherent and well connected to children's previous knowledge.	Lessons focus on discrete skills.
	The concept/skill is narrow.
Lessons teach identifiable concepts and are focused on understanding.	Concepts/skills are presented as an isolated set of facts or skills to be learned.
Children are active participants in instructional conversations, with the teacher soliciting children's questions, ideas, solutions, and interpretations.	The teacher focuses on facts and procedural knowledge.
	Assignments are repetitive.
Activities are connected with a substantive, unifying concept.	The teacher controls classroom conversation.

Adapted from Stipek, D., & Byler, P. (2004). The early childhood classroom observation measure. *Early Childhood Research Quarterly, 19,* pp. 386, 387, 394.

of a positive classroom climate, as identified in the research literature. Positive classrooms help students feel safe, respected, supported, and ready to learn. Intentional teachers can foster positive classroom environments by building relationships with and between their students, offering positive physical and verbal communication, and showing respect for everyone in the class. Positive classroom environments are the foundation upon which all other intentional teaching practices rely in order to flourish.

The Professional Development Activities section that follows describes two LEARN IT activities that are essential to use in replicating LEARN IT. Through this LEARN IT institute, implementation and mentoring session, and supportive learning community meeting, educators will develop a deep and actionable understanding of intentional teaching. The first activity is focused directly on intentional teaching strategies and the second on a well-known research-based practice, dialogic reading (Whitehurst, 2008). Collectively, these activities reveal the structure used throughout LEARN IT to enhance early childhood educators' instructional practices. Subsequent chapters emphasize the other intentional teaching practices explored with the educators through the LEARN IT professional development program.

In positive classrooms, educators work to build relationships with their students through respectful, warm physical and verbal communication, including smiling, eye contact, and engaging conversations.

Intentional Teaching Basics

As described in Chapter 1, the initial LEARN IT institute focused on developing and supporting educators' understanding and use of LEARN. This part of LEARN IT focuses on developing educators' basic intentional teaching strategies. Even though this entire book focuses on intentional teaching strategies, educators initially need to learn the basics. This LEARN IT activity delineates the approach that should take place at the start when using this model. Educators will engage in a facilitated institute, implementation and mentoring session, and supportive learning community. The activity that follows can be replicated and adapted, building on the individual interests and strengths of early educators and addressing their specific interests, abilities, and needs.

LEARN IT Institute

This LEARN IT institute explores the essential aspects of intentional teaching. Prior to the institute, educators should read the Foundations section in this chapter, a chapter from Copple and Bredekamp's (2009) *Developmentally Appropriate Practice in Early Childhood Programs Serving Children Birth Through Age 8,* and at least one of the articles presented in the Intentional Teaching Basics Resources text box. These readings enable participants to gain initial understanding of the interconnected aspects of intentional teaching. Throughout the LEARN IT institute, the information in the articles is used to introduce and develop the information presented in the Foundations section on intentional teaching.

INTENTIONAL TEACHING BASICS RESOURCES

Reading:

Copple, C., & Bredekamp, S. (2009). To be an excellent teacher. In C. Copple & S. Bredekamp (Eds.), *Developmentally appropriate practice in early childhood programs serving children birth through age 8* (3rd ed., pp. 33–50). Washington, DC: National Association for the Education of Young Children.

Articles:

Gronlund, G., & Stewart, K. (2011). Intentionality in action: A strategy that benefits preschoolers and teachers, *Young Children, 66*(6), 28–33.

Jung, M., & Conderman, G. (2013). Intentional mathematics teaching in early childhood classrooms. *Childhood Education, 38,* 173–177.

Sackes, M. (2014). How often do early childhood teachers teach science concepts? Determinants of the frequency of science teaching in kindergarten. *European Early Childhood Education Research Journal, 22,* 169–184.

Tepylo, D. H., Moss, J., & Stephenson, C. (2015). A developmental look at a rigorous block play program. *Young Children, 70*(1), 18–25.

Wright, C., Diener, M. L., & Kemp, J. L. (2013). Storytelling dramas as a community building activity in an early childhood classroom. *Early Childhood Education Journal, 41,* 197–210.

After completing the readings to develop their basic understandings of intentional teaching, participants will view, analyze, and critically reflect on video segments that depict intentional teaching. One possible video is NAEYC's *The New Developmentally Appropriate Practice* (2009); however, any video that illustrates aspects of intentional teaching strategies may be utilized. Worthwhile video exemplars emphasize teacher–child learning and development contexts through which participants can examine multiple aspects of intentional teaching.

The videos should include evidence of the following aspects of intentional teaching, as presented in Burns, Kidd et al. (2012) and discussed earlier in this chapter:

- Designing learning opportunities to meet the individual needs, interests, and prior knowledge of all children

- Using ongoing assessment practices to make informed curricular decisions and plan instructional strategies and activities

- Involving children in curricular explorations grounded in rich content (e.g., in science, creative arts, and social studies)

- Engaging in high-quality, high-quantity, reciprocal, codirected conversations with each child rather than a select few in learning centers, small groups, and individual teaching moments

- Establishing a positive classroom climate

To ensure aspects of intentional teaching are clear before watching the video, educators can use Handout 2.1 as a video-viewing and notetaking guide. Before showing the video, facilitators and participants should discuss the aspects of intentional teaching emphasized on the handout. Participants then watch the video and complete the viewing guide on their own before discussing it with the group. This experience of viewing a relevant video and filling out the guide can be repeated as needed to reinforce and develop particular aspects of intentional teaching.

Once participants have completed the handout on their own, they can discuss their handout answers in group of four. Participants should consider the aspects of intentional teaching observed in the video. Facilitators can work with the small groups to clarify aspects of intentional teaching and correct misunderstandings.

After the small-group discussions, participants gather as a whole group to promote further examination of the intentional teaching dialogues that occurred within the small-group contexts. Writing one at a time, participants post the five intentional teaching strategies evident in the video segments on chart paper at the front of the room. The small groups can then share their thoughts and ideas with the larger group of educators. Gathering again as a whole group allows the professional development team to continue to mediate any remaining inaccuracies and ensure all educators have the opportunity to refine their thinking, ask questions, and reflect across all aspects of intentional teaching. During this discussion, participants consider additional intentional teaching strategies that they believe would also be effective within the classroom observed. Participants can also discuss similar experiences in their own classrooms and evaluate these experiences in light of the newly learned intentional teaching practices. Participants share examples of effective intentional teaching within a real context and consider their situation and the aspects of intentional teaching realized.

This activity may be repeated numerous times with different videos until participants identify aspects of intentional teaching strategies accurately on their individual handouts. Alternatively, written case study examples may also be used instead of videos. The goal of either medium is for educators to gain confidence in identifying aspects of intentional teaching and to begin to use their understanding to analyze their own classroom practices.

Video Review for Intentional Teaching Strategies

1. What aspects of a *positive classroom environment* did you observe? _____
_____
_____
_____
_____
_____

2. In observed *conversations between children and teachers in center or small-group activities,* jot down some notes on ones in which the conversations were *reciprocal* with both the child and adult directing the conversation. _____
_____
_____
_____
_____
_____
_____

3. List examples of *rich curriculum content* observed. _____
_____
_____
_____
_____
_____
_____

4. Jot down notes on observations when you notice that the teacher is *gathering information on the learning and development* of the children and using that information to present or change *instruction.* _____
_____
_____
_____
_____
_____

5. Jot down notes on observations in which the teacher addresses students' *individual needs, interests, or prior knowledge.* _____
_____
_____
_____
_____
_____

Implementation and Mentoring

Upon completion of the previously described LEARN IT institute that introduced intentional teaching, educators should identify a situation within their own classrooms that they want to approach with intentional teaching practices in mind. Throughout LEARN IT, participants will use the implementation and mentoring form introduced in Chapter 1 (Figure 1.2), in which they identify a classroom need that they think could be enhanced if intentional teaching practices were applied. Participants should fill out this form, Handout 2.2, before meeting with their mentors.

Once they have completed the form, participants set up time to meet individually with their mentor. As discussed in Chapter 1, in the implementation and mentoring component, mentors provide guidance, support, and feedback as educators enact, assess, and reflect on new knowledge and teaching strategies. Mentors and participants work closely to explore the chosen intentional teaching practice and to identify and implement specific intentional teaching strategies in the classroom.

For example, educators Joan and Hector, the participants mentioned in the opening of this chapter, elected to focus on encouraging a more positive classroom climate and ensuring play centers were based on children's needs, interests, and prior knowledge. Joan and Hector's form is presented in Figure 2.2.

Concerned about the amount of time they spend managing and redirecting behaviors during center time, Joan and Hector elected to focus on two aspects of intentional teaching that they hoped would encourage a more positive classroom climate. Specifically, Joan and Hector wanted to focus on engaging children in high-quality conversations and ensuring play centers are based on children's needs, interests, and prior knowledge. Joan and Hector reasoned that if they created a means to help children plan their play, they could enhance their intentional teaching within the context of their own classroom. Setting up play planning then became a goal for the mentor, Marie, working with Joan and Hector. Marie looked at research and best practices in this area (e.g., Bowman et al., 2000; Burns, Johnson et al., 2012) and discussed with Joan and Hector whether the play-planning procedures designed by High Scope (Hohmann, Weikart, & Epstein, 2008) or *Tools of the Mind* (Bodrova & Leong, 2007) could be adapted for their classroom so that intentional teaching strategies could be consistently used. After these discussions, an adapted version of play planning was developed. Joan, Hector, and Marie each used a copy of the poster they developed to represent classroom learning/play centers (see Figure 2.3). The educators worked with small groups of six children to help them to decide what they wanted to accomplish during play time and think through the center that could be used to reach their goal.

Play centers themselves were developed using intentional teaching principles focused on promoting high-quality reciprocal, codirected conversation between educators and children and rich curriculum contexts (see Chapter 3 for more details). Even though centers were depicted on the planning poster, educators and children focused their planning on what children wanted to accomplish during play and then selected a center in which this could be done. In dialogue with the educators, the children understood that their personal goals could be reached in a number of different centers. For example, if children wanted to play with cars and pretend they were driving to their grandma's home, they could accomplish this goal in several ways: 1) make roads in the block center and drive there using the cars available in the block center, 2) make roads on paper in the art center and use the little cars to drive on them, or 3) pull chairs together in the imaginative play center and pretend they are a car and act out going to grandma's home. Following planning conversations, children

Implementation and Mentoring Form

Educator's name _____ Mentor _____

Site _____ Date _____

Identify the **intentional teaching strategy** you want to **enact**. Select one child to interact with during ☐ center time ☐ small group ☐ individually. Describe the support you would like from your mentor to help you implement the **intentional teaching strategy**.

Intentional teaching strategy of focus:

Culturally Responsive Practice

☐ Choose an area and set it up to reflect children's cultures

☐ Account for child's interest-background and use child's prior knowledge

☐ Inspire child to complete the idea/activity by connecting it to his/her home culture

☐ Provide specific feedback to extend child's play in that area

☐ Question to promote higher-level thinking

Interactional Reading

From *Bringing Words to Life*

☐ Choosing vocabulary words

From Dialogic Reading

☐ Prompt
  o Completion prompt
  o Recall prompt
  o Open-ended prompt
  o Wh- question prompt
  o Distancing prompt

☐ Evaluate the child's response

☐ Expand the child's response

☐ Repeat–child repeats the expanded response

Expanded Vocabulary

☐ Math vocabulary (5 words)

☐ Science vocabulary (5 words)

Assessment and Instruction

☐ Follow child's interest

☐ Observe and record child learning behaviors

☐ Initiate conversations and write plans with child

☐ Provide meaningful learning opportunities informed by assessment

Extending Play

☐ Redirect play to replace violent play

☐ Plan play

☐ Act out stories

☐ Dramatic use of the constructions child makes

Inclusion

☐ Adapt environment

☐ Adapt routines

☐ Adapt materials and activities

☐ Adapt requirements

☐ Adapt instruction

Continue on back if needed

Focus child _____

Elaborate on how you will implement the intentional teaching strategy. _____

_____

_____

What type of in-class support do you think will help you?

☐ Modeling while you take notes

☐ Assistance with co-teaching the child

☐ Feedback after observation

☐ Other _____

Use back if needed

Figure 2.2. Joan and Hector's in-class Implementation and Mentoring Form for intentional teaching strategies.

went to their play centers for a minimum of 40 minutes. Once the children were established in their centers, the educators followed the previously established classroom method for ensuring centers were not overpopulated with children.

A positive classroom climate was maintained as educators encouraged children's social play with peers. The educators' intentional teaching continued as they worked with and observed children in play centers. Children were redirected as needed to meet the play plans they selected before play. Redirection took place through reciprocal, codirected conversations while educators remained mindful of the need to be involved but not interrupt play. Educators also expanded on individual children's development and learning needs as they did ongoing assessments of children. Photos and quick notes were documented on cell phones for later reflection if needed. When play was complete, children and educators again came together in their small groups and reviewed the activities that all children participated in during play. Emphasis was given to whether individual children met their goals.

Joan, Hector, and Marie discussed how this same procedure could be implemented if the educators each took half of the students into their small group. They also put the planning process on the agenda for an upcoming supportive learning community meeting so that they could share their experiences thus far with the new play plan and gain insight from peers who could provide feedback on their efforts and offer examples of similar procedures used in their own classrooms.

Blocks

Science

Pretend play

Puzzles

Math

Art and writing

Books

Figure 2.3. Play planning poster center.

This planning activity is one that mentors should keep in mind when providing support for implementation for the educators in LEARN IT. It relates directly to intentional teaching and, in most classrooms, is an area in need of improvement.

Supportive Learning Communities

Mentors and educators work together in supportive learning communities to refine their understandings surrounding intentional teaching. To get started, participants reconvene in their small groups from the first LEARN IT activity.

In this supportive learning community gathering, educators share their experiences implementing intentional teaching strategies and seek advice on other ways they might enhance their work with young children. Educators also reflect strategically on their efforts to infuse intentional teaching practices; they may choose to bring video clips of themselves teaching, to share with their peers in the supportive learning community. Willing participants record a 10- to 15-minute segment for their supportive learning community to view. Participants video record during centers time, with one educator as the focus. Not all participants are comfortable sharing videos, so we do not recommend making this a required component. With each supportive learning community having between four to eight members, each community should have several videos to examine for aspects of intentional teaching, even if some educators opt out of bringing their own.

Participants use Handout 2.3 to take notes during and immediately after viewing the peer video clips. After they have written down their individual observations, participants work in pairs. One educator should serve as the interviewer and the other as the interviewee. The interviewers ask the interviewees to identify the intentional teaching strategies they see most frequently in the video. The interviewer should record the strategy on a poster or chart

Supportive Learning Community Video Review for Intentional Teaching Strategies

1. What aspects of a *positive classroom environment* did you observe? _____
_____
_____
_____
_____
_____

2. In observed *conversations between children and teachers in center or small-group activities*, jot down some notes on ones in which the conversations were *reciprocal,* with both the child and adult directing the conversation. _____
_____
_____
_____
_____
_____

3. List examples of *rich curriculum content* observed. _____
_____
_____
_____
_____
_____

4. Jot down notes on observations when you notice that the teacher is *gathering information on the learning and development* of the children and using that information to present or change *instruction.* _____
_____
_____
_____
_____

5. Jot down notes on observations in which the teacher addresses students' *individual needs, interests, or prior knowledge.* _____
_____
_____
_____
_____
_____

paper. The pairs then switch roles and the new interviewer prompts the interviewee to identify other intentional teaching strategies observed. Once the teaching strategies have been recorded by each pair, participants post them on a whiteboard or chalkboard for further discussion with the entire supportive learning community.

During the whole-group discussion, mentors should work to underscore aspects of intentional teaching strategies that promoted children's interests, interactions, and individual needs. Moreover, the mentors should use this time to reveal additional strategies for the participants to consider. Participants review their list of teaching strategies and revise, change, or add to the list of intentional teaching strategies, based on the new knowledge learned from the discussion. To wrap up the supportive learning community meeting, the participants read, discuss, and reflect on the intentional teaching strategies listed on each chart paper in a carousel fashion around the room.

To conclude the supportive learning community session, participants view additional videos of their peers and complete the activity directing teachers to consider how intentional teaching would work within their school context. Participants keep their curricular goals and diverse student populations in mind during this process. This networking, which includes collaborative discussions of intentional teaching strategies among teaching teams, increases the frequency of their implementation and helps with sustained focus on aspects of intentional teaching.

Figure 2.4 is a checklist of this LEARN IT strand, presented so that the professional development team can assess whether they implemented all aspects of the intentional teaching strategies module. This checklist serves as a tool to assess fidelity of implementation and guide the process. All aspects of LEARN are utilized across this strand of LEARN IT. Participants engage in learning knowledge and skills specific to intentional teaching strategies. They have multiple opportunities to enact, assess, and reflect on specific intentional teaching strategies. They participate in this learning within the context of a supportive learning community that includes mentors and colleagues interested in intentional teaching.

Checklist for Intentional Teaching Basics

	LEARN IT institute	Implementation and mentoring	Supportive learning communities
Learn	❐ Facilitators presented research and best practice related to intentional teaching strategies.	❐ Mentors taught methods to help children plan so that participants could use intentional teaching strategies in organizing centers time.	❐ Mentors provided supports so that participants could videotape a segment of their teaching to be examined by their supportive learning community.
Enact	❐ Facilitators presented video or case study in which intentional teaching strategies were presented in an early childhood education classroom.	❐ Mentors supported participants as they implemented planning time in the classroom.	❐ Mentors provided an opportunity for participants to view and discuss a video in which intentional teaching strategies were implemented.
Assess	❐ Facilitators scaffolded participants' identification and analysis of intentional teaching strategies and their underlying characteristics.	❐ Mentors and participants assessed whether the implementation of planning time made it possible for them to use more intentional teaching strategies during that time.	❐ Mentors scaffolded participants' identification of intentional teaching strategies that each teacher or instructional assistant used most frequently in his or her classroom video.
Reflect	❐ Facilitators provided opportunities for participants to share understandings about the observed intentional teaching strategies in small groups and with the whole group and to discuss additional intentional teaching strategies they believed would have been effective in the classroom observed.	❐ Mentors and participants determined how planning time can be used every day in class and how to think through use of intentional teaching strategies during planning and centers time.	❐ Mentors supported discussion of participants' more advanced understanding of intentional strategies and considered additional intentional teaching strategies they might also use in their classroom.
Network	❐ Facilitators implemented session in which participants discussed similar instructional contexts in their classrooms and shared instructional teaching strategies that were relevant and materials that were particularly helpful.	❐ Mentors provided the opportunity for participants to share their experiences regarding planning with the community of learners in their school at community meetings and got feedback to help make planning time a sustainable classroom practice.	❐ Mentors presented additional videos of peers to provide feedback and critically addressed the feasibility of using intentional teaching strategies on a regular, sustained basis given their program curriculum and policies.

Figure 2.4. Checklist for Intentional Teaching Basics.

Promoting Intentional Teaching: The LEARN Professional Development Model for Early Childhood Educators
by Julie K. Kidd, M. Susan Burns, and Ilham Nasser.
Copyright © 2019 by Paul H. Brookes Publishing Co., Inc. All rights reserved.

Dialogic Reading: An Example of an Intentional Teaching Practice

In LEARN IT professional development, the use of many research-based strategies helps participants understand that intentional teaching and numerous research-based strategies are complementary practices. In this next activity, one such research-based strategy, dialogic reading (Whitehurst, 2008), is presented as provided within LEARN IT professional development. In this type of reading, the focus is on the dialogue between the book reader and the child being read to. The child participates in the dialogue, as together the educator and child talk about the book and the meaning of the written text. Other complementary research-based strategies are embedded throughout Chapters 3 through 7.

LEARN IT Institute

Before the Dialogic Reading LEARN IT institute, participants should read the articles listed in the Dialogic Reading Resources text box. These articles will allow participants to explore background information and become more familiar with the strategies associated with dialogic reading. Facilitators should also divide participants into three peer-teaching groups and assign each group one article from the text box. During the institute, educators will teach the information from their assigned article to their peers. Before the institute, educators should read their article, contact peers, and begin to formulate a presentation plan. Materials that educators might need for teaching include access to computers and Power-Point; a LEARN IT facilitator who is very familiar with the readings is made available to each team. Participants may also choose to create their own handouts or activities to aid in teaching the article they will present. Participants can also consider integrating Handouts 2.4 and 2.5 into their presentations.

DIALOGIC READING RESOURCES

Group 1

Whitehurst, G. J. (2008). Dialogic reading: An effective way to read to preschoolers. Retrieved from http://www.readingrockets.org/article/400

Group 2

McIlwain, M. J., Burns, M. S., & White, C. S. (2016). The implementation and study of dialogic buddy reading in a Head Start classroom. *Dialog, 18,* 85-90.

We also shared the following article with this group as a support in understanding the chosen article:

McIlwain, M. J., Burns, M. S., & White, C. S. (2016). From research to evidence-based practice: An account of the scientific implementation of dialogic buddy reading. *Dialog, 18,* 47-71.

Group 3

Beck, I. L., McKeown, M. G., & Kucan, L. (2013). *Bringing words to life: Robust vocabulary instruction* (2nd ed.). New York, NY: Guildford Press.

Use excerpts to help teachers learn how to choose vocabulary words to teach based on their students' learning needs.

To begin the institute, the peer-teaching groups should finalize their plan to teach their peers about the content in their reading. Once teaching plans are finalized and materials produced, the peer-teaching groups can begin their prepared presentation of the article.

After presentations are complete, the large group should discuss and examine the basic knowledge presented, as related to dialogic reading. Next, working in small groups, the participants use the information read and discussed to conduct an initial review of a children's book. Specifically, the small groups should use books from the kit *Read Together, Talk*

Dialogic Reading: An Effective Way to Read to Preschoolers

Please read the article on dialogic reading:

Whitehurst, G. J. (2008). Dialogic reading: An effective way to read to preschoolers. Retrieved from http://www.readingrockets.org/article/400

Your goal in this activity is to present the main ideas of Dialogic Reading to your colleagues here today. You have 10 minutes to read this document and put notes on the report chart paper. You will then have 5 minutes to report to the whole group.

You may use the following prompts to help guide your preparation.

1. Why is reading to children important? _____
_____
_____
_____
_____

2. What is the purpose of dialogic reading? _____
_____
_____
_____
_____

3. What is the PEER sequence and how is it used? _____
_____
_____
_____
_____

4. What are the CROWD prompts and how are they used? _____
_____
_____
_____
_____

5. Why is dialogic reading important? _____
_____
_____
_____
_____

Bringing Words to Life

Beck, I. L., McKeown, M. G., & Kucan, L. (2013). *Bringing words to life: Robust vocabulary instruction* (2nd ed.). New York, NY: Guilford Press.

Part 1

Your goal in this activity is to present the main ideas of *Bringing Words to Life* to your colleagues here today. You might want to do some of the activities in this handout and/or on the web page with the others as a part of your report. Read this document and put notes on the chart paper. You will then report to the whole group.

Begin by retrieving the web page *Vocabulary in Practice* at http://www.readingrockets.org/teaching/reading101-course/modules/vocabulary/vocabulary-practice.

On this web page, scroll down and review the information in the following sections:

- *How well do my students need to "know" vocabulary words?*

- *Are there different types of word learning?*

- *Choosing words to teach*

Use this chart from Beck, McKeown, & Kucan (2013, p. 18) to rate your knowledge of the words listed.

Word	Know it well, can explain it, use it	Know something about it, can relate it to a situation	Have seen or heard the word	Do not know the word
tyranny				
surreptitious				
grapnel				
purport				
sensitive				
dubious				

Part 2

Your goal in this activity is to present the main ideas of *Bringing Words to Life* to your colleagues here today. You might want to do some of the activities in this handout with the others as a part of your report. Read this document and put notes on the chart paper. You will then report to the whole group.

Retrieve the web page Choosing Words to Teach at http://www.readingrockets.org/article/choosing-words-teach.

On this web page, scroll down and review the information in the following sections:

- *Identifying Tier Two words in texts*

- *An example for young children*

- *In summary*

(continued)

Using one of the passages on the web page or a book you have with you, list six new words for your class that meet the criteria for identifying Tier Two words.

_____   _____

_____   _____

_____   _____

Use the three points in the *In summary* section to further evaluate whether the words meet the criteria for Tier Two words.

1. How is each word listed generally useful? _____

_____

_____

_____

_____

_____

_____

_____

_____

2. How do the listed words relate to words and ideas familiar to the students? _____

_____

_____

_____

_____

_____

_____

_____

_____

_____

3. What role does each word play in the context of the text? _____

_____

_____

_____

_____

_____

_____

_____

_____

_____

Together (Pearson Early Learning Group, 2005). Based on the dialogic reading research, the kit contains a collection of children's books to guide teachers' facilitation of dialogic reading with young children. Each member of the small group reviews a different children's book and associated materials from *Read Together, Talk Together*. Participants can use Handout 2.6 to guide the review. The handout encourages participants to connect to the peer-taught lessons. Upon the completion of Handout 2.6, individual group members share a bit about their book and a section of their findings on the handout with the other members of their small group.

After everyone has a chance to share within the small groups, the whole group should join together again to capture ideas from across the smaller group discussions. As participants share their ideas with the whole group, facilitators can reframe and clarify any misunderstandings the educators articulate, as they discuss their evaluations of the materials in the kit in relation to the new knowledge gained through the peer-taught lessons. Educators should draw on their expertise from the preassigned article readings to extend the dialogic reading discussion. As peer teachers further share their knowledge of their article, colleagues are more likely to regard them as knowledgeable resources and problem-solving collaborators. This allows the LEARN IT facilitators to play a supporting role in educators' growth.

To support their synthesis of the information, participants complete Handout 2.7, writing a reflection on the appropriateness of dialogic reading for their classroom. After participants record their individual thoughts about dialogic reading in practice, they meet in their supportive learning communities to discuss the benefits of this practice for their school. This final reflective discussion initiates a dialogue the educators will continue in their supportive learning community meetings at their school-based sites.

Supportive Learning Communities

Given the nature of book reading inspired by dialogic readings, educators should meet with their school-based supportive learning communities *before* engaging in the implementation and mentoring session on this topic. To focus the meeting, educators should bring their materials from the LEARN IT institute, including their personal reflections recorded on Handout 2.7, along with a children's book in English. Educators who are fluent in another language and use that language regularly to promote the fluency of young learners in their class can bring a second book in that language as well. Educators should number the pages of their children's book in preparation for the supportive learning community activity that follows.

To begin the meeting, participants review the knowledge gained in the LEARN IT institute and discuss how they believe book reading inspired by dialogic reading would work in their classroom. Then educators complete Handout 2.8, Preparing Books for Dialogic Reading, which is designed to prepare participants for the future reading to their students of a particular book, using the dialogic reading strategies. As they work on the handouts, educators add specific prompts using a book they brought to the supportive learning community. The prompts will be assessed for accuracy throughout the work session. After completing this handout, the educator will have the instructional plan needed to take part in dialogic reading with a child or small group of children. This resource makes them able to participate in a dialogue as together they talk about the book and the meaning of the written text.

An example of a completed dialogic reading form is included below in Figure 2.5. It is based on the book *The Old Man and His Door* (Soto, 1996b). If participants have numerous children with home languages of Spanish in their class, they also use the Spanish version of the book, *El viejo y su puerta* (Soto, 1996a). Participants prepare their form and prompts in

Review of *Read Together, Talk Together*

Pick a book from the kit and the associated Teacher's Notes. Read the book if you are not familiar with it. Read the Teacher's Notes and answer the following questions about the Teacher Notes.

What book and Teacher's Notes are you examining?

_____

Pages 1 and 2: Jot down notes that further clarify about Dialogic Reading from Group 1. _____

_____

_____

_____

_____

_____

_____

_____

_____

_____

Page 3: Give 2 examples from the teacher notes about your chosen book that are consistent with what you learned from the McIlwain et al. articles addressed by Group 2. _____

_____

_____

_____

_____

_____

_____

_____

_____

_____

Page 4: Considering the vocabulary examples presented on page 4 and the Beck et al. material presented by Group 3, do you think the vocabulary provided was the best? What additional vocabulary word would you include based on the Beck information? Why you would include the particular vocabulary word? _____

_____

_____

_____

_____

_____

_____

_____

_____

_____

Dialogic Reading in My Classroom

Please take a few minutes to think through how this activity can be useful in your practice in your particular class-room. Jot down notes. These notes are for your own use and not shared with the LEARN IT facilitators. Consider the following:

1. How does book reading inspired by dialogic reading align with your chosen school curriculum? _____
_____
_____
_____
_____
_____

2. What resources are available in your school for the purchase of necessary books? _____
_____
_____
_____
_____
_____

3. How will book reading inspired by dialogic reading be shared with parents? _____
_____
_____
_____
_____
_____

4. What times of the day afford the opportunity for you to read in this manner with a small group? _____
_____
_____
_____
_____

5. Other notes: _____
_____
_____
_____
_____
_____

Preparing Books for Dialogic Reading

Book Title: _____

Author: _____

Read the book to students at least once so they are familiar with it. Do this in your usual manner, addressing print concepts and giving any needed information regarding meaning. Ask recall questions after finishing the book.

Example Recall Questions

1. _____

2. _____

3. _____

4. _____

Reread the book numerous times. This is where you will use the PEER sequence with the CROWD prompts based on dialogic reading.

Pick up to eight vocabulary words of focus. Remember, they can be part of the story or shown in the picture. They can be objects or actions. Space the words throughout the book. Word choice is based on *Bringing Words to Life: Robust Vocabulary Instruction* (Beck, McKeown, & Kucan, 2013).

1. _____   5. _____

2. _____   6. _____

3. _____   7. _____

4. _____   8. _____

Finally, write out a list of questions for each of the vocabulary words. Use a variety of types of prompts given the CROWD prompts and write the type of prompt. Be sure to include the page number where the vocabulary word appears as well.

Vocabulary word	Question	Prompt	Page number

HANDOUT 2.8.

Preparing Books for Dialogic Reading

Book Title: _The Old Man and His Door_

Author: _Gary Soto_

Read the book to students at least once so they are familiar with it. Do this in your usual manner, addressing print concepts and giving any needed information regarding meaning. Ask recall questions after finishing the book.

Example Recall Questions

1. _What is the title of this book?_

2. _What did the man bring to the barbeque?_

3. _What are some things the door was used for?_

4. _Do you think it was good that the man brought the door?_

Reread the book numerous times. This is where you will use the PEER sequence with the CROWD prompts based on dialogic reading.

Pick up to eight vocabulary words of focus. Remember, they can be part of the story or shown in the picture. They can be objects or actions. Space the words throughout the book. Word choice is based on _Bringing Words to Life: Robust Vocabulary Instruction_ (Beck, McKeown, & Kucan, 2013).

1. _barbeque_	5. _lake_
2. _dizzy_	6. _ramp_
3. _buzzed_	7. _piñata_
4. _balanced_	8. _made a table of the door_

Finally, write out a list of questions for each of the vocabulary words. Use a variety of types of prompts given the CROWD prompts and write the type of prompt. Be sure to include the page number where the vocabulary word appears as well.

Vocabulary word	Question	Prompt	Page number
Barbeque	What is a barbeque?	Wh- prompt	3
Dizzy	The wife was dizzy. What does dizzy mean?	Wh- prompt	7
buzzed	What is happening in this picture? What noise do the bees make?	Open-ended	14–15
balanced	The mom balanced the honey on the door. What does balanced mean?	Wh- prompt	16
lake	The water is called a lake. Have you seen a lake before?	Distancing prompt	20
ramp	Where is the "ramp" in this picture?	Wh- prompt	23
piñata	A piñata hung from the tree. What is a piñata?	Wh- prompt	25
made a table of the door	What is happening in this picture? What does it mean to make "a table of the door"?	Open-ended	28–29

Figure 2.5. An example of a completed dialogic reading supports handout.

Spanish. This can be done for any language spoken by educators and children. For example, when we implemented LEARN IT with Head Start educators, we had a number of children with Arabic as their home language. The Arabic-speaking teachers translated their copies of the books into Arabic and prepared their form and prompts in Arabic for use with their Arabic-speaking children.

After working to create prompts for the books they selected, participants role-play, reading the books to each other in pairs. In each pair, one participant acts as the teacher, the other as the student. During this time, participants and LEARN mentors work together to revise any prompts that are not working as expected during the role play. Collaboratively, the LEARN mentors and participant pairs work to provide feedback to each other on the prompts and readings. Feedback includes ways to make answers more accessible for different children; for example, an educator might have a child act out actions or draw his or her own pictures to represent the new vocabulary word and post it in an appropriate learning center for the child's peers to use.

The experiences during the supportive learning community meeting continue to support educators' considerations of how book reading inspired by dialogic reading could be used in their classroom. To conclude this supportive learning community session, educators reflect on changes in understandings they had, given the experiences they completed with their supportive learning community members, as compared to their reflections they captured after the LEARN IT institute. To further support the collaborative nature of the supportive learning community, educators can share the results of their dialogic reading handouts with their fellow supportive learning community members. Participants end this session poised to begin implementing dialogic reading strategies within their own classrooms.

Implementation and Mentoring

To initiate the implementation and mentoring session for dialogic reading, educators fill out an implementation and mentoring form (Handout 2.2), identifying the intentional teaching strategy they want to enact, and submit it to their mentor. Mentors should then meet with participants to create a plan for implementing dialogic reading in their classroom.

In considering dialogic reading, we return to Lillie, who was highlighted in the vignette that opened Chapter 1. After attending a LEARN IT Institute and supportive learning community meeting, Lillie tested out dialogic reading strategies with two of her students. Lillie also networked with her peers to clarify her practice and followed up on her colleague's suggestion to invite her LEARN IT mentor, Janet, to engage in a co-planning and co-teaching in-class mentoring session. However, she remained concerned that she was not seeing the increase in students' vocabulary that she had anticipated with the incorporation of this intentional teaching strategy. Subsequently, Lillie followed up with Janet to schedule another implementation and mentoring session, aiming to work strategically with her to enhance her incorporation of dialogic reading strategies. In Figure 2.6, we include Lillie's mentoring request form asking to be observed and provided with feedback on her storybook reading. We present this case of Lillie to provide the framework that can be used when providing mentoring in this area.

To begin to address Lillie's concerns, Janet first reviewed the dialogic reading plan Lillie had developed to teach the lesson in light of what she had learned in previous LEARN IT sessions. As it turned out, when Janet reviewed the lesson plan, there were a few enactment problems. First, Lillie's plan revealed that she was electing to embed all of the dialogic reading strategies as a part of her large-group read-aloud time. As they reviewed the

To be completed by early educators

Implementation and Mentoring Form

Educator's name *Lillie*   Mentor *Janet*

Site *Pre-K*   Date

Identify the **intentional teaching strategy** you want to **enact**. Select one child to interact with during ❑ center time ❑ small group ❑ individually. Describe the support you would like from your mentor to help you implement the **intentional teaching strategy**.

Intentional teaching strategy of focus:

Culturally Responsive Practice	Interactional Reading	Expanded Vocabulary	Extending Play
❑ Choose an area and set it up to reflect children's cultures	From *Bringing Words to Life*	❑ Math vocabulary (5 words)	❑ Redirect play to replace violent play
❑ Account for child's interest-background and use child's prior knowledge	☑ Choosing vocabulary words	❑ Science vocabulary (5 words)	❑ Plan play
	From Dialogic Reading	**Assessment and Instruction**	❑ Act out stories
❑ Inspire child to complete the idea/activity by connecting it to his/her home culture	☑ Prompt	❑ Follow child's interest	❑ Dramatic use of the constructions child makes
	o Completion prompt	❑ Observe and record child learning behaviors	**Inclusion**
❑ Provide specific feedback to extend child's play in that area	o Recall prompt	❑ Initiate conversations and write plans with child	❑ Adapt environment
	o Open-ended prompt		❑ Adapt routines
❑ Question to promote higher-level thinking	o Wh- question prompt	❑ Provide meaningful learning opportunities informed by assessment	❑ Adapt materials and activities
	o Distancing prompt		❑ Adapt requirements
	☑ Evaluate the child's response		❑ Adapt instruction
	☑ Expand the child's response		
	☑ Repeat—child repeats the expanded response		

Continue on back if needed

Focus child _____

Elaborate on how you will implement the intentional teaching strategy. _____
_____
_____
_____

What type of in-class support do you think will help you?
❑ Modeling while you take notes
❑ Assistance with co-teaching the child
☑ Feedback after observation
❑ Other _____

Use back if needed

Figure 2.6. Lillie's in-class Implementation and Mentoring Form for book reading.

methods described at the LEARN IT institute and supportive learning community, Lillie and Janet realized that dialogic reading methods would be very difficult to implement with a group larger than three or four children. Therefore, Lillie and Janet concluded that Lillie would continue with her plan to complete the whole-group read-aloud sessions so all of her students had the opportunity to become familiar with the book and were confident answering recall questions. Accordingly, Lillie repeated the reading of the book for at least 2 days. During her whole-group read-aloud sessions, she continued to reflect on dialogic reading practices and realized that she could not reliably provide correct CROWD and PEER prompts (see Whitehurst [2008]) and monitor the full group of 18 children. In an analysis of her own classroom context, Lillie elected to modify her incorporation of dialogic reading strategies by changing part of the lesson plan to provide the CROWD and PEER prompts to a group of three or four children during centers time. To test out her new approach, Lillie decided to use a set of prompts and book plan developed during her supportive learning community meeting for *Whistle for Willie* (Keats, 1964). The book plan and prompts are shown in Figure 2.7.

During her implementation, Lillie assessed children's understanding of the identified vocabulary words using an informal checklist completed after each small group. See the Example of Quick Assessment text box for an example. She used this information to help her decide on the focus of the next CROWD and PEER prompts to be completed in small groups. While working with small groups and with the assessment, she was able to determine more accurately whether children were learning the new vocabulary words.

HANDOUT 2.8.

Preparing Books for Dialogic Reading

Book Title: _Whistle for Willie_

Author: _Ezra Jack Keats_

Read the book to students at least once so they are familiar with it. Do this in your usual manner, addressing print concepts and giving any needed information regarding meaning. Ask recall questions after finishing the book.

Example Recall Questions

1. _What did Willie want to learn?_

2. _Why did he want to learn to whistle?_

3. _Why do you think he put on his father's hat?_

4. _Was Willie successful in learning how to whistle?_

Reread the book numerous times. This is where you will use the PEER sequence with the CROWD prompts based on dialogic reading.

Pick up to eight vocabulary words of focus. Remember, they can be part of the story or shown in the picture. They can be objects or actions. Space the words throughout the book. Word choice is based on _Bringing Words to Life: Robust Vocabulary Instruction_ (Beck, McKeown, & Kucan, 2013).

1. _straight_   5. _graffiti_
2. _dizzy_   6. _persistent_
3. _barber pole_   7. _raced_
4. _practice_   8. _errand_

Finally, write out a list of questions for each of the vocabulary words. Use a variety of types of prompts given the CROWD prompts and write the type of prompt. Be sure to include the page number where the vocabulary word appears as well.

Vocabulary word	Question	Prompt	Page number
Straight	Here (point) the dog runs straight to the boy. What does it mean to run straight?	Wh- prompt	3
Dizzy	(Reread the text and point to the pictures of Peter.) Look, Peter was dizzy. What does dizzy mean?	Wh- prompt	4, 5, 6
Barber pole	(Point to the picture.) What is this? Why is there a barber pole in front of a store?	Wh- prompt	11
Practice	What is happening in this picture? (Can reread text if needed, but move children to address practice.) What does practice mean?	Open ended	14
Graffiti	Look at the wall behind Peter. Describe what you see. Did you know these types of painting are often called graffiti? Where have you seen graffiti before?	Distancing	17, 18
Persistent	Peter "blew and blew and blew. Suddenly, out came a real whistle!" He practiced and worked at learning to whistle. He was persistent. What does persistent mean?	Wh- prompt	21
Raced	"Willie raced straight to him." When have you raced before? What do you do when you race? What did Willie do?	Distancing	24
Errand	(Read page 27. Point out the word errand.)	Distancing	27

Figure 2.7. Lillie's completed dialogic reading supports handout.

EXAMPLE OF QUICK ASSESSMENT

Insert a check when child knows vocabulary word.

Children's names

Vocabulary

❏ 1. straight

❏ 2. dizzy

❏ 3. barber pole

❏ 4. practice

❏ 5. graffiti

❏ 6. persistent

❏ 7. raced

❏ 8. errand

Throughout this process, Janet worked strategically with Lillie to help her see additional opportunities to refine her intentional teaching practices through the incorporation of dialogic reading strategies. Janet observed the large group and small groups in order to provide feedback. Together, Lillie and Janet reviewed children's progress, working to make some new prompts for children who might need more support acquiring the new vocabulary. They also developed strategic scaffolds for some children that Lillie had noticed were having difficulty responding to initial recall questions. In addition, Lillie and Janet decided to keep the small groups heterogeneous as much as possible until children mastered the new vocabulary, so that peers supported each other's learning. To further promote the children's acquisition of new vocabulary, they decided to encourage children's continued exploration of the book content with teacher support by placing additional copies of the focus book in the independent reading center.

After working with Janet during the 2 weeks before the supportive learning community meeting, Lillie identified a set of questions that she wanted to bring to the meeting for further exploration. At this point, she wondered about the decision process involved in adding a new book for dialogic reading in the classroom: How would children handle two or more books of focus being used at the same time? How should she encourage peers to be more involved with each other on the dialogues about the books? Feeling confident in her instructional refinements, Lillie was excited about returning to her supportive learning community to focus on these ongoing issues related to book reading inspired by dialogic reading.

Figure 2.8 is a checklist of this LEARN IT strand that the professional development team can use to assess whether they implemented all aspects of dialogic reading across LEARN IT. Those facilitating a LEARN IT activity can use this checklist as a tool to guide the process and ensure that they are working through each step. All aspects of LEARN are utilized across this strand of LEARN IT. Participants engage in learning knowledge and skills specific to dialogic reading strategies. They have multiple opportunities to enact, assess, and reflect on specific aspects of dialogic reading. They participate in this learning within the context of a supportive learning community that includes mentors and colleagues interested in dialogic reading.

Checklist for Book Reading Inspired by Dialogic Reading

	LEARN IT institute	Implementation and mentoring	Supportive learning communities
Learn	❐ Facilitators presented research and best practice related to dialogic reading and to implementing it in day-to-day teaching.	❐ Mentors helped participants identify particular needs they have implementing dialogic reading using knowledge learned through the institute and supportive learning community.	❐ Mentors reviewed information on dialogic reading and provided materials to participants so that they could apply their learning to one particular book.
Enact	❐ Facilitators provided opportunities for participants to apply learned information with *Read Together, Talk Together* using Handout 2.2.	❐ Mentors supported participants as they implemented dialogic reading in the classroom, both during the planning phase and again during implementation with a small group of children.	❐ Mentors established parameters for participants to role-play dialogic reading strategies.
Assess	❐ Facilitators gave participants an opportunity to report answers on the handout and receive corrections from facilitators on any misunderstandings.	❐ Mentors guided participants to assess children on their understanding of target words through expressive and receptive vocabulary questions and used this information to assess the effectiveness of the strategy they implemented.	❐ Mentors provided corrective feedback during role play activities.
Reflect	❐ Facilitators provided opportunities for participants to consider how this practice could be used in their classrooms.	❐ Mentors promoted reflection on why this type of instruction might be a necessary addition to the types of book reading the participants provide their students.	❐ Mentors supported discussion of the use of dialogic reading in their classrooms.
Network	❐ Facilitators implemented a session in which participants met in groups based on their site/school and considered the benefits of this practice for their site/school.	❐ Mentors provided participants the opportunities to network with peers and follow up in community meetings.	❐ Mentors copied accurate dialogic reading notes and prompts and shared them with the entire group.

Figure 2.8. Checklist for Book Reading Inspired by Dialogic Reading.

SUMMARY

In Chapter 2, intentional teaching, the focus of our professional development, was highlighted as central to all areas of development and learning. Intentional teaching was presented as a construct that is key to effective interactions that promote young children's learning. We discussed what has been written about intentional teaching and shared our definition of intentional teaching from research we conducted. We then focused on LEARN IT by linking the background information to practical knowledge that teachers can use to implement intentional teaching in their classrooms. Accordingly, we offered two activities that guide educators to reflect intentionally on current classroom practices and engage in the strategic implementation of new practices to enhance learning experiences for individual children.

In these activities, we integrated the information in Chapter 1 into its practical use in the intentional teaching content presented in Chapter 2. Together, these chapters provide the foundation for specific topical areas related to the intentional teaching strategies presented across Chapters 3 through 7. Our task in those chapters is to present our activities and experience in providing LEARN IT, as described in Chapter 1, across various aspects of intentional teaching in early childhood education. The specific areas we emphasize in those chapters are 1) learning through play, 2) including each child, 3) culturally responsive practice, 4) assessing diverse young children, and 5) intentionally linking assessment with curriculum and instruction. We believe these areas are of central concern when addressing intentional teaching across areas of development and learning central to the academic success of young children.

Learning Through Play

Educator Katie is a participant in the LEARN IT project. She has worked in the same classroom for many years and has a rigid curriculum that she has to follow, which focuses on specific learning outcomes. For example, Katie is given strict instructions on ways to utilize learning centers. As a result, she is very strict in her approach to managing children's behaviors. When the LEARN IT mentor, Isabella, visited the classroom, Katie asked her to focus on one child, Lora, whom Katie struggled with because the child did not follow directions and was easily distracted. Isabella played with Lora on the days she came in for the implementation and mentoring session. Isabella quickly discovered that Lora needed more guidance and redirection than she was getting. In one of the sessions, Lora wanted to move some housekeeping toys to the block area, and Isabella went along with that. Katie, the lead teacher, immediately stopped her because those toys belonged in the housekeeping center. Lora had a meltdown. As Isabella observed, she saw a teacher being very rigid and a little girl being denied her outside-the-box thinking.

Later, Katie explained that the curriculum strictly dictates the setup of the play centers. Also, Lora's parents had asked Katie to closely monitor their child's behavior, as she tended not to follow directions. Katie believed that moving toys around would encourage Lora's inappropriate behaviors. When asked whether other children in her classroom move toys around from one center to another, Katie immediately said no, because this creates chaos and more work for all in the classroom. With further discussions and reflections, Katie and her supportive learning community team at her school explored the benefits and challenges associated with flexible use of materials and the ways this may be used to extend learning opportunities in play situations.

Very often, preschool teachers worry about interfering too much in children's self-directed play and, as a result, miss the opportunity to guide their young students who may be in need of guidance to enrich and extend learning. Some argue against adults' interventions in play situations based on an educational philosophy and belief in free engagement in child-led play that is uninterrupted. Nevertheless, in cases such as the one described here, the child Lora became bored and easily distracted. Katie was challenged to consider more flexible play choices for this child. Early childhood educators need to be intentional about their play centers and the way they are inviting play situations. Furthermore, they sometimes need to directly and intentionally guide children who may require more adult intervention to maximize learning and interactions.

WHAT TO EXPECT
IN THIS CHAPTER

This book weaves the importance of play into all aspects of learning across chapters. Previous chapters also explore intentional teaching and describe it as teaching that takes place when educators engage children in planned instructional activities intentionally designed to address children's prior knowledge, interests, abilities, and needs (Burns, Kidd, Nasser, Stechuk, & Aier, 2012). Intentional teaching means including each child in early childhood classrooms, tailoring instruction to individual abilities and linguistic and cultural backgrounds. Later chapters will highlight the importance of embracing ongoing assessment strategies that enable educators to flexibly modify children's instructional plans according to their needs.

Learning through play is an essential component of intentional teaching. This chapter shares foundational knowledge about play and outlines professional development activities that build educators' practical knowledge about play. This chapter

- Focuses on intentionally extending learning experiences of young children through play activities

- Highlights the importance of providing children with freedom in play, in addition to structuring play in intentional ways that promote learning

- Shares LEARN IT activities that support educators as they plan play and extend learning through play

FOUNDATIONS: LEARNING THROUGH PLAY

The play landscape has changed dramatically for modern children; indoor spaces are replacing outside play and structured playgrounds are replacing play in neighborhood streets. More recently, virtual play on computers and other electronic devices has entered the natural play spaces in schools and in public spaces, especially as smart devices became more accessible. This new version of play is threatening the more classical views of play. Most known is Plato's assertion that educators should not "keep children to their studies by compulsion but by play" (Dickey, Castle, & Pryor, 2016, p. 111). Kernan (2007) noted that "since the time of the classic Greek philosophers, play has been considered the expression of the natural spirit of the child and thus a key defining feature of childhood" (p. 5). In these quotes, the message is clear to let children play freely and in natural settings. More recently, Miller and Almon (2009) suggested that play includes "activities that are freely chosen and directed by children and arise from intrinsic motivation" (p. 15).

Early childhood classical theorists also point out the importance of play in a child's life. According to Maria Montessori, "play is the child's work." Others such as Piaget (1962) stated that play is a natural way to learn; play develops the child's cognitive abilities, facilitating learning (Elkind, 2007). Piaget systematically studied play and saw it progress through three stages: practice of functional play, symbolic play (constructive and dramatic), and, finally, play with rules. Vygotsky disagreed with Piaget about play stages but agreed that play stimulates the development of abstract thought. In addition, Vygotsky advocated for the significance of symbolic play for social and language development. He argued that children learn about the world by interacting with adults and peers around them.

Intentional play interactions elevate children's learning to their higher potential. Similar to the psychoanalytic tradition of Freud and Erikson, who suggested that play is a way for children to fulfill their wishes and work through their conflicts, Vygotsky proposed that play is a means of gratifying impossible desires. Psychologists such as Parten and Kagan, and anthropologists such as Mead and Goodall, studied the socialization aspects of play and advocated for its importance in gaining social skills such as cooperation, tolerance, and patience (Bodrova & Leong, 2003). Their work supported Vygotsky's assertion that children conform to the implicit rules of the play situation, which supports self-regulation skills in children. As the 21st century began, the movement toward free and internally motivated play was superseded by more structured and standard-driven play. Intentionality, in this case, supports teachers' awareness and attempts to balance teacher-directed and child-directed play interactions.

Basic Characteristics of Play

According to Parten (1932), there are social participation stages of play in early years that follow a developmental pattern parallel to Piaget's stages of cognitive development. Those develop at a typical age of appearance starting at age 2 and ending at around age 5, and include the following:

- *Unoccupied behavior:* little interest in anything around the child

- *Onlooker behavior:* watches peers but does not participate

- *Parallel play:* engages in side-by-side play

- *Associative play:* interacts with others often but keeps own theme of play

- *Cooperative play:* play theme is coordinated with other peers

These age-appropriate play characteristics allow educators to identify typical and atypical behaviors, observe for developmental red flags and unique differences, and utilize play to provide young children with new knowledge and materials, skills such as literacy and numeracy, and dispositions such as working together and problem solving.

There are further characteristics to keep in mind as educators plan for play, and these vary according to the perspectives provided earlier. For example, Hirsh-Pasek, Golinkoff, and Eyer (2003), who follow a Piagetian perspective, identified five basic elements in children's play that are important to consider:

- *Play must be pleasurable and enjoyable.* Anyone who has watched children playing recognizes the delight on their faces and can see the pure joy of the experience as they form new friendships and solve problems.

- *Play must have no extrinsic goals.* There is no prescribed learning that must occur and no expectation that must be met. Only the play matters.

- *Play is spontaneous and voluntary.* Children choose to play without someone telling them to do so. In fact, adults who tell children what to play take the fun out of the experience. It is no longer a spontaneous activity and is now directed play.

- *Play involves active engagement on the part of the player.* Often, the active engagement is with objects that are directed by the child. Children may also interact with others in play. Actively manipulating blocks in some way is playing; building a tower of five blocks during a mathematics lesson is not.

- *Play involves an element of make-believe.* Very often, in play situations, children seem serious about the roles they take because for them play is real. In a housekeeping play scenario, they are cooking for real and they want others to drink and eat with them for real. They are playing roles inspired by real-life events that are relevant to them.

Elkonin (2005), on the other hand, emphasized the social origin of play and challenged theories that conceptualized play as biological in nature and driven by internal instincts. Elkonin believed that play is characterized by an "elaborated and developed form of role playing" (p. 34) that was not addressed by Piaget. Elkonin explained, "Piaget stops at its [role playing] threshold; he studies some prerequisites for its occurrence, but goes no further" (p. 33). Elkonin instead draws upon Vygotsky's work that supports his belief that make-believe or sociodramatic play is the essence of children's play. Bodrova and Leong (2015) build upon Vygotsky's work to identify three characteristics of socio-dramatic play:

- Children construct make-believe situations.

- Children assume roles that they then act out.

- Children follow rules that are determined by the roles they assume.

As children engage in make-believe play, these features influence children's thought processes and promote higher levels of cognitive functioning (Bodrova & Leong, 2015; Vygotsky, 1978). Bodrova and Leong noted that play promotes cognitive development because 1) children move from relying on objects to using symbolic thought in their play, 2) play promotes intentional behavior, and 3) children exhibit signs of being able to generalize emotions. They explained that as children engage in make-believe play, they use objects that represent people and things that are part of the story, learn to curb their impulses as they plan what roles they will play in the imaginary situation, and follow rules that guide the role play. For example, a girl taking on the role of the mother may pick up a doll and use a stick or a block as a bottle. As the girl feeds the baby the bottle, she will intentionally hold the baby in her arms and insert the bottle into the baby's mouth, thereby following the rules of the role she has undertaken. If the baby becomes sick, the girl will take on the concern that she knows a mother feels when a child is sick and will use these generalized feelings to comfort the baby. If the girl does not follow the rules, other children engaged in the role play will attempt to correct the girl or choose to exclude her from their play.

Drawing from Elkonin's work, Bodrova and Leong (2003, 2015) addressed the developmental nature of play and made the distinction between immature and mature play. Mature play appears after age 4 and includes characteristics such as imaginary situations, multiple roles, clearly defined rules, flexible themes, and longer periods of play (Bodrova & Leong, 2003). Vygotsky (1978) viewed play along a continuum that begins with imaginary situations that are similar to real situations and reproduce what happens in real life. For example, a child feeding a baby doll recreates the real world. As children develop, their play becomes more imaginative and more novel in nature.

Vygotsky described these more advanced levels of play in examples of children using a stick for a horse or a block of wood as a doll. He contended that as children's play matures, rules rather than objects influence their actions. According to Bodrova and Leong (2015), Elkonin built on Vygotsky's ideas and identified four levels of mature play:

Level 1: Object-oriented play in which routines are played out in stereotypical ways that do not reflect real life. For example, children may play restaurant; however, they do not name the roles they are playing. Instead, they may serve the food routinely in the same way, but not take orders, wait for the food to be cooked, or clean up the plates after the meal has been eaten. They may even perform the tasks out of order and serve the food before taking the order. When a child does not play according to the rules, other children typically do not object or explain what is wrong.

Level 2: Object-oriented play in which the play reflects real life. At this level, children initiate play and then take on a role, for example, of server, cook, or patron. The objects, the food on the plates in this role-play, are still the main focus. However, children carry out the routines in ways that more accurately mimic real life. For example, children as patrons may sit down at a table, the server will take the order and get the food, and the patrons will eat. If a child does not follow the rules, other children may not like it, but they do not tend to provide an explanation of what is wrong.

Level 3: Role-oriented play that determines actions. Children initiate play by assuming roles and using these roles to determine what they will do and say during the make-believe play. The actions become more varied, and the speech generated during the sociodramatic play uses real-life words, inflection, and level of formality. The server, for example, will take the patrons' orders, serve the food, and bring a check. The conversation between the server and the patrons will sound more like a real-life conversation. In addition, children expect others to play by the rules and will speak out if others are not following the rules. Children who break the rules will try to correct their mistake.

Level 4: Role-oriented play in which relationships among roles reflect real life. At this level, the relationship among the characters takes on a higher level of significance. Children take on a role before play initiates and stay in that role throughout the role play. They perform their role and interact and talk with others in their roles in ways that are well defined, logical, and consistent with real life. For example, the server is expected to interact with the patrons in specific ways and in particular sequences that mimic real life. If a child breaks a rule by not performing consistent to real life, others will not only correct the child but will explain why the rule exists.

Because early educators' understandings of play influence how they approach play-based learning in their classrooms, the characteristics of play discussed here are important to consider. LEARN IT takes a sociocultural approach to providing play opportunities in prekindergarten and kindergarten that draws upon the work of Vygotsky and Elkonin. LEARN IT emphasizes the role educators can play in providing opportunities for sociodramatic play and supporting development and learning through play opportunities.

Benefits of Play

Previous studies show links among play and important skills and domains in early childhood development, such as memory, self-regulation, oral language skills, successful school adjustment, and better social skills (Koralek, 2004). According to Singer, Golinkoff, and Hirsh-Pasek (2006), play has a positive effect on social skills as well as on academic skills such as mathematics and literacy. In addition, research has repeatedly suggested that engagement in play promotes gains in social skills, cognitive skills, and emotional maturity (Burns, Johnson, & Assaf, 2012; White, 2012). Children learn ways to socialize and communicate with others through play, as it allows them to relax and learn new knowledge and practice new skills in a stress-free environment. These types of interactions in play situations support higher academic achievement because children feel safe to take risks and challenge themselves (Sherman, 2014). This is critically important, especially in situations in which intentional play opportunities are in limited availability to children outside the school doors.

These benefits of play provide support for a movement to bring play back to the classroom, as it represents authentic learning and encourages imagination and other developmental skills. Sherman (2014) also suggested making play, such as acting and storytelling, part of a teacher's daily repertoire. Utilizing play illustrates the teacher's understanding of young children's needs and the use of a child-sensitive approach (Perlmutter & Burrel, 1995). An early childhood education rich with play opportunities that are both structured and unstructured allows learning to happen. When children play, they have opportunities to work with and combine concepts they have been previously taught. Play is also beneficial for developing tendencies and approaches to learning, important in making the transition to kindergarten.

An interesting way to think about the benefits of play is to think about play deprivation. According to Dickey et al. (2016), there are consequences in all domains of development when children are deprived of play. For example, in the physical domain, "play deprivation in early years may lead to obesity, restlessness, abnormal brain development, etc. In socioemotional domain, play deprivation may lead to inadequate social skills, lack of self-control, helplessness, depression, aggression, anxiety, and stress" (p. 113). It is true that longitudinal studies are needed to examine the long-term impact of play deprivation, but there is enough evidence to document benefits of play in early childhood. According to Eliason and Jenkins (2016, p. 21), play facilitates much-needed skills and attitudes, including the following:

- Learning

- Development

- Motivation

- Thinking and problem solving

- Social development and social awareness

- Flexibility

- Skill development

- Sensory awareness

- Attention span and listening

- Language acquisition and communication

- Physical and motor development

- Healthy emotional development

- Autonomy

- Imagination

- Metacognition (thinking about one's own thinking)

Adults Facilitate Play

Teachers' support is essential for learning and enhancing play characteristics and benefits discussed in the previous section. Gmitrova and Gmitrov (2003) provided evidence in their study of child-directed play and teacher-directed play. They suggested that cognitive gains were attained when teachers were involved. The results of the study showed an increase in cognitive behavior during child-directed play combined with teacher-directed play. This is a shift in thinking about play; the field moved from totally free and unstructured play, to no play due to a focus on academic readiness, to a compromise wherein play may occur with teacher assistance and without. This is where intentional and purposeful (called "thoughtfully supported play" by Bodrova & Leong, 2012) planning of play situations and environments is essential in bringing play back into the early childhood classroom.

In play-based learning environments, adults may provide an individual challenge to extend children's thinking and to help individual children move forward from their present learning to the next step to reach their highest potential. For instance, if a child shows interest in a question or a topic, such as rocks and shells, the teacher can plan activities and set up a rocks and shells center that allows that child to explore further and interact/play with the materials while learning about texture, colors, and smells of rocks and shells. Of course, intentional teachers understand that play should align with a child's interest while also sparking interest in other questions and topics during play interactions.

The intervention in children's play can also be viewed as a continuum between indirect planning of play to direct involvement in the play situation by an adult. At one end of the continuum, adults adopt the role of managers as they organize the time, space, and resources that promote play. When adults mediate or interpret the play that occurs, they become more and more involved. Direct involvement occurs when adults adopt an active role in the play, such as the movement from engagement in parallel play to co-playing and ending with play tutoring, as described by Dockett and Fleer (2002). The task of the early educator is to choose the most suitable strategies to use based on knowledge of the individual children; the particular context; and the broader cultural, ethical, and equity considerations. Such a continuum of adult involvement in children's play is also suggested in the findings of the Effective Provision of Pre-School Education (EPPE) project by Sylva, Melhuish, Sammons, Siraj, and Taggart (2004).

The Researching Effective Pedagogy in the Early Years (REPEY) group of studies in the United Kingdom also provide evidence that adult and child involvement, such as in cognitive engagement and sustained shared thinking between adults and children, are essential (Kernan, 2007). In an additional study by White (2012), the concept of guided play has been suggested to offer more direction during free play to enrich the play experience. According to the study, in this form of guided play, "parents or other adults can scaffold children's play by joining in the fun as co-players, asking thoughtful questions, commenting on children's discoveries, or encouraging further exploration or new facets to the child's activity" (White, p. 7). Of course, this does not mean that the child is not intrinsically motivated and that play is not fun and child-directed; rather, it is an opportunity for adults to provide guided play experiences. In other words, educators must provide intentional interventions to extend play and, as a result, learning in all its forms. Intentionality in this approach comes in to enrich, enhance, and elevate as needed.

Families Facilitate Play

Families as significant partners to teachers have an important role in encouraging children to play and actually playing with their children. Play creates stronger bonds between parents and their children. Play also reduces stress and allows parents to see the uniqueness of their children (Anderson-McNamee & Baily, 2010). Mothers and siblings have an essential role in developing children's play skills. Mothers help their children in facilitating the process of play and expressing discoveries and feelings while playing. Siblings, on the other hand, help with developing collaboration skills (Howe & Bruno, 2010). Teachers can take a major role in encouraging extending play activities to the home. This can be done by teachers reaching out to parents and informing them of benefits of play at school and at home. The following are a few tips to partner with families around play and its benefits:

- Create a common understanding with families on the importance of play for learning and for life. For example, create a newsletter on play that you can share with parents on your philosophy and the benefits of play discussed in this chapter.

- Share with parents formally and informally how you set up free play and intentional and directed play situations.

- Make explicit the connections among play situations and literacy and numeracy whenever you can in conversations with parents. For example, drawing and painting are precursors for writing.

- Invite parents to set up and participate in play situations.

- Provide parents, when possible, with play ideas at home and ways they can use play to bond with children.

Play and Learning Environments

A recent body of research has developed around play and the importance of creating intentional environments for enhancing play behaviors in young children. According to Bodrova and Leong (2003), play that is guided by teachers moves children's creative play into a more mature level in which teachers can act intentionally on enhancing their centers to allow higher levels of thinking and learning. They suggest providing children with access to ample amount of multipurpose props that they can make meaning of and decide on use on their own. This will allow for open-ended possibilities of play (Bodrova & Leong).

Intentionally setting up learning centers is recommended by Bredekamp and Copple (1997) to promote learning, higher-level thinking, and engagement. Unfortunately, some early childhood educators misuse the recommendation and neglect to invest in setting goals and objectives for their centers. According to Stuber (2007), engaging centers can actually increase the efficiency of engagement in learning. She added, "Centers help teachers put the child at the center of their decision making—where children should be" (Stuber, p. 59). Setting up stimulating classroom environments that support children's learning can influence children's learning and developmental outcomes. A classroom with a rich environment that provides props, for example, to encourage use of language will support varied spoken vocabulary (Burns & Kidd, 2016). Similarly, thoughtful use of manipulatives and the presence of books and writing materials across all learning centers can encourage meaningful numeracy and literacy. In essence, effective and intentional learning centers are set up carefully, so that children learn and develop and are monitored to make sure such learning is taking place. Educators are interacting with children and are active in promoting learning and development, but they are also intentional in the way they interact with each child and all children.

When examining play from the child's perspective, Kernan (2007) documented accounts of child's play in various settings, including informal and outside school settings, where children preferred the following activities: 1) constructing, such as play with open-ended materials; 2) creating small spaces such as farms and buildings; 3) transporting and carrying cars around; 4) playing with water; 5) engaging with work using real tools and using all body movements to reenact socially and culturally valued activities; 6) engaging in storytelling; and 7) having a sensitive adult close by who values play and who can offer support at key moments. These key priorities help in understanding cases in which children are engaged and educators provide support as needed.

The teacher is ultimately responsible for the learning environment. When teachers ensure that the classroom space and environment are interesting, inspiring, safe, challenging, and inviting, children will flourish. This does not necessarily mean that teacher-directed activities are not important; instead, they should be left to a minimum in some cases and increased in others, depending on the child's needs and interests. The teacher needs to be intentional about each activity and each learning situation (Burns et al., 2012). Eliason and Jenkins (2016) added that regardless of whether play is child-guided or teacher-directed, activities should be age-based, and materials and activities should be individualized and adaptable to children with disabilities. Materials should be culturally and linguistically appropriate, and authentic assessments should be used.

Learning Through Play

As discussed in previous sections, there is documented support for the importance and benefits of play, the intentional role of the adults, and intentionality when setting the learning environment. The LEARN IT professional development approach focuses on planning intentional dimensions of play and fostering quality play as essential aspects of preschool learning. The LEARN IT strategies and activities encourage educators to pay special attention to extending play opportunities, especially through the use of the intentional strategies described in the following subsections.

Planning Play and Reflection There is wide agreement that planning has an important role in enhancing children's play and learning. Advanced planning helps children get their ideas out and prolong playtime. Epstein (2003) confirms that when children are engaged in planning steps, they score better in language, mathematics, and science. Chapter 2 offered an activity that provides guidance on planning with children and encouraging teachers to be more intentional in asking open-ended questions and allowing children to plan, play, and reflect. The use of planning and reflection in many programs has been limited and has lacked the intentionality of the child. According to Epstein, "Planning is more than making choices. Planning is choice with intention" (p. 29). Chapter 2 also named resources and suggestions on planning instruction in early childhood research reviews (e.g., *Eager to Learn: Educating Our Preschoolers* [Bowman, Donovan, & Burns, 2000]) and application to practice books (e.g., *Preschool Education in Today's World: Teaching Children With Diverse Backgrounds and Abilities* [Burns et al., 2012]).

There is support in the research that, in order to promote thinking and reasoning in children, there are two important curriculum components: planning and reflection. Teachers need to be purposeful in planning and selecting strategies that support children's use of problem-solving skills and development of reflection skills (Stuber, 2007). Teaching children to plan and reflect supports achieving child outcomes and behaviors such as participation, increasing ability to set goals and develop and follow through on plans. Planning allows for the increase in capacity to concentrate over time on a task, such as the use of a process wherein the child and the teacher plan their play activities together. First, they plan, such as the child deciding to play in blocks area that day. Then the child plays freely. When done, the child and the teacher review what was done and learned during play in the block center.

Recent work by Diamond, Barnett, Thomas, and Munro (2007) demonstrate the potential for a prekindergarten rich in planning to set up the stage for children's capacity to succeed later in school. According to Kernan (2007), play in early childhood settings tends not to be planned the same way academic work is planned. Some of the features of play, such as freedom, spontaneity, fun, and ownership, do not always sit happily or naturally within educational and curriculum-driven programs; Katie's classroom, discussed in the opening vignette, is an example of such a curriculum-driven program. In some contexts, these features of play are marginalized and are limited to the outdoor break. They are also viewed as the nonteaching time, where a distinction is made between the outdoors as the space for nonserious play, recreation, or running around and indoors as the space for serious work and learning (e.g., quiet and sitting down) (Evans & Pellegrini, 1997; Kernan, 2006; Pellegrini, 2005). Nonprescribed play may be difficult to manage within educational contexts because play can change the nature of power relationships—the control is with the children rather than with the teacher (Brown & Freeman, 2001; Wood & Attfield, 2005). In the vignette, the child Lora pushed the limits of prescribed play and the educator Katie had to keep control of the situation by preventing Lora from thinking outside the box. Katie, like many early childhood teachers, is burdened by a prescriptive curriculum that does not allow the flexibility young children need. Intentional teaching reinforces the need for planning so that play situations are self-driven by the child unless teacher guidance is needed.

Integrating Play Into the Curriculum   Some educators oppose early learning guidelines and benchmarks and view them as limiting the young child's creativity as well as the educator's creativity. According to Kagan, Scott-Little, and Frelow, 2009, a framework is needed for play that explains and brings together early development guidelines with the pedagogy of play. This means that educators can see play not as just an activity, but rather as a strategy that will promote development guidelines. If the guideline is, for example, to promote social skills and self-help, educators can use play situations to address these skills and provide materials that allow children to learn (e.g., tying shoelaces in housekeeping). This is true for other sets of skills, such as sorting and counting in math, that may be addressed in block center and others. According to Kagan et al.,

> To blend play and early learning guidelines, thinking must shift from considering play as simply something children do naturally and something that is "good" for them, to also thinking of play as a strategy for providing children with experiences where they can learn specific skills or knowledge articulated in the early learning guidelines. (Kagan et al., 2009, p. 23)

Educators must intentionally provide the materials that children need to make progress on specific goals and guidelines as they play. Educators must also be involved during the play to promote activities and interactions that provide opportunities for children to practice specific skills. For example, in the blocks area, a teacher might also provide pencils and paper for children to draw designs of roads and buildings before starting to build.

Redirect Play to Replace Violent Play   According to Carlson (2011), rough play is part of the early childhood development and it should be supported and supervised. The author also asks teachers to distinguish between big body play (e.g., chasing each other and rolling on the ground together) and fighting. Real fighting causes children to cry. Carlson explained, "In appropriate rough play, children's faces are free and easy, their muscle tone is relaxed, and they are usually smiling and laughing. In real fighting, the facial movements are rigid, controlled, stressed, and the jaw is usually clenched" (p. 20). One of the suggestions the author made to supervise and redirect play is to enforce the rules and intervene to help children communicate verbally rather than nonverbally during play. For example, in cases where children misuse toys and materials, the teacher stops the play and reminds children of the safe use of toys. In play situations, children are encouraged to create those rules and roles they all take on. Katie's student Lora may be one who may enjoy taking on roles and changing that role based on the play situations. As Leong and Bodrova (2013) pointed out, children who may be seen as aggressive and loners may show positive leadership roles when guided in outdoor play situations. For instance, when children on the playground play intense games, such as role playing as fire fighters and emergency medical staff, redirection can be a key strategy. Many of the fast and "rough" but helping behaviors are allowed in this type of play, while friends save and take care of their friends on the playground. No one gets hurt; rather, they get helped (Bodrova & Leong, 2003, 2015).

The Professional Development Activities section that follows describes two LEARN IT activities that are specifically planned to enhance educators' knowledge and skills in planning play situations and engaging in intentional play interactions. In these two activities, we allocate time to discuss knowledge and literature on play and its benefits to continue the support for play in early childhood education classrooms curriculum and instruction. Even though play is integrated throughout LEARN IT, it is important to give enough time and space to gain new knowledge and reflect on planning intentional play to extend learning. For veteran educators, this is a way to refresh recent and applicable knowledge. For novice educators, the activities increase theoretical knowledge with applicable ideas and skills.

Learning Through Planning Play

The learning through planning play strand of LEARN IT professional development attempts to clarify the connections between play and learning. It exposes educators to activities and recent knowledge that will support thinking more intentionally about play. Educators will engage in the institute, implementation and mentoring session, and supportive learning communities to help them master the intentional teaching strategy of planning play.

LEARN IT Institute

Prior to the institute, participants read the Foundations section at the beginning of this chapter and the article in the Learning Through Planning Play Resources text box. During the institute, educators will view the video in the text box.

LEARNING THROUGH PLANNING PLAY RESOURCES

Reading:

Leong, D. L., & Bodrova, E. (2013). Chopsticks and counting chips: Do play and foundational skills need to compete for the teacher's attention in an early childhood classroom? *Young Children, 58*(3), 10-17. Available at *https://www.publichealthbaron.info/uploads/7/1/0/3/71038325/play_article_1.pdf*

The following video will be viewed during the institute: *Play: A Vygotskian Approach with Ph.D.s Elena Bodrova and Deborah J. Leong.* (26 minutes).

To begin the institute, educators discuss key takeaways from the assigned readings. They engage in a group discussion to increase their current knowledge on the topic and to activate their prior knowledge on play. When the discussion winds down, participants view a video on play that provides a provocative and closer look at children's behaviors during play. We recommend using *Play: A Vygotskian Approach With Deborah J. Leong, Ph.D., and Elena Bodrova, Ph.D.* to promote learning and discussion. This particular video introduces a Vygotskian approach to play and elaborates on ideas about it based on the research by Bodrova and Leong (2003). Participants use Handout 3.1 as a viewing guide; the handout summarizes the main ideas of the video. After viewing in the large group, participants form small groups and discuss their observations of the main ideas gained from the video. They assess whether these behaviors during play described in the film are evident in their students' behaviors.

Next, in the same small groups, participants share responses to the "Chopsticks and Counting Chips" article by Leong and Bodrova (2013) that was assigned prior to the institute. Educators share insights on the article's range of strategies to enhance play based on the Vygotskian approach. This article complements the information provided in the *Play* video by the two authors who translated Vygotsky's philosophy and approach into practical strategies. For example, Leong and Bodrova suggest integrating play in mathematics and literacy activities and promoting play as a way to support the social and emotional development of young children.

As those conversations wrap up, participants should work in small groups to assess the strategy of providing children with opportunities to act out stories, as proposed in the Leong and Bodrova (2013) article. This strategy allows for a broad range of reading comprehension through the dramatic use of children's construction of their own meaning. Acting out stories provides various learning modalities and increases learning opportunities through interaction and communication with peers and adults. This strategy may be implemented when children are in a dramatic play setting, where they learn how to cooperate and communicate

Play: A Vygotskian Approach

With Deborah J. Leong, Ph.D., and Elena Bodrova, Ph.D.

(26 minutes)

Davidson Films, Inc.

668 Marsh Street, San Luis Obispo CA 93401

Tel.: 805.594.0422   Fax: 805.594.0532

E-mail: dfi@davidsonfilms.com Web: www.davidsonfilms.com

Introduction

This video was filmed in two preschool classrooms and in homes and neighborhoods.

The video is based in part on a paper that Lev Vygotsky wrote in 1933. He reviewed the literature of play before going on to make some new insights.

BENEFITS OF PLAY

Affective/Emotional

- The psychoanalytic tradition of Sigmund and Anna Freud and Erik Erikson suggests that play is a way of children fulfilling their wishes. It is also a therapeutic way of working through their conflicts.

- Vygotsky proposed that play is a means of gratifying impossible desires.

Cognitive

- Piaget systematically studied play and saw it progress through three stages:

  1. Practice of functional play
  2. Symbolic play (constructive and dramatic)
  3. Play with rules

- Vygotsky disagreed with Piaget about the stages but agreed that play stimulates the development of abstract thoughts.

Social

- Psychologists Mildred Parten, Jerome Kagan, and Caroline Howe and anthropologists George Herbert Mead and Jane Goodall studied the socializations aspects of play.

- Vygotsky and his student Daniel Elkonin studied how play stimulates self-regulation skills in children.

Children must conform to the implicit rules of the play situation

- The play situation supports self-regulation skills in a child. S/he is able to operate in the upper level of his/her zone of proximal development in terms of social development.

VYGOTSKIAN DEVELOPMENTAL PATH TO PLAY

A. Necessary components:

- Imaginary situation

- Defined roles

(continued)

- Rules

- Use of language

B. Age-related description of play and development

- Infancy: Emotional attachment is the necessary precursor to learning.

- Children learn to respond to language

- Toddlerhood: Children use objects in a pretend way

- Take on assigned roles

- Early Childhood: Play is the leading activity

- Later childhood: Play loses its primary position but remains valuable

C. Fostering quality play

- Redirect play to replace violent play

- Assure sufficient time for play

- Help plan play

- Provide stimulating, but multipurpose, props

- Help reluctant children enter play by giving them roles

- Encourage dramatic use of the constructions children make

- Help children act out stories

- Model ways of settling disputes

---

through role play or pretend play (Myck-Wayne, 2010). Acting out stories and engaging in dramatic play move the child from immature play, as discussed in the *Play* video, to a mature form of play (Davidson, 2003). It makes stories come to life; for example, when they are reading a book about animals, children will act out the various animals in the book.

Next, participants review books, such as *Brown Bear, Brown Bear, What Do You See?* and role-play situations that allow for dramatic play of stories. Educators act out characters in the stories, considering prompts they might use to have children in their class do the same.

To conclude the institute, participants consider the questions in Handout 3.2 and discuss them in their small group. Likewise, these questions should aid in their personal reflections. These LEARN reflection questions allow the small groups to see how the knowledge from the article and the role plays may support the intentional design of such opportunities in their classrooms. They also spur a thorough examination of what needs to change in their environment to allow for dramatic story telling.

Implementation and Mentoring

In the play implementation and mentoring session, educators will examine actual opportunities to extend intentional planning of play. As in previous implementation and mentoring sessions, educators first fill out Handout 3.3, the mentoring forms on which they indicate their needs and preferences, and submit it to their mentor. Mentors should review the form and provide guidance and feedback as the educator enacts and evaluates intentional play strategies in the educator's classroom. To begin planning play, educators observe the play behaviors of the child in their class and plan play opportunities that match her or his interests. Educators videotape play interactions they have with a specific child as they act out stories based on what they learn in the LEARN IT institute. Videotaping themselves is a challenge for many educators, as they see themselves behaving, reacting, and interacting in ways they never noticed before. Still, over time, and with the help of mentors, educators internalize the importance of this strategy and feel comfortable enough to share the video recording with the mentor.

For example, returning to this chapter's opening vignette, mentor Isabella worked with educator Katie, who refused to allow Lora, a student in her class, to move toys around. After attending the Learning Through Planning Play institute, Katie set a goal to extend intentional play opportunities for each child in her class. To achieve this goal, Isabella guided Katie to videotape her play interactions. Although Katie was initially uneasy about recording herself, Isabella shared the importance of watching play interactions through a different lens and offered to be present in the room during the taping. Katie felt encouraged and filmed several video segments, which she asked Isabelle to provide notes on.

In the implementation and mentoring session, Isabella and Katie went over the mentoring form and discussed whether needs were met. By taking the time and going through the mentoring form, Isabella assisted Katie in reflecting on ways to modify the teaching segment on acting out stories to increase participation, individualization, and interactions with Lora and other children. Later, Katie shared her video-recorded lesson with her peers. She was more confident about her strengths and areas of improvements and was able to articulate that in the supportive learning community. She was also certain that her peers would provide her with constructive feedback to help her improve her practice.

LEARN Planning Play Reflection Questions

L: What new knowledge did you gain from watching the video and reading the article? _____

_____

_____

_____

_____

_____

_____

E: What practical ideas did you get that you can apply in your classroom? _____

_____

_____

_____

_____

_____

_____

A: How are "play" activities planned in your classroom and how do you assess their effectiveness? _____

_____

_____

_____

_____

_____

_____

R: Thinking about becoming an intentional teacher? How can you plan "play" opportunities to enhance learning (e.g., language, social skills) in your classroom? What modifications can you make based on the observations? _____

_____

_____

_____

_____

_____

N: How do others do it? _____

_____

_____

_____

_____

_____

_____

Implementation and Mentoring Form

Educator's name _____ Mentor _____

Site _____ Date _____

Identify the **intentional teaching strategy** you want to **enact**. Select one child to interact with during ☐ center time ☐ small group ☐ individually. Describe the support you would like from your mentor to help you implement the **intentional teaching strategy.**

Intentional teaching strategy of focus:

Culturally Responsive Practice

☐ Choose an area and set it up to reflect children's cultures

☐ Account for child's interest-background and use child's prior knowledge

☐ Inspire child to complete the idea/activity by connecting it to his/her home culture

☐ Provide specific feedback to extend child's play in that area

☐ Question to promote higher-level thinking

Interactional Reading

From *Bringing Words to Life*

☐ Choosing vocabulary words

From Dialogic Reading

☐ Prompt
  o Completion prompt
  o Recall prompt
  o Open-ended prompt
  o Wh- question prompt
  o Distancing prompt

☐ Evaluate the child's response

☐ Expand the child's response

☐ Repeat–child repeats the expanded response

Expanded Vocabulary

☐ Math vocabulary (5 words)

☐ Science vocabulary (5 words)

Assessment and Instruction

☐ Follow child's interest

☐ Observe and record child learning behaviors

☐ Initiate conversations and write plans with child

☐ Provide meaningful learning opportunities informed by assessment

Extending Play

☐ Redirect play to replace violent play

☐ Plan play

☐ Act out stories

☐ Dramatic use of the constructions child makes

Inclusion

☐ Adapt environment

☐ Adapt routines

☐ Adapt materials and activities

☐ Adapt requirements

☐ Adapt instruction

Focus child

Elaborate on how you will implement the intentional teaching strategy.

_____

_____

Continue on back if needed

What type of in-class support do you think will help you?

☐ Modeling while you take notes

☐ Assistance with co-teaching the child

☐ Feedback after observation

☐ Other _____

_____

_____

Use back if needed

Promoting Intentional Teaching: The LEARN Professional Development Model for Early Childhood Educators by Julie K. Kidd, M. Susan Burns, and Ilham Nasser.

Supportive Learning Communities

In their next supportive learning community, educators review and reflect on the importance of fostering and promoting quality play. They will focus on the three components that promote intentional play: planning play, integrating play into the curriculum, and redirecting certain types of play, along with ways to enhance it. To begin this supportive learning community meeting, educators write the three components on a whiteboard and share their understanding and opinions on these. Educators discuss their own experiences with planning, integrating, and redirecting play.

Next, participants complete Handout 3.4, the Self-Assessment of Play Strategies. In completing this handout, educators assess their level of comfort with the strategies and to what extent they are able to utilize them in planning intentional play in their classrooms. The play strategies are part of the knowledge of intentional play in the classroom gained from Bodrova and Leong (2003). Participants then discuss the self-assessments as a large group.

After discussing their self-assessments, participants form pairs and choose two of the strategies from the self-assessment form. The pairs role-play the chosen strategies, focusing on planning play, integrating play into the curriculum, and redirecting certain types of play. For example, they might create a multipurpose center with props that will help a reluctant child enter play using a guided process of planning, playing, and reviewing along with the teacher. After each role play, the supportive learning community assesses the value of each, to promote intentional play planning as the educators relate to the children in their classrooms. Likewise, participants share ideas and reflections with each other.

Figure 3.1 is a checklist of this LEARN professional development strand that the professional development team can use to assess whether they implemented all aspects of the learning through play module. While planning and implementing the LEARN IT activity on planning play, facilitators can use this checklist as a tool to guide the process. All aspects of LEARN are utilized across this strand of LEARN IT. Participants engage in learning knowledge and skills specific to play strategies. They have multiple opportunities to enact, assess, and reflect on specific play strategies. They participate in this learning within the context of a supportive learning community that includes mentors and colleagues interested in learning about play.

Self-Assessment of Play Strategies

1- Strategy	Score (1 to 5) 1–Not at all 2–A little 3–Some 4–Comfortable 5–Very comfortable
Providing stimulating and multipurpose props	
Helping reluctant children to enter play by giving them roles	
Encouraging dramatic use of the constructions children make	
Creating imaginary situations for kids	
Integrating different play roles and themes	
Sustaining play situations	

Promoting Intentional Teaching: The LEARN Professional Development Model for Early Childhood Educators
by Julie K. Kidd, M. Susan Burns, and Ilham Nasser.

Checklist for Learning Through Play

	LEARN IT institute	Implementation and mentoring	Supportive learning communities
Learn	❏ Facilitators provided opportunities for participants to learn new knowledge on best practice and effective ways to plan play interactions. Facilitators provided opportunities for participants to learn information on the types of play and setting up a classroom so that play can happen in natural ways.	❏ Mentors engaged participants in further exploring the knowledge learned in the institute and provided additional information on good books to use and ways to enhance acting out stories.	❏ Mentors reviewed the three strategies that were introduced: planning play, integrating play into the curriculum, and redirecting certain types of play. Mentors reviewed the Plan, Do, Review strategy and others in Chapter 2 as part of planning play as a way to increase intentionality.
Enact	❏ Facilitators provided an activity in which participants acted out stories as a strategy to extend play based on the new knowledge they gained.	❏ Mentors encouraged participants to videotape interactions with children during play. Mentors supported participants and provided guidance on interactions with children.	❏ Mentors provided an opportunity to choose two out of a list of strategies generated and role-play them to illustrate ways they use those to enhance the Plan, Do, Review process.
Assess	❏ Facilitators encouraged participants to examine their ideas on which play strategies addressed are part of their daily classroom routines. Facilitators engaged participants in reviewing children's books that would be good examples to use in situations of reading and acting out stories.	❏ Mentors worked with participants to watch the video and identify moments of success and growth while working with the focus child. Mentors worked with participants to review the mentoring form and assess whether they met the need identified on the form.	❏ Mentors provided an opportunity for participants to go through the process of planning play, integrating play into the curriculum, and redirecting certain types of play. Mentors provided an assessment (Handout 3.4) of certain instructional strategies to enhance intentionality in play situations.

Figure 3.1. Checklist for Learning Through Play.

(continued)

Figure 3.1. *(continued)*

Checklist for Learning Through Play

	LEARN IT institute	Implementation and mentoring	Supportive learning communities
Reflect	❐ Facilitators provided opportunities for participants to reflect on the practices they engage in to promote play, the application of role plays and acting out stories in their classrooms, and ways they can enhance skills such as the quality of book reading experiences. Facilitators encouraged participants to share insights they gained from enacting the activities.	❐ Mentors debriefed with participants and reflected on modifications needed in the next play interaction participants will have with children.	❐ Mentors encouraged participants to reflect on the Plan, Do, Review process and ways various strategies extend play and support children's growth and learning through play.
Network	❐ Facilitators provided opportunities for participants to share reactions, attitudes, and challenges they face in play situations and the application of the strategies learned in their classrooms and to share lists of good books to use (e.g., animal books).	❐ Mentors provided guidance, support, and feedback and encouraged participants to engage with the supportive learning community in enacting the play situation and strategy.	❐ Mentors provided opportunities for participants to work with peers to come up with a list of strategies and to share among themselves ideas on what works for them. Mentors encouraged participants to post further ideas to share with others on an online platform that some use.

LEARN ACTIVITY

PROFESSIONAL DEVELOPMENT ACTIVITIES

Integrate Intentional Play to Extend Learning

In this strand, educators further explore the planning of intentional play and ways it can be integrated in the curriculum. This strand builds on the first and focuses on planning play and integrating it in the curriculum. Educators will engage in the institute, implementation and mentoring, and supportive learning communities to master fully and intentionally integrating play.

LEARN IT Institute

Prior to the institute, participants read the article in the Integrate Intentional Play to Extend Learning Resources text box.

INTEGRATE INTENTIONAL PLAY TO EXTEND LEARNING RESOURCES

Seitz, H. J. (2006). The plan: Building on children's interests. *Beyond the Journal: Young Children on the Web.* Retrieved from https://www.brandeis.edu/lemberg/employees/pdf/seitzbuilding.pdf

---

Educators in this strand of LEARN IT participate in an activity that is focused on learning formats and learning centers. It starts by gathering all the prior knowledge in the room about learning formats. This activity is helpful because it assists participants in assessing their practice and classroom play interactions, once changes are made to enact the knowledge learned on intentional play from the previous strand. Participants gather in small groups and create a table with a column listing various familiar learning formats. For example, participants might list 1) large group, 2) small group, 3) play/learning centers, and 4) daily routines. Then, in the second column, they write examples of what they do routinely in each format and reasons why they do it in this manner. Educators reflect on the question, "What do I do routinely in large groups?" and record it in the first row. When the chart is complete, they evaluate the benefits of what they do and whether there are other ways that may be more beneficial. This activity also helps educators examine the various teaching strategies they utilize and increases their intentionality in planning daily routines.

Next, the focus moves to learning centers. Before the session, the facilitator prepares colored strips of paper that have names of the various learning centers. Participants select a strip that reflects a learning center they have in their classrooms, such as dramatic play, art, science blocks, sand/water/sensory table, and classroom library. Then the groups tell, draw, or role-play ideas of how they may effectively use an intentional teaching strategy with children engaged in play in specific learning centers. Participants model the activity at a learning center, provide a modification to make the learning center more effective, or tell about a teaching technique that they found to work effectively with children. For example, it may make sense to add pencils and paper to the dramatic play center so that children can write and/or draw scripts and stories.

In the same small groups, participants discuss the assigned article, "The Plan." Through reading and discussion, they learn new information on how to intentionally plan play and other activities, keeping in mind the interests and needs of each child. This article proposes ideas on including play planning in the curriculum and across content. For example, planning for several small groups of children in the classroom who share similar interests or planning for individual children that is woven into the large-group planning process. The institute format allows for exploring various planning methods that teachers use themselves and working with the group to create others.

Implementation and Mentoring

This implementation and mentoring focuses on developing educators' use of intentional teaching strategies during play and on empowering and supporting educators in taking a

86

risk. Before the session, participants fill out Handout 3.5, reflecting on areas in their classroom, along with Handout 3.3, the Implementation and Mentoring Form. Participants share both with their mentor before or at the start of their next implementation and mentoring session. Through the reflection questions, each educator has a chance to assess the area that works best and share reflections with the mentor on what makes it work. During the debrief, the mentor should ask further reflective questions and discuss with the educator effective learning environments that promote play. After this discussion, the mentor and educator should focus more closely on the strategy that the educator wishes to implement. The mentor should provide guidance and feedback as the educator enacts, integrates, and reflects on play strategies.

For example, educator Katie used the mentoring form to indicate where further support is needed in her classroom and to make sure she was implementing play to extend learning in an efficient and intentional way. During the time Katie had with her mentor, Isabella, the conversation focused on Katie's ways of setting up centers and the flexibility allowed within the boundaries she sets or is forced to set. Isabella and Katie explored variations of play centers that may be mobile and flexible and meet the needs of Lora, Katie's student. For example, the housekeeping center may have a bucket of plastic and pretend fruits and vegetables that is mobile and Lora may move to the blocks area where she may build a store or a house in which to store them. Isabella also worked with Katie on identifying power struggles that may have been part of the dynamic with Lora; she noted how important it was to name that dynamic and be aware of it. Lora was pushing the boundaries, and Katie responded from a place of control and refused the challenge. This was not an intentional act and was not driven with Lora's needs in mind.

Supportive Learning Communities

Intentional teachers repeatedly think of ways to enhance play experiences and reinforce learning. In the supportive learning communities, educators focus on ways to do so. In particular, the group focuses on being intentional about outdoor activities. Outdoor play is as important as indoor play and usually is a neglected area in curriculum planning. Offering outdoor play that is structured and intentional helps prevent behavioral issues and provides outdoor options for those who need it. During the supportive learning communities, participants have an opportunity to explore intentional teaching strategies during outdoor play. Participants bring their weekly or monthly plans to the meeting. As a group, they brainstorm ideas to enhance outdoor play. Then, participants work in pairs and exchange ideas. The pairs intentionally plan one outdoor learning center that allows for free play, for each of their lesson plans. For example, if an educator has an art activity planned, he or she may consider taking out easels, paper, and markers or other available indoor materials that can transfer easily to the outdoors.

As a second activity, participants draw a map of ways they might structure an outdoor thematic play session and outline strategies to set one up. Once they establish structure, participants list ways that the structure allows for a safe flow of children playing and interacting with the centers, a safe setup of materials outdoors, and ways to avoid accidents or angry children. Finally, as a group, educators discuss and share additional challenges that might stem from the outdoor space, materials, or other challenges.

Figure 3.2 is a checklist of this LEARN IT strand for the professional development team to use to assess whether they implemented all aspects of integrating intentional play to extend learning. Facilitators use the checklist as a tool to guide the planning and implementation process of their LEARN IT professional development program. All aspects of LEARN are utilized across this strand of LEARN IT. Participants engage in learning knowledge and skills specific to integrating intentional play to extend learning. They have multiple opportunities to enact, assess, and reflect on specific strategies that integrate play to extend learning. They participate in this learning within the context of a supportive learning community that includes mentors and colleagues interested in learning about integrating intentional play to extend learning.

Reflecting on Your Classroom

Please answer the reflection questions below and share them with your mentor at your next implementation and mentoring session.

1. What is one area in your classroom that works well, in relation to play? _____ .

_____

_____

_____

_____

_____

_____

_____

_____

_____

_____

_____

_____

2. Why is this area successful? _____

_____

_____

_____

_____

_____

_____

_____

_____

_____

_____

_____

_____

Checklist for Integrating Intentional Play to Extend Learning

	LEARN IT institute	Implementation and mentoring	Supportive learning communities
Learn	☐ Facilitators provided opportunities to learn new knowledge on learning formats and how they work and on learning centers and how to enhance them. Facilitators provided information on planning play in ways that address needs of children as a group and individuals and ways to integrate play during daily routines.	☐ Mentors provided further knowledge related to information learned in the institute and gave participants additional information on identifying areas of the classroom that really worked well.	☐ Facilitators reviewed the ways to design and plan outdoor play as part of the curriculum and ways to enhance outdoor play.
Enact	☐ Facilitators engaged participants in an activity in which they told, drew, or role-played strategies to enhance play in learning centers, including ways to adapt.	☐ Mentors encouraged participants to observe in their classrooms and identify the areas that worked well, especially the centers that promote intentional play.	☐ Facilitators asked participants to come up with ways to design a learning center that can be carried on outdoors based on the theme in the curriculum and ways and strategies to activate it.
Assess	☐ Facilitators encouraged participants to examine their ideas as well as new ones on play strategies in various learning formats and in various play centers. Facilitators provided an opportunity for participants to try out the planning process described in the article and ways to improve integration of the group needs and individual children's needs.	☐ Mentors encouraged participants to assess the various centers and how they worked. Mentors reviewed the mentoring form with participants and determined whether they met the need identified on the form.	☐ Facilitators asked participants to draw a map with information on where to locate the outdoor learning center and how to ensure the safe flow of activities.

Figure 3.2. Checklist for Integrating Intentional Play to Extend Learning.

(continued)

Figure 3.2. *(continued)*

Checklist for Integrating Intentional Play to Extend Learning

	LEARN IT institute	**Implementation and mentoring**	**Supportive learning communities**
Reflect	❏ Facilitators provided opportunities for participants to reflect on the practices they engage in to promote play and the application of these in their classrooms and ways they can integrate play in their curriculum and existing routines.	❏ Mentors debriefed with participants and encouraged them to reflect on modifications needed to make other centers in the classroom work well.	❏ Mentors encouraged participants to reflect on the plan to enhance the outdoor play components in the curriculum and the need to integrate that in the weekly or daily plans.
Network	❏ Facilitators encouraged participants to share successes and challenges they face in the various learning centers and ways they integrate play with each other.	❏ Mentors provided guidance, support, and feedback and on the enhancement of learning centers and play interactions.	❏ Mentors provided participants with an opportunity to work with peers on developing outdoor plans and sharing ideas on learning centers that work outdoors.

SUMMARY

This chapter on play aimed to provide insights and new knowledge on play and the importance of teachers being intentional even when they plan free play. We recommended various activities on how to utilize play to enhance learning and growth in all domains. The design of the LEARN IT activities around play provides guidance on planning professional development opportunities and ways to enhance educators' practice. This chapter also provided guidance and tips on planning play environments and collaborating with families.

Including Each Child

4

With Leah S. Muccio

As mentioned in Chapter 2, Joan is a Head Start educator who works with an instructional assistant, Hector. Their class has three children with IEPs, two male and one female. Although they have quite different abilities, interests, and disability diagnoses, these children—Gavin, Faith, and Javier—have positive one-on-one interactions with their peers and teachers. Each student succeeds during one-on-one instruction with teachers, in which they are provided with appropriate learning opportunities such as multiple representations when new material is presented (e.g., storybooks with puppets or action figures to act out stories to develop listening comprehension). They all have difficulty in social interactions with their peers, especially during centers time, though their delayed language and social skills isolate them in large- and small-group activities, too. All have English as their home language. Joan finds it challenging to provide them with high-quality learning opportunities and relies primarily on the special education teacher who delivers push-in services to meet their learning needs. This chapter focuses on Joan's three young students with IEPs.

Gavin has an intellectual disability with general delays in all areas of development. He is a strong swimmer and would spend all of his time in his community pool with his mother, if he could. Most of the time, he plays by himself, and his play is somewhat repetitive. He and his classmates have not yet learned how to play together. Occasionally, Gavin tries to initiate play with others but is mostly rejected by peers. This motivation to play with his peers and his common interest with some of his peers in superheroes are strengths that Joan and Hector want to build upon. Still, both educators have difficulty meeting Gavin's needs given all the other needs of their students.

Faith has language delays with no intellectual or physical disabilities. She loves painting at the easel and often paints pictures for her baby sister. She has some social problems during more structured learning activities and in play, but it is unclear if the problems stem from social-emotional sources or language problems. When activities have ample visual cues, she can participate successfully with peers, but miscommunication can happen. If misunderstood by peers or adults in the classroom, she gets frustrated and resists being redirected. She can have physical outbursts that seem unprovoked. Hector believes the outbursts are provoked by Faith's frustration given her language/communication problems. Joan and Hector have observed times in which Faith's visual strengths have been a source of help to other students in the class; for example, in completing puzzles.

Javier loves to run on the playground and play with puppets and stuffed animals in the puppet theater. He is extremely active and easily distracted. He is also large for his age, and this makes his unregulated behavior seem more disruptive. His behavior was worse this year. Others in the program believe his grandmother's death has greatly affected him. He is able to develop the skills and knowledge from most lessons presented to him, when Joan or Hector can pull his attention to the activity at hand. Joan and Hector mention that he quickly picks up on new concepts that grab his attention; for example, types of race cars. He is caring about his peers and teachers but often bangs into them or interrupts their play (e.g., knocks over blocks in children's construction) by accident. Joan and Hector also are mindful that, at times, Hector hits or screams at other children when engaged in interactions that include one or more of his classmates.

Joan's goal is to have the skills needed to make necessary adaptations so that she can include the children with disabilities in all the learning experiences in her inclusive classroom. She wants the children with disabilities to feel a sense of belonging in the classroom and wants to contribute to the children meeting their IEP goals. For example, when interacting with children during center time, she might take the opportunity to draw several children into the activity and promote their positive interactions. She wants to be able to direct Hector to best meet the children's needs. Hector would like to spend less time redirecting inappropriate behavior and more time interacting with all the children together. Both Joan and Hector find that there are times when they need more strategies to support the children with disabilities to be fully included in their classroom.

WHAT TO EXPECT IN THIS CHAPTER

Many early educators, like Joan and Hector, engage in professional development to enhance the quality of the instruction they provide for each individual child in their classroom, including children with disabilities. They are seeking professional development that focuses on the supports, adaptations, and accommodations that promote the success of each child. When professional development does not address the strengths and needs of the particular children in their classrooms, they are left wondering how to adapt what they have learned for each child in their classroom. LEARN IT professional development is focused on including each child in classroom interactions. Intentional instruction can provide the knowledge and strategies that educators need to make informed instructional decisions that benefit each individual child. This chapter

- Provides foundational information on *including each and every child,* with a special focus on children with disabilities

- Addresses *empirical work as well as wisdom from the field* on inclusion and adaptations for children with disabilities, focusing on children in preschool and kindergarten. (These are the areas we emphasize, as we believe the participants in the professional development should already possess foundational knowledge of various disabilities, the law, and professional standards for early childhood special education. If this is not the case, we suggest they read about this in an introductory text, such as

Preschool Education in Today's World: Teaching Children With Diverse Backgrounds and Abilities [Burns, Johnson, & Assaf, 2012]).

- Discusses the importance of intentional interactions, and outlines two LEARN IT professional development activities with a focus on the following:

  - *Learning* by linking the background information to practical knowledge teachers can use to include each child and family in their classrooms

  - *Enacting* and providing strategies for including each child in the classroom

  - *Assessing* the effectiveness of the strategies enacted

  - *Reflecting* to make informed and intentional instructional decisions

  - *Networking* with colleagues and mentors and sharing ideas for making these strategies work in their early childhood education classrooms

FOUNDATIONS: INCLUSIVE EARLY CHILDHOOD EDUCATION

Including children with disabilities is a key aspect of intentional teaching (Soukakou, Winton, West, Sideris, & Rucker, 2014) and a core value in early education and care (Guralnick & Bruder, 2016). Inclusive early childhood education teachers actively address the diverse developmental needs of children with disabilities (Dinnebeil, Boat, & Bae, 2013) within a general education setting, so that children with and without disabilities learn and play together. Although for children with and without disabilities, sharing the same physical space in an early childhood classroom is requisite, educators have to go further for successful inclusion of young children with disabilities; inclusive classrooms instead require specialized instructional practices (Barton & Smith, 2014; Nguyen & Hughes, 2012). Including each child means ensuring that all children have high-quality, individualized interactions with adults in the classroom (Cate, Diefendorf, McCullough, Peters, & Whaley, 2010; Hebbeler & Spiker, 2016). Although inclusion takes different forms, the outcomes of successful inclusion for children with disabilities and their families are a sense of belonging and membership, active participation in classroom activities, and access to positive social relationships, so that the children can reach their full potential within a diverse society (Division for Early Childhood of the Council for Exceptional Children & National Association for the Education of Young Children [DEC/NAEYC], 2009; National Professional Development Center on Inclusion, 2009; Odom, Buysse, & Soukakou, 2011).

Successful inclusion of children with disabilities in early childhood settings remains a challenge for teachers and assistant teachers (Barton & Smith, 2015). Most early childhood teachers, administrators, and parents express positive attitudes toward inclusive education (Guralnick & Bruder, 2016; Hsieh & Hsieh, 2012) and believe that inclusive settings provide benefits for children with and without disabilities (Guo, Sawyer, Justice, & Kaderavek, 2013). However, concerns persist about the ability of programs like Head Start to fully meet the needs of children with disabilities (Muccio & Kidd, 2018). Both preservice and in-service early childhood teachers often feel uncomfortable or unprepared to fully meet the needs of children with disabilities in their classrooms (e.g., Carrington, Berthelsen, Nickerson, & Nicholson, 2016; Rakap, Cig, & Parlak-Rakap, 2015). In a recent study, Head Start professionals indicated that they did not have the needed supports in place to facilitate successful inclusion of all children (Muccio, Kidd, White, & Burns, 2014). They were concerned that they did not possess the specialized knowledge and skills needed to work with children with varying abilities. Not having access to quality professional development focused on including each child can serve as a barrier for successful inclusion; therefore, professional development that integrates specific knowledge and skills related to inclusion is needed (Muccio et al.). According to Yang and Rusli (2012), "the key to making inclusion successful is the availability of effective inclusion strategies and teacher training" (p. 54).

Why Inclusion for Each Child?

Inclusion for children with disabilities in preschool and kindergarten settings is supported by legal mandate, increasing societal acceptance for ability diversity, and a large body of research that demonstrates that inclusion benefits children with and without disabilities (Guralnick & Bruder, 2016; Odom et al., 2004; Warren, Martinez, & Sortino, 2016). The Individuals with Disabilities Education Improvement Act (IDEA) of 2004 (PL 108-446), a United States federal law introduced in its initial form in 1975, expanded to include preschool-age children in 1986, and most recently reauthorized in 2004, guarantees children with disabilities a free and appropriate public education in the least restrictive environment. The least restrictive environment means that children with disabilities have the opportunity to be placed with children with typical development whenever it is possible and beneficial (Barton & Smith, 2015). In addition to meeting legal mandates, inclusion of children with disabilities yields positive academic, social, affective, and developmental benefits for children, families, and communities (Barton & Smith; Odom et al., 2011).

Young children in inclusive programs do as well as or better than children in self-contained programs or in programs without children with disabilities (National Professional Development Center on Inclusion, 2009). For children with disabilities, research has indicated that children in inclusive settings are better able to learn (e.g., Lee, Yeung, Tracey, & Barker, 2015), have higher levels of active engagement in classroom activities (e.g., Jolivette, Stichter, Sibilsky, & Ridgely, 2002), make significant progress in academic skills such as language and literacy development (e.g., Stanton-Chapman & Brown, 2015), and develop friendships and social skills (e.g., Hollingsworth & Buysse, 2009). For children with typical development, research has indicated that these children also benefit from inclusive settings (Odom et al., 2011). Benefits of inclusion for children with typical development include the following:

- Positive attitudes toward ability diversity (e.g., Rafferty, Boettcher, & Griffin, 2001)

- Improved leadership and autonomy in the classroom (e.g., Fuchs, Fuchs, & Burish, 2000)

- Increased self-esteem and confidence (e.g., Katz & Chard, 2000)

- Improved prosocial behaviors based on a sense of fairness and equity (e.g., Diamond & Hong, 2010)

Furthermore, research confirms that children with typical development

• Make developmental gains in inclusive programs equal to those in programs without children with diagnosed disabilities (e.g., Odom, DeKlyen, & Jenkins, 1984)

• Build positive knowledge and attitudes about children with disabilities (Diamond & Huang, 2005)

• Develop voluntary and mutually enjoyable friendships with children with disabilities (e.g., Buysse, Goldman, & Skinner, 2002)

• Learn compassion and empathy (Cross, Traub, Hutter-Pishgahi, & Shelton, 2004).

However, research also indicates that in order for children to experience these benefits, the quality of the inclusive practices in these settings is an important factor (Barton & Smith, 2015; Soukakou et al., 2014) and that specialized approaches to adapt and differentiate instruction to best meet the individual needs of children with disabilities contribute to higher-quality environments for young children with disabilities (Division for Early Childhood, 2014; Grisham-Brown, Pretti-Frontczak, Hawkins, & Winchell, 2009; Strain & Bovey, 2011).

Adapting and Differentiating Instruction for Children with Disabilities

The joint position statement from DEC/NAEYC defines early childhood inclusion as

> The values, policies, and practices that support the right of every infant and young child and his or her family, regardless of ability, to participate in a broad range of activities and contexts as full members of families, communities, and society. The desired results of inclusive experiences for children with and without disabilities and their families include a sense of belonging and membership, positive social relationships and friendships, and development and learning to reach their full potential. (DEC/NAEYC, 2009, p. 2)

The position statement focuses on the key factors for successful inclusive experiences for infants, toddlers, and preschool-aged children with disabilities. Access, participation, and supports are the components that characterize high-quality inclusive early childhood programs.

Access is evident in early childhood programs where "a wide range of learning opportunities, activities, settings, and environments" (DEC/NAEYC, 2009, p. 2) are available to children with disabilities. The participation and support dimensions of the definition move beyond enrollment to encompass coordinated systems, specialized services, and individualized accommodations that enable children with disabilities to participate fully in play and learning experiences and for all children to experience a sense of belonging in these settings. The authors asserted that "having a common understanding of what inclusion means is fundamentally important for determining what types of practices and supports are necessary to achieve high quality inclusion" (DEC/NAEYC, 2009, p. 1). The DEC/NAEYC early childhood inclusion definition provides practitioners and researchers with a framework to successfully implement and evaluate the inclusion of young children with disabilities in preschool and kindergarten classrooms and has proved valuable in the professional development.

The National Professional Development Center on Inclusion (2011) provided a compilation of evidence-based practices that support early childhood inclusion, divided into the features of high-quality inclusion defined in the position statement, access, participation, and supports (DEC/NAEYC, 2009). The practices that support access and the practices that support participation fall under the broader umbrella of adaptations and differentiated instruction. The broadest concept is differentiation. According to Tomlinson (2000), "Whenever a teacher reaches out to an individual or small group to vary his or her teaching in order to create the best learning experience possible, that teacher is differentiating instruction" (p. 2). Adaptations are the specific actions the teachers take in the classroom to differentiate their instruction. Adaptations "promote children's learning and development by allowing children to more effectively participate in activities and routines in their natural environments" and "function as a 'bridge' or a mediator between the skills that a child can currently perform and the requirements or expectations of an activity or routines" (Milbourne, 2009, p. 1). The goal is for teachers to provide adaptations that cause the least disruption or make the children who are getting extra supports stand out the least from the other children in the group. Table 4.1 details the quality inclusive practices related to differentiation and adaptations in early childhood settings.

The Professional Development Activities section that follows describes two LEARN IT activities that are specifically planned to enhance educators' knowledge and skills in inclusion. The first activity focuses on including each child and the second focuses on adapting and differentiating instruction. Each activity allocates time to discuss the knowledge and literature on including each child and engages educators in multifaceted professional development.

Table 4.1. Inclusive practices

Practices that support access	Universal design (UD)/universal design for learning (UDL)	UD and UDL support access to early care and education environments through the removal of physical and structural barriers (UD) and the provision of multiple and varied formats for instruction and learning (UDL).
	Assistive technology (AT)	AT interventions involve a range of strategies to promote a child's access to learning opportunities, from making simple changes to the environment and materials to helping a child use special equipment. Combining AT with effective teaching promotes the child's participation in learning and relating to others.
Practices that support participation	Embedded instruction and other naturalistic interventions	Embedded instruction and intervention strategies address specific developmental or learning goals within the context of everyday activities, routines, and transitions at home, at school, or in the community.
	Scaffolding strategies	Scaffolding strategies are structured, targeted approaches that can be used with children who require more intensive supports across a wide variety of teaching and learning contexts and in combination with other approaches. Scaffolding strategies include modeling, response prompting, variations of prompting and modeling, peer supports, and corrective feedback.
	Tiered models of instruction/intervention	Tiered models of instruction offer a framework that can be used in early childhood to help practitioners connect children's formative assessment results with specific teaching and intervention strategies.

Including Each Child

This strand of LEARN IT helps early childhood educators select and develop adaptations to classroom practices that increase a child's independent participation with the least amount of hands-on assistance by the teacher. As discussed earlier in this chapter, less intrusive adaptations allow children to more successfully interact with their peers. Therefore, during the LEARN institute, implementation and mentoring, and supportive learning communities, educators will develop their understandings of what it means to include each child. Educators must also learn skills to enact effective, evidence-based strategies that result in positive learning outcomes for each child.

LEARN IT Institute

Before the LEARN IT institute convenes, participants should read the Foundations section of this chapter along with one of the articles listed in the Including Each Child Resources text box.

INCLUDING EACH CHILD RESOURCES

Cross, A. F. (2004). Adaptations to support development and membership. *Early childhood center inclusion research series: Children with significant disabilities in inclusive community settings.* Bloomington, IA: Indiana University, Indiana Institute on Disability and Community, Early Childhood Center. Retrieved from https://www.iidc.indiana.edu/styles/iidc/defiles/ecc/inclres-adaptations.pdf

Milbourne, S. A., & Campbell, P. H. (2012). *CARA's kit: Creating adaptations for routines and activities.* Philadelphia, PA: Child and Family Studies Research Programs, Thomas Jefferson University. (Read pages 1–4.)

Sandall, S. R. (2003). Play modifications for children with disabilities. *Young Children, 58*(3), 54–57.

The first institute on including each child will begin with an introductory movement activity (Catlett, 2009). To set up, facilitators should post signs on the wall with the following text. Include one sign for each of the following bullets:

- Pull off the road, move under a streetlight, and change the tire on my own.

- Take off the old tire, take a break, and then put on the spare tire.

- Use a tire patch kit to plug the hole, and drive to a service station.

- Call a friend to walk you through the process step-by-step, and change the tire.

- Flag someone down to help, give him or her the spare tire and jack, and watch as that person changes the tire.

- Call the road service to get the tired changed or get the car towed to a service station.

When signs are posted and participants arrive, participants read the following scenario:

Imagine that you are driving at night, when you blow a tire. What will you do?

Participants review each of the posted signs and place themselves on the continuum by going to stand under a sign taped on the wall that describes the action they would most likely take.

The continuum is organized by most to least independent solutions. Everyone along the continuum will achieve the goal of getting that tire changed. Educators should discuss what is different for each of the choices (the level of support). Educators further discuss how they feel to be at the top end of the continuum of solutions, where they are independent, or at the bottom, where they are totally dependent on others. They explore how everyone has different abilities and needs levels of support in different areas and how abilities change when provided different levels of support. Further, participants discuss the level of support needed from others and the stigma of dependency. Participants leave the discussion with a renewed sense of what people with disabilities might experience when they are dependent upon others to function. They will also take away the idea that the adaptations that teachers provide can significantly affect children's ability to complete a task. Within the tire changing continuum, as the levels of support increase, the focus is on adapting the situation to be able to change the tire rather than fixing a participant's skill deficit. This has meaningful implications for participants' work with children with disabilities. By focusing on what diverse children can do with the appropriate supports, teachers can begin to more effectively promote participation and enhance learning activities for all children.

Next, participants discuss the preassigned readings. In small or large groups, participants relate the knowledge they learned from the reading and connect it to planning instruction that includes each child. Then, participants review Handout 4.1 and discuss the meaning of the adaptations continuum. The adaptations continuum describes each type of adaptation from least intrusive to most intrusive (Milbourne & Campbell, 2012).

The least intrusive adaptation along the continuum is to adapt the environment, both to adapt the room set-up and to adapt or select the appropriate equipment. Adaptations to the environment require changes to the classroom setting. Examples of adaptations to the environment include 1) rearranging the classroom furniture to ensure there are accessible pathways so a child in a wheelchair or crutches can move around freely and 2) providing slant boards and table lamps at the art center to support children with reduced visual acuity.

The next adaptation is to adapt the activity or routine. Specific activities or routines can be added or modified during the school day. Examples of adaptations to activities and routines include 1) providing opportunities for movement during story reading for children who have difficulty paying attention or 2) reviewing a visual schedule during circle time for children who are supported by predictable routines.

The next adaptation along the continuum is to adapt the materials. Materials used in an activity or routine are changed to support a child's participation. These adaptations are increasingly intrusive because other children may notice if a child is using special materials. Examples of adaptations to materials include 1) using a rubber band around the blades of scissors to make it easier for a child with fine motor challenges to cut or 2) elevating the sand table to an appropriate height so children in wheelchairs can use it.

The next adaptation is to adapt the requirements or instruction. Changes to what children should do during an activity or routine or to the way a teacher provides instruction to them can support their participation. Examples of adaptations to requirements or instruction include 1) ensuring that a child completes each step of a multistep activity before providing the next direction or 2) allowing a child with sensory issues to use gloves to play with clay.

The final and most intrusive adaptation along the continuum is to provide assistance. It involves another child or an adult actually helping the child to participate in the activity or routine. Examples of assistance include 1) providing a child with hand-over-hand support while he or she is writing or 2) having a child help a peer to put on dramatic play clothes.

To further this exploration, participants review the CARA's Kit (Milbourne & Campbell, 2012) reading. CARA stands for Creating Adaptations for Routines and Activities, and it provides a tool for teachers to implement effective adaptations to promote children's participation in everyday activities and routines and to enhance opportunities for children to learn in a natural environment. The goal of using the adaptations continuum is to create a situation more conducive to participation and learning while the children participate as independently as possible. Educators should align the level of intrusion depicted in Handout 4.1

Adaptations Continuum

Least intrusive → Most intrusive

Adapt environment
- Adapt room set-up
- Adapt/select equipment

Select or adapt activity or routine

Adapt materials

Adapt requirements or instruction

Provide assistance

Notes:

Source: Campbell, P. H., Kennedy, A. A., & Milbourne, S. A. (2012). *CARA's Kit for Toddlers: Creating Adaptations for Routines and Activities.* Baltimore, MD: Paul H. Brookes Publishing Co.

with the "flat tire" experience they enacted in the LEARN IT institute. They should consider the continuum of tire-changing choices and discuss what they notice. Each action on the tire continuum is an example of one type of adaptation on the adaptation continuum in *CARA's Kit*. Working with a partner, participants then decide which action on the tire continuum matches the different levels of adaptations on the adaptations continuum. To review this information, participants return to the large group and call out the adaptation (e.g., "Pull off the road, move under a streetlight, and change the tire on my own" is an example of an adaptation of the environment). Participants note that the tire continuum has examples of each type of modification in the adaptations continuum, from least to most intrusive.

Next, participants complete Handout 4.2, Adaptations in My Own Class. After they have completed the form, they should divide into small groups. For this activity, a count-off strategy is useful so that participants become acquainted with a wide range of peers in the professional development program and interact with participants who teach children with different disabilities and needs. Group size should be determined by the number of professional development facilitators available; at least four people should be in each small group.

Participants share their examples of adaptations and their reflection on why this represents a particular level of intrusiveness. Participants' responses serve as a basis for a discussion of each of the adaptations. As the conversation evolves, facilitators correct any misunderstandings of an adaptation presented by participants to be confident that each participant understood multiple exemplars of each level of adaptation. Participants can make changes on their handout as needed, so that they have them for future use.

Implementation and Mentoring

In the LEARN IT professional development strand of including each child, the focus is to provide educators with support to implement adaptations and to differentiate their instruction and interactions with the children. Mentoring will highlight practices that support access and participation in their classrooms. As with previous mentoring and implementation sessions, educators first fill out the Implementation and Mentoring Form, Handout 4.3, and submit it to their mentor. The mentor's aim is to address the most significant challenges identified by participants, in order to enable them to better meet the needs of each child in their classroom, particularly focusing on the children with disabilities. Mentors provide feedback and guidance to support educators as they enact, assess, and reflect on the strategies learned in the institute and through the readings.

To exemplify a mentor supporting educators as they implement strategies to support all children, we return to Joan's Head Start classroom, discussed earlier in the chapter. In Joan's classroom, she and Hector found that the children loved games and were beginning to develop the turn-taking and self-regulation skills needed to play simple games such as Hi Ho Cherry-O and Connect 4 as well as teacher-created board games. As part of the classwide behavior system, children elected to have special time to play games at the end of the day as their reward. As mentioned in the vignette in the beginning of this chapter, Javier is one of the three children in Joan's classroom who has an IEP. Javier, who has been diagnosed with emotional and behavior issues and received support from the program behavioral specialist following his grandmother's death last year, eagerly wished to join in on the game playing. However, when he entered a game, he was not able to follow the rules and found it especially challenging to wait for his turn. It got to the point where the other children did not want him to play games with them. Even as an observer to the games, Javier often disrupted them by knocking over the board or pieces, hitting or kicking other children, or screaming in the children's faces.

Adaptations in My Class

Review the information about the types of adaptations and the level of intrusiveness of the different types of adaptations. Jot down notes about one adaptation you use at each of the levels below. Although you may use many adaptations throughout the day, list only one in each area for this activity. We will discuss them in small groups after you complete this form.

1. Adapt environment (adapt room set-up)

2. Adapt environment (adapt/select equipment)

3. Select or adapt activity or routine

4. Adapt materials

5. Adapt requirements or instruction

6. Provide assistance

To be completed by early educators

Implementation and Mentoring Form

Educator's name _____   Mentor _____

Site _____   Date _____

Identify the **intentional teaching strategy** you want to **enact**. Select one child to interact with during ☐ center time ☐ small group ☐ individually. Describe the support you would like from your mentor to help you implement the **intentional teaching strategy.**

Intentional teaching strategy of focus:

Culturally Responsive Practice

☐ Choose an area and set it up to reflect children's cultures

☐ Account for child's interest-background and use child's prior knowledge

☐ Inspire child to complete the idea/activity by connecting it to his/her home culture

☐ Provide specific feedback to extend child's play in that area

☐ Question to promote higher-level thinking

Interactional Reading

From *Bringing Words to Life*

☐ Choosing vocabulary words

From Dialogic Reading

☐ Prompt
  ○ Completion prompt
  ○ Recall prompt
  ○ Open-ended prompt
  ○ Wh- question prompt
  ○ Distancing prompt

☐ Evaluate the child's response

☐ Expand the child's response

☐ Repeat–child repeats the expanded response

Expanded Vocabulary

☐ Math vocabulary (5 words)

☐ Science vocabulary (5 words)

Assessment and Instruction

☐ Follow child's interest

☐ Observe and record child learning behaviors

☐ Initiate conversations and write plans with child

☐ Provide meaningful learning opportunities informed by assessment

Extending Play

☐ Redirect play to replace violent play

☐ Plan play

☐ Act out stories

☐ Dramatic use of the constructions child makes

Inclusion

☐ Adapt environment

☐ Adapt routines

☐ Adapt materials and activities

☐ Adapt requirements

☐ Adapt instruction

Focus child _____

Elaborate on how you will implement the intentional teaching strategy. _____

_____

_____

Continue on back if needed

What type of in-class support do you think will help you?

☐ Modeling while you take notes

☐ Assistance with co-teaching the child

☐ Feedback after observation

☐ Other _____

Use back if needed

As Joan saw that the once-cherished game time was often ending in tears and frustration, she decided to focus on providing intentional adaptations to this classroom activity to work toward Javier's successful participation. She wanted this to be an enjoyable time for all the children. In discussing this situation with her mentor, Marie, she admitted that she had begun to dread game-playing time and found that her assistant teacher, Hector, would frequently find reasons to leave the room during that time. Hector's stress and frustration were evident, and Joan admitted she felt the same stress and frustration; she also believed that the other children did not deserve to be mistreated by Javier. She found herself resorting to sending Javier to another classroom during game play. She thought she was spending excessive time redirecting his negative behavior.

After attending the LEARN IT institute on including all children, Joan elected to apply the approaches in order to promote Javier's more successful inclusion into classroom learning activities, specifically working toward enabling him to play games with the other children. During a mentoring meeting to plan the next steps, Marie, Joan, and Hector collectively decided it would be a long-term process to try out (enact) and evaluate (assess) the impact of the adaptations to support Javier during game time. They agreed that Marie would observe and document with anecdotal notes at least once, as first Joan, then Hector, implemented their adaptations with Javier. They also agreed that Joan and Hector would jot down their thoughts about implementation before Marie came back to the classroom the following week, to provide an opportunity to assess and reflect on the adaptations implemented.

During the planning meeting, Joan, Hector, and Marie worked to define an appropriate short-term goal for Javier's behavior and decided to focus first on Javier participating as an observer to the games without any harmful or disruptive behavior. This would allow the other children to begin to accept him and would allow Javier to gradually move toward playing the games. They decided that it would be helpful if Joan or Hector facilitated Javier's game observation to promote the safety of the other children. With Marie's support, Joan and Hector decided to try this in combination with the least intrusive adaptation of changing the environment. They thought that moving the game from the floor to the table might give the activity a bit more structure. By being a bit removed from the busier and noisier environment of the children playing on the carpet, Javier would be able to focus on maintaining his self-control during the game. Rather than excluding Javier from the game playing, the goal was to provide him with the needed supports to enable him to be in the room peacefully with other children while they played the games.

During the first day that Joan implemented the new adaptations, Javier quickly became frustrated, knocking over his chair. Joan needed to physically block him from hitting one of the other children at the table. During the remainder of the week, Joan and Hector reported to their mentor that Javier continued to exhibit challenging behavior during the game-playing sessions. Javier struck Joan during one of these interactions, and she and Hector reported being discouraged because the adaptations were not having their intended impact. Although they wanted to return to excluding Javier from game playing and the behavior specialist also wanted to remove Javier from the classroom, after a discussion with Marie, the educators determined that they needed to provide a more comprehensive intervention. In increasing the level of intervention, Joan and Hector hoped that with more support, Javier might be able to decrease his undesirable behavior.

Together, they adapted the materials by introducing Javier to Waiting Walter, a stuffed animal walrus for Javier to hold to occupy him as he waited. They created a social story for Javier about turn-taking that incorporated Waiting Walter. Social stories are individualized short stories used when a child is experiencing challenges in a specific situation. The purpose of using social stories is to provide children with a better understanding of the expectations in a situation, along with repeated opportunities to review them (Head Start Center for Inclusion, n.d.). They read Javier the story in the morning and introduced the stuffed animal to him. See Figure 4.1 for the Waiting Walter social story. Marie sat with Joan and Javier as she introduced the story and the stuffed animal and provided feedback to Joan, including the recommendation for Javier to associate Walter specifically with game playing.

Joan told Javier that Walter would come out to help him to wait his turn during game-playing time. She sent home a copy of the social story for Javier to read with his aunt, who is his custodial parent. Joan sent an e-mail to Marie relating that during the afternoon, Javier had thrown Walter at another child during game-playing time, and she expressed concern that this adaptation was not working. However, Marie replied to Joan and encouraged her to persist with this strategy and to continue reading the story with Javier each day.

During her next classroom visit the following week, Marie noted that Javier was carrying around the social story and he told her in detail about Walter. Javier was able to observe the game-playing without interrupting or having an outburst. Marie noticed that Javier squeezed the stuffed animal very tightly during the game when he seemed to be frustrated, but that the toy seemed to provide him with an outlet for his frustration. After the game-playing session, Marie was encouraged. Joan and Hector provided Javier with very positive feedback that he and Walter could wait their turn.

Figure 4.1.   Waiting Walter social story.

Throughout the semester, Joan and Hector both supported the game-playing activity and assessed and reflected on the impact of the adaptation of the materials. Some days were better than others, but overall, Javier was moving toward much more appropriate behavior. By the end of the semester, along with the support of a sand timer for him to see how much time would elapse during each turn, Javier was able, at first, to play Connect 4 with Joan or Hector, and then to play the game with one other child under Joan or Hector's supervision. The other children began to interact with Javier in more positive ways, including him and Walter in other play. Although some negative behavior continued, Javier was able with adaptations of the appropriate intensity to engage in game-playing and build his social and emotional skills. Joan and Hector shared these experiences in their learning community. As modeled by Joan, Hector, and Marie, mentors and educators must work closely together to enact, assess, reflect, and adapt intentional teaching strategies to include all children.

Supportive Learning Communities

The goal of this supportive learning community is to allow educators to share their experiences implementing adaptations in their classroom. The activities in this supportive community will highlight adaptations that increase children's independent participation, with the least amount of hands-on assistance by the educator. The focus of this activity is to use LEARN IT to develop adaptations for a morning sign-in activity based on the children in Joan and Hector's class. To begin, educators read Handout 4.4, Making an Identifying Mark for Attendance. Then, working in two groups, educators discuss and complete the activity. As part of this activity, each group creates a sign-in plan that will work for Joan and Hector's class and that will include Gavin, Faith, and Javier. The goal is to move each child in the class toward successful completion of an assessment task that consists of the individual children writing their name and drawing a picture of themselves. Facilitators can also consider creating other vignettes given feedback from participants.

In their small groups, educators engage in in-depth discussions of their current differentiation practices and the adaptations they provide, getting feedback from their peers as to possible next steps. Then, with the other educators in their classroom (e.g., the teacher and teacher assistant), they plan a sign-in structure and procedure that will work for their individual class. Throughout discussions, participants reflect on their ideas for the activity, making sure decisions are based on best practices for inclusion, the needs of their students with and without disabilities, and the possibilities given their classroom environments. They should consider the physical structure of their classroom, the languages of students in class, the number of children in the class, and how many adults are available. Each classroom group should outline their final sign-in plan on large chart paper.

To wrap up the activity, participants share the plans across the two groups. During this time, participants should think critically about inclusion practices and the levels of adaptation, so that the sign-in activities require the least intrusive adaptations for all children. The groups should present and defend their proposal, while other participants make suggestions and share further ideas. Facilitators can list suggestions on a blank piece of chart paper.

Figure 4.2 is a checklist of this LEARN IT strand for the professional development team to assess whether they implemented all aspects of the intentionally including each child module. All aspects of the LEARN framework are utilized across this strand of LEARN IT. Participants engage in learning knowledge and skills specific to intentionally including each child. They have multiple opportunities to enact, assess, and reflect on specific intentional teaching strategies to implement adaptations in their classroom. They participate in this learning within the context of a supportive learning community that includes mentors and colleagues interested in intentional teaching to implement adaptations in their classroom.

Making an Identifying Mark for Attendance

As part of children learning about communicating using print and how it functions and with the goal to intentionally use classroom routines to help the children build their self-regulation skills, Joan has implemented a plan in which children sign in as they enter their classroom each morning.

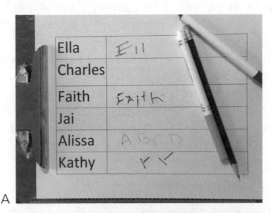

A

B

For the three students with individualized education programs (IEPs), Joan and Hector identified the following adaptations:

Gavin: Joan and Hector want to implement a sign-in procedure that will meet Gavin's developmental and learning needs. Gavin's delayed development in fine motor, intellectual, and social development necessitates adaptations of the sign-in. How do they develop a sign-in plan that is usable for the entire class with adaptations that are the least intrusive for Gavin? As with all of the children in Joan and Hector's class, Gavin will need to learn to stop and complete the sign-in activity each morning. When looking at the examples in Figures A and B, the educators believe Gavin could trace over the letter G as depicted in Figure C, or circle his picture, should Joan offer a sign-in like the one depicted in Figure D.

(continued)

C

D

Faith: Faith can recognize and copy her name for the sign-in activity as depicted in Figures A and E and can trace her name or beginning letter as depicted in Figures C and D. She will need nonverbal reminders, such as a picture card in her cubby, to complete the sign-in activity each morning.

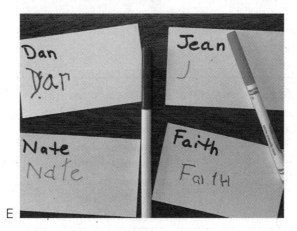

E

Javier: Javier can easily use the example of a sign-in format in Figure B. He can print most of his first name in a form that is recognizable. The challenge for Javier will be remembering to sign in, waiting his turn if other children are signing in at the same time, and doing so without interfering with the process used by the other children.

As part of this activity, create a sign-in plan that will work for their class and that will include Gavin, Faith, and Javier. The goal is to move each child in the class toward successful completion of an assessment task that consists of the individual children writing their name and drawing a picture of themselves. We want all students to have an opportunity to demonstrate the best of their capabilities and for the sign-in activity to be constructed in such a manner as to allow for children's growth and development.

Checklist for Including Each Child

	LEARN IT institute	Implementation and mentoring	Supportive learning communities
Learn	❏ Facilitators presented research and best practice related to intentionally including each child in the context of day-to-day teaching.	❏ Mentors helped participants use knowledge learned through the institute to identify particular support they need to include a child in classroom activities.	❏ Mentors reviewed information learned through the workshops and the mentoring.
Enact	❏ Facilitators provided opportunities for participants to apply learned information through activities to understand how adaptations can be the least intrusive.	❏ Mentors supported participants as they planned and implemented strategies to provide adaptations to include a child in the classroom using the least intrusive intervention.	❏ Mentors established parameters for participants to complete the sign-in activity.
Assess	❏ Facilitators asked participants to report adaptations they use in their class based on the level of intrusiveness and provided feedback for accuracy from a professional development mentor.	❏ Mentors guided participants to assess interventions to ascertain effectiveness or need to modify the adaptations.	❏ Mentors helped participants make corrections to the sign-in activity developed with peers and mentor.
Reflect	❏ Facilitators provided opportunities for participants to consider the adaptations they use in their practice/classrooms.	❏ Mentors encouraged participants to determine the impact of the intervention on the children and why this type of instruction might be useful for their ongoing teaching practice.	❏ Mentors supported discussion on suggestions for the sign-in activity and how they were based on best practices for inclusion.
Network	❏ Facilitators implemented a session in which participants met in groups based on their site/school and considered the benefits of this practice for their site/school.	❏ Mentors provided participants with opportunities to network with peers and follow up in community meetings, including with the special education team.	❏ Mentors made sure that activities developed by peers were shared and discussed in terms of how and why they were enacted.

Figure 4.2. Checklist for Including Each Child.

Adapting and Differentiating Instruction

The focus of this strand of LEARN IT is on adapting and differentiating instruction for each child. Prior to the LEARN IT institute, participants should review their copy of *CARA's Kit* (Milbourne & Campbell, 2012), which was introduced in the previous institute. Through this strand and the previous one, participants become deeply familiar with additional information in *CARA's Kit,* with a focus on the personal and practical perspectives on inclusion. They also make connections between the previous strand on inclusion and the new learning presented in this strand. In this strand of LEARN IT, educators enhance their skills in adapting and differentiating instruction.

LEARN IT Institute

To begin the institute, participants share their current understandings of inclusion and adaptations, based on what they learned from the prior reading and from the prior institute, implementation and mentoring, and their supportive learning communities. The facilitator can record main ideas on the whiteboard or chart paper throughout the discussion. To end the discussion, participants share interests for new learning. Facilitators should record this discussion on the chart paper as well and then ask participants to review so that their interests and needs are incorporated into the current activities. Facilitators can make an electronic file of the full groups' interests and needs; they should refer back to that file frequently to account for and incorporate the ideas captured into the rest of the institute day, implementation and mentoring, and supportive learning communities.

Next, participants explore their own experiences and connections to people with disabilities. Because research has indicated that teachers' attitudes toward inclusion of children with disabilities can affect their practices (e.g., Leatherman & Niemeyer, 2005; Mitchell & Hedge, 2007), the goal of this discussion is for participants to explore their attitudes toward inclusion and the experiences they have had that shaped their perspectives. Educators discuss the influence of these experiences on their current practices in adapting and differentiating instruction for young children with disabilities. To extend this discussion, educators can use fun and interesting materials, such as markers, clay, playdough, pens, crayons, and paper, to individually represent their first experiences with someone with disabilities. After they create these reflections, participants turn to the person next to them and share their experiences in pairs.

To expand the discussion, participants form small groups, counting off so that they get to know others in the large group. Facilitators should participate with each group, facilitating a discussion in which all group members have a chance to speak. Participants should bring their drawing, clay, or writing to the small group as a reference point. In these groups, participants discuss the differences and similarities between experiences, including when they had the experience, the nature of the disability, what they thought about it, and their relationship with the individual with disabilities. They should consider as well how other adults and children acted around the person with the disability and how their actions influenced the participants. Participants conclude the discussion with connections to the present day; how do those experiences influence their current practices as a community member, in the classroom, and in adapting and differentiating instruction? Participants may share concerns as to what they tell their students about children with disabilities and whether they think it is "fair" for a child with a disability to have accommodations. They should reflect on how to move past their personal and professional barriers to providing adapted and differentiated instruction. Participants must step back from their assumptions and worries to look at inclusion with a fresh perspective about providing all children with the support they need. Facilitators can link back to the tire activity from the previous institute and ask the participants to consider how the strengths-based perspective can help them to better meet the needs of the children with disabilities in their classrooms. After concluding this discussion, educators engage in a transition break, such as a group game, transition activity, or snack.

When the group gathers back together, participants explore examples of the key components of early childhood inclusion: access, participation, and supports (DEC/NAEYC, 2009). *Access* is providing children with disabilities with opportunities to engage in high-quality early childhood settings, environments, and experiences. *Participation* is a sense of belonging and engagement for children with and without disabilities. *Supports* are systems-level structures that sustain inclusive learning opportunities. Through group discussion, educators develop a better understanding of how adaptations are used to include children with disabilities in classroom activities. They learn new information focused on personal experiences with learners with disabilities and adapting and differentiating instruction. Specifically, educators should focus on the following:

- Understanding access, participation, and supports as the defining features of inclusion that can be used to identify high-quality early childhood programs and services

- Understanding adaptations (i.e., something that is changed or changes so as to become suitable to a new, special use or individual situation) with the goal to facilitate the participation of children in activities, and routines and to enhance children's development and success

- Clarifying that the forms of adaptations (i.e., changes along a continuum, including, from least to most intrusive, adapt environment, select or adapt activity or routine, adapt materials, adapt requirements or instructions, or provide assistance) are selected and implemented to make sure that children can participate as independently as possible while reducing the direct assistance provided to the least amount necessary

- Increasing participants' capacity to facilitate participation in activities and routines for each child, particularly children with disabilities

- Developing adaptations to meet the needs of students in their classroom and addressing classroom situations with individual children

- Learning skills to evaluate the effectiveness of adaptations and modifying them as needed

With these learning goals and associated information in mind, participants watch the video *Foundations of Inclusion Birth to Five* (CONNECT, 2013; 11 minutes). The video, embedded within modules developed by CONNECT: The Center to Mobilize Early Childhood Knowledge, is available as part of a free online module on the foundations of inclusion that can be found on the Project CONNECT course series web site: http://connect.fpg.unc.edu/connect-course-foundations-inclusion. A direct link to the video can be found at http://community.fpg.unc.edu/connect-modules/resources/videos/foundations-of-inclusion-birth-to-five.

Participants break into small groups, determined by their school/community setting. They create their own brochure containing key information from the video to "sell" their classrooms as inclusive, by including key information from their learning. At a minimum, the brochure should include the three points listed on Handout 4.5. Participants use this handout as a brainstorming guide to get started on their brochure.

Group Brochures

Create your own brochure to "sell" your classrooms as inclusive. Include key information from the video along with prior readings and institutes. At a minimum, your brochure should cover the three elements below. Use the blank space to brainstorm how you will discuss each of these elements in your brochure.

- The definition of early childhood inclusion

- The key aspects of early childhood inclusion (access, participation, supports)

- Examples depicting how there is evidence of each of the aspects of early childhood education inclusion in your practice

Participants can complete the brochure with hands-on materials or electronically, depending on the materials and technology available (e.g., printer) and the approach the participants wish to take. Participants share the brochures with the whole group using a poster session format in which half of the participants stay in their group to present their brochure and the other half move through the groups, listening to them describe their brochure, asking questions, and giving feedback. Participants reference Handout 4.5 to ensure that each group's brochure has the three key elements included. They should ask group members questions about each of the key elements.

The session ends with Adaptations Bingo. To prep for this activity, facilitators create a variety of Adaptation Bingo cards. See Figure 4.3 for a sample card; please note that the activity requires multiple versions with the levels of adaptations (environment, activity and routine, materials, routine and instructions, and assistance) placed in different boxes. To begin the activity, participants should take out *CARA's Kit* (Milbourne & Campbell, 2012) and review the levels of adaption on the adaptation continuum on page 4. The facilitator should hand out a Bingo card to each participant along with Bingo daubers or chips. The group should review the adaptations on the card and then read the Adaptation Bingo rules that follow:

- LEARN IT facilitators act out an example of an adaptation.

- Participants mark the level of adaptation being modeled.

- When participants get three in a row, they win and call out "Bingo."

- LEARN IT facilitators ask one of the winners about the intrusiveness of the adaptations they marked.

The group plays until everyone wins. To wrap up, educators review the information shared and the activities conducted during the institute. Facilitators may also use this time to solicit participants' feedback on anonymous comment cards about the institute's effectiveness. In summary, the activities in this institute review and build depth of knowledge in the participants' understanding of adaptations and differentiating instruction for successful inclusion of children with disabilities.

Implementation and Mentoring

This implementation and mentoring session will provide the participants with support to implement adaptations and to differentiate their instruction and interactions with specific

Assistance	Free	Requirements/instructions
Activity	Environment	Materials

Figure 4.3. Sample adaptation Bingo card.

children. Participants focus on the practices that support access and participation in their classrooms. To get started, participants fill out the Implementation and Mentoring Form, Handout 4.3, to identify the inclusion strategy that they wish to work on with their mentor. Mentors should aim to address the most significant challenges identified by the educators, in collaboration with the special education team. The goal of the session is to enable educators to better meet the needs of each child in their classroom, particularly focusing on meeting the needs of the children with disabilities.

In the previous implementation and mentoring on including all children, educators Joan and Hector worked through the development of a successful way to include the student Javier in their class' much-loved simple game activity. As they became more familiar with adaptations, they wanted to make a plan to include another student, Gavin. They discussed next steps in their inclusive practice with their mentor, Marie. Soon, the discussion turned to Gavin. Marie asked if game time might also be a useful time to provide adaptations to help increase Gavin's participation. After attending the institutes and completing the assigned readings, Joan and Hector readily agreed to work to provide Gavin with the supports he needed to participate during game time.

In the opening vignette, we described Gavin as having general delays in all areas of development and we noted that he plays by himself. He and his classmates have not learned how to play together; occasionally, Gavin tries to initiate play with others but is mostly rejected by peers. Joan and Hector realized that Gavin would need a more intrusive adaptation to participate in game playing. However, they wanted to figure out if they could prompt a peer to provide the intensive assistance so Gavin would have more experience with peer interactions. In addition, the classmate would also learn how to appropriately interact with Gavin. Joan and Hector also realized that their games would need to be adapted. They chose to adapt Hi Ho Cherry-O because they thought it was the most easily adapted. They asked another student, Ella, if she would be willing to help teach the game to Gavin because she was calm when eating lunch near Gavin. She also interacted with him in more structured situations, due to their shared love of superheroes and superhero fantasy play.

Joan and Hector adapted the game before involving Ella and Gavin. Due to Gavin's intellectual and fine-motor delays, a new game board was purchased. The new game board was the plastic one available from Hasbro to provide more support to stabilize the game for play. In addition, larger cherries were used, replacing the small plastic cherries with pom-poms, and five were used instead of the usual 10 small cherries that come with the game. Figure 4.4 provides a photo of the modified game. The spinner was changed, as can be seen in Figure 4.4. Spinner options to take cherries off the tree were set at 1, 2, or 3, and there was only one possibility for putting cherries back on the tree. In addition, the spinner was fastened to the table with masking tape for ease of play.

Prior to playing the game in class, Ella and Gavin were taught the new version of the game. In addition, Ella learned numerous ways to invite Gavin to play the game and help him with participation (see English, Goldstein, Kaczmarek, & Shafer, 1996; Stanton-Chapman, Denning, & Jamison, 2012). During the simple game time, the original and adapted forms of Hi Ho Cherry-O were set up on one table. Ella was instructed to invite Gavin to play with her using the adapted version. Two other children played the game at the same table. Joan and Hector supported the play of all children, including Gavin, as needed. The adapted game worked well. As it turned out, other children wanted to sometimes play the adapted version, so it became regularly played at simple game time. Joan and Hector learned how to adapt materials and provide differentiated instruction to allow all the children in their class to participate at simple game time. They also gained additional experience with adapting class

Figure 4.4. Game board adapted.

activities and providing differentiation that can be generalized to additional class activities and routines.

Supportive Learning Communities

The goal of this supportive learning community is for teachers to share their experiences implementing adaptations and differentiating instruction in their classroom, to increase their children's independent participation. At this meeting, participants apply the information in *CARA's Kit* (Milbourne & Campbell, 2012) to students in their class. To get started, educators sit in their class teaching pairs. Each pair chooses a child or group of children in their class with a disability who could most benefit from adaptations to address a challenging situation. They identify all possible adaptations along the continuum and develop their own as well. Educators use *CARA's Kit,* which suggests adaptations based on a situation, for guidance. Educators can talk through each adaptation using the following guiding questions:

- What would it look like in our classroom?

- What it would it look like if it were successful?

- What would it look like if you need to move on to another strategy?

Throughout the process, participants should jot down notes so that they have them for future reference.

After answering these questions, participants choose an adaptation that they would like to try with a particular child and justify it in terms of an appropriate level of intrusiveness. They delineate a plan that focuses on what they need to do before, during, and after implementation. When they're ready, the pairs share their adaptation and plan with the rest of the group to receive critical feedback. Other participants give their thoughts on the appropriateness of the adaptation for the particular child or group of children. In this activity, educators carefully critique the plan and give feedback regarding whether it will work with the focus child and all of the other children in the class, as well as the other adults teaching in the classroom.

Figure 4.5 is a checklist for this LEARN IT strand that the professional development team can use to assess whether they implemented all aspects of program. Facilitators can use the checklist as a tool as they plan and implement the adapting and differentiating instruction module. All aspects of LEARN are utilized across this strand of the professional development. Participants engage in learning knowledge and skills specific to adapting and differentiating instruction. They have multiple opportunities to enact, assess, and reflect on specific intentional teaching strategies for including all children, including children with disabilities. They participate in this learning within the context of a supportive learning community that includes mentors and colleagues interested in intentional teaching.

Checklist for Adapting and Differentiating Instruction

	LEARN IT institute	Implementation and mentoring	Supportive learning communities
Learn	❏ Facilitators reviewed information participants learned from the previous institute and presented research and best practices related to intentionally adapting and differentiating instruction.	❏ Mentors helped participants use knowledge learned through the institute to identify particular support they need to adapt and differentiate instruction for a child in their class.	❏ Mentors reviewed information learned to examine adaptations using *Cara's Kit* and developed a deep knowledge of developing and providing adaptations.
Enact	❏ Facilitators provided opportunities for participants to apply learned information through activities to help them identify and move beyond their personal barriers to providing adapted and differentiated instruction. Facilitators provided an opportunity for participants to participate in a brochure development experience and shared it with the rest of the group.	❏ Mentors supported participants as they planned and implemented strategies to provide adapted and differentiated instruction.	❏ Mentors led enactment of teacher learning to adapt and differentiate instruction.
Assess	❏ Facilitators led participants to identify their current needs for understanding regarding adapting and differentiating instruction, identify their own personal experiences that affect adapting and differentiating instruction, and assess whether they understood the new information.	❏ Mentors and participants determined whether the adaptations allowed the specific children to enjoy the game time in class and analyzed why this type of instruction might be useful for their ongoing teaching practice.	❏ Mentors supported development of criteria to decide how to assess whether an adaptation is successful.
Reflect	❏ Facilitators provided opportunities for participants to consider the practices they use in their classroom adapting and differentiating instruction.	❏ Mentors provided an activity so that participants thought of this experience as a model of how they can include children with disabilities in many aspects of their class.	❏ Mentors supported discussion of participants' suggestions for how they will modify adaptations if they find they are not working successfully.
Network	❏ Facilitators implemented a session in which participants supported each other as they developed their understanding of equity by adapting and differentiating instruction.	❏ Mentors provided participants with opportunities to network with peers and follow up in community meetings, including with the special education team, to help make using adaptations a sustainable classroom practice.	❏ Mentors made sure that that participants reviewed each other's selected adaptations for a particular child or group of children and considered how the adaptations can be implemented in their own classroom.

Figure 4.5. Checklist for Adapting and Differentiating Instruction.

Promoting Intentional Teaching: The LEARN Professional Development Model for Early Childhood Educators by Julie K. Kidd, M. Susan Burns, and Ilham Nasser.

SUMMARY

The first part of this chapter introduced three preschool children in Joan and Hector's class who have IEPs: Gavin, Faith, and Javier. We shared the challenges Joan and Hector face and discussed their goals for each of these children. We presented current research on inclusive early childhood education and discussed the importance of intentionally including each child, including children with disabilities, in preschool and kindergarten classrooms. We shared evidence-based strategies for adapting and differentiating instruction for children with disabilities. Then we described two strands of professional development activities: 1) intentionally including each child and 2) adapting and differentiating instruction. In each of these strands, we provided examples of activities that are used during the LEARN IT institute, implementation and mentoring, and supportive learning communities that promoted participants' understanding and enactment of various evidence-based strategies. In Chapter 5, we continue to examine educators' intentional teaching as we explore educators' culturally responsive practice.

Implementing Culturally Responsive Practice

5

Elsa, a preschool educator participating in LEARN IT professional development, was reading a book to children in her classroom about airplanes. Means of transportation was a unit in the curriculum. She started by pointing out pictures of airplanes and made a connection with one of the children in the group, who had flown on an airplane during the summer break to visit grandparents in Morocco. Elsa asked the child how long the trip took and asked the other children to guess the length of the flight. The children were so interested in the topic that, after the reading, she continued to create a chart with all the guesses of the children.

She then showed a map of the world and asked children to help her find out the route that the airplane took from the United States to Morocco. The children were fascinated by the distance and time traveled. They pointed out water and land, as they traveled with their fingers on the maps. Following the conversation, Elsa and the children came up with a few questions to answer about Morocco: What languages do they speak and what sports do they play? What did the grandparents do during the day and how did their friend spend his time while in Morocco? What places did he visit? What foods did he eat and what were his favorite desserts? What do children in Morocco like about school? As the children came up with more questions, Elsa thought some of the questions would be perfect to send home with the child for the family to answer. This was a perfect entry to many math, science, and literacy concepts that she needed to teach as part of her curriculum.

Elsa was very happy that she had seized a teachable moment and that her children were so engaged when she highlighted the culture of one of her students. She believed she should do more to celebrate other children and their cultures in her classroom. As a preschool educator, Elsa values the importance of respecting all cultures. She is a strong believer in engaging families and their cultural practices and values in the classroom. She makes an effort to reach out as often as she can. Recently, she has been thinking about ways to support and celebrate a new Vietnamese student in her classroom, Kim, who is shy, is an English language learner, and plays alone. After talking to her colleagues during their supportive learning community meeting, Elsa was excited about the prospect of utilizing the advice she was given to support Kim.

As a way to celebrate Kim and her Vietnamese culture, Elsa organized a day about Vietnam; she bought and prepared Vietnamese food and hung art decorations in the hallway leading to her room. She invited Kim's family to participate, but to her surprise, when they arrived, they seemed very upset. They claimed that the teacher had made their child look different from others and that she had singled Kim out. Elsa was upset and felt bad for not coordinating ahead of time with her student's family. She did not realize then that being sensitive to someone's culture does not necessarily mean celebrating it one day of the year.

When her LEARN IT mentor, Isabella, came to her classroom, Elsa told her what had happened and asked for further guidance with children in her classroom who have cultural backgrounds different from hers. Specifically, she wanted to know ways to make them feel welcomed. Isabella suggested Elsa start by examining previously held values and beliefs she carries about children and what is good for them. Elsa also raised the issue during her next supportive learning community meeting. She asked the group for advice on how to be more intentional in developing her cultural sensitivity and responsiveness to her students and their families. She used the network of professionals at her school to assess her responses to the events described here and to reflect on what she might do differently in the future. Elsa knows she has some way to go to find answers to this question, but she also knows that she will have multiple opportunities to learn, enact, assess, and reflect on this topic. She will also continue to network with her peers informally and at the next supportive learning community meeting at her school.

WHAT TO EXPECT IN THIS CHAPTER

Like Elsa, most early educators may believe that culturally responsive practices are essential to ensuring that learning is enhanced for each child, including children with diverse cultural, linguistic, and socioeconomic backgrounds. However, implementing practices that are responsive to the diverse children and families in the classroom may be a challenge. Professional development focused on exploring children's and teachers' cultures, and ways they play a role in the learning and teaching process, provides opportunities for early educators to recognize their own assumptions and biases and make culturally responsive instructional decisions.

In this strand of LEARN IT professional development, the emphasis is on expanding and discussing the key role that culturally responsive practice plays in considering intentional teaching of each young child, regardless of the child's ethnic, linguistic, or socioeconomic background. This chapter

- Highlights the role that cultural beliefs and values play in the classroom, especially when those affect educators' practices and interactions with children and families

- Encourages educators to deeply examine and reflect on their own cultural perspectives, perceptions, and belief systems and how they come into play in interacting with young children and their families

- Focuses on intentionally planning and executing lessons and instructional activities that are culturally responsive and take into consideration the cultural background of each young child in the preschool or kindergarten classroom

- Promotes intentionality in implementing strategies that educators may already know about culturally responsive practice, such as those currently used by early childhood professionals

- Discusses the importance of intentional interactions that are culturally responsive

- Provides practical ideas and resources for developing and implementing culturally responsive instruction

- Describes LEARN IT activities that focus on developing early educators' culturally responsive practice

FOUNDATIONS: DEFINING CULTURALLY RESPONSIVE PRACTICE

In various studies, the term *culturally responsive practice* has been used to describe the alignment between the home culture and the school's goals for children. It is often described in other terms that mean the same exact phenomena; *cultural pedagogy, cultural compatibility,* and *cultural relevancy* are often used to describe culturally responsive practice and its importance for learning (Bui & Fagan, 2013; Phuntsog, 2001). When developing a unique definition of culturally response practice for LEARN IT, our team examined many different ways in which *culture* has been defined. For example, according to Griswold (2012), culture is a way of life and includes a group's morals, customs, beliefs, and knowledge. Culture, according to Seefeldt, Castle, and Falconer (2014), "determines the way in which each person thinks, feels, and behaves" (p. 163).

As LEARN IT was developed, significant time was spent discussing current views and definitions of all concepts related to the professional development, including culturally responsive practice. The definition that reflected the team's own knowledge, experiences, and views was the following:

> Cultural responsiveness means teachers utilize, embrace, develop, and foster children's appreciation and understanding of their cultural and ethnic backgrounds. The awareness gained from learning about and connecting to each child's and family's cultural/ethnic background is used to form authentic, responsive learning environments and relationships where the curriculum is developed through the children's home culture, prior knowledge, and lived experience. (Kidd, Burns, Nasser, Assaf, & Muccio, 2009)

Knowing the complexity of cultures and cultural responsiveness, this definition assumes the proactive roles that teachers play in meeting the needs of children from various cultural backgrounds. The main assumption here is that cultural responsiveness is not a burden on teachers, but rather a way to enrich the experiences of everyone in the learning situation. The definition addresses educators' ability and readiness to "utilize, embrace, develop, and foster children's appreciation and understanding of their cultural and ethnic backgrounds" (Kidd et al., 2009). It asks a lot of the teacher. However, more important, it focuses on intentionality in planning, executing, and assessing every activity and daily routine.

Others define cultural responsiveness based on the importance of culturally responsive practice to academic gain, to students' success, and to opening doors for culturally different students to reach their highest potential (Ford, 2010). Learning should be a meaningful experience for students, and for that to happen, the educator's role should go beyond the role of a technician (Sherman, 2014). With students of diverse backgrounds, educators should avoid teaching with a single mindset (Yang, Hsiao, & Hsiao, 2014) and expand their skill sets to include strategies that will promote learning for each student. There is evidence in studies with older children that culturally responsive pedagogy is a pathway to social justice in schools. For example, Esposito and Swain's (2009) study in urban schools suggested that "by adhering to the tenets of culturally relevant pedagogy (e.g., personal accountability and cultural critique), participants [teachers] helped their students think critically about how social injustices affected their lives" (p. 38). The implication of that, according to Esposito and Swain, is that teachers were able to help prepare students to have an "impact [on] change in their communities and the larger society" (p. 38). Social justice is on the radar when educators examine the long-term benefits of the use of culturally responsive practice as, according to Banks (2004), social justice and diversity go hand in hand with the creation of global citizenship and participation.

The Context and Need for Culturally Responsive Practice

In this era of massive global migration, the United States, especially in large cities, is in a state of constant change, with various ethnic groups, religions, and languages coexisting (Zhao, 2010). This cultural diversity brings with it celebrated differences that exist among the various cultures and languages. At the same time, many educators, who are creating and shaping the vision for a future America, are not adequately prepared to manage the differences that stem from having immigrant and minority students in their classrooms (Garcia, Arias, Murri, & Serna, 2010).

Recent statistics on demographic shifts show that 44% of children in U.S. schools are nonwhite, whereas 85% of the teaching force is white and female (Ford, 2010). This may cause anxieties in some circles; in others, it may also be seen as a new and renewed opportunity for interconnectedness and engagement. In either scenario, many good, well-meaning teachers put pressure on children by trying too hard to be responsive while lacking the knowledge and strategies to meet the needs of children who are different from themselves. In one of the LEARN IT meetings on culturally responsive practice that we conducted with Head Start teachers, one educator questioned whether she should call child protective services because a family would not allow their 7-year-old daughter to eat meat. Questions such as these challenge teachers to go out of their comfort zone and learn more about religious, cultural, and family practices different from their own.

Starting in preschool or even before, the process of acculturation and exposure to mainstream American culture intensifies as young children are introduced, along with their families, to school rituals and practices that are unfamiliar, such as parent–teacher conferences and national holidays and celebrations. Intentional teachers must start with an examination of their own intentions for a child who is a newcomer to this country and the classroom. Some of these questions, for example, relate to strong personal beliefs about who is considered an American and who is not and to the need to support newcomers in understanding and sharing the basic values that make us Americans. Some early childhood educators may question practices observed in students and their families (Sirin, Ryce, & Mir, 2009), as in the example of the girl who did not eat meat. Nevertheless, intentional teachers value diversity and the richness it brings to the classroom, although they may face discrepancies between their values and those of their students and must determine the best ways to deal with this.

Early educators, who are mostly white and female, typically know how to guide young children in an assimilation process through celebrations, values, and foods, but need support in guiding children's development of ethnic and cultural identities. Intentional educators are aware of this issue because being culturally responsive requires a deep belief in the importance of maintaining the home culture of individual children and blending it with the new American one (Banks, 2004). Intentional teachers respect and accept differences and authentically transmit this attitude to children. Educators must expand their understanding of who is an American and accept various variations of that. They have to challenge their own belief systems and decide where to draw their boundaries. When one educator described how a Pakistani family with whom she worked fasts for 30 days during Ramadan (the Muslim month of fasting), only eating or drinking before sunrise or after sunset, her mentor asked her what she thought about that, and her reply was, "Well, that is their tradition and I can't do anything about it." When the mentor questioned whether she thinks it is acceptable not to eat or drink during the day for 30 days, she responded that this is their way and she respects that without further research and investigation. This example draws teachers' attention to situations where cultural responsiveness stands against the educator's belief of what is good for children, and what she or he believes are developmentally appropriate practices, while taking into consideration the fluid definition of healthy child development across contexts.

Many teachers and educators are challenged by the desire and necessity to engage in culturally responsive practice (Sleeter, 2011). Very often, teachers realize that taking small measures, such as having some dolls representing different ethnic groups in the housekeeping center and labels in different languages to mark learning centers, does not always respond to the various and pressing needs of their students. However, going further or deeper may challenge the core of teachers' belief systems. Educator Elsa's attempt to make a Vietnamese child feel included, detailed in the opening vignette of the chapter, reflects a sincere effort to be more aware and more proactive about culturally responsive practice. However, her good intentions did not mesh well with the family's goals. Her understanding of being culturally responsive differed from the family's expectations. In some instances, communicating expectations and goals to the family is a challenge; the teacher needs to reach out and foster nurturing and authentic relationships with students and their families. This requires an investment in understanding practices and religious traditions of those communities that are different from one's own.

Benefits of Culturally Responsive Practice

Culturally responsive practice requires taking responsibility in teaching, which according to Sherman (2014) means educators interact with their students on a daily basis to plant dispositions that are critical for learning and good citizenship. Cultural sensitivity is one of those dispositions that needs to be included in the learning benchmarks and curriculum. Symbolic curriculum, according to Gay (1995), includes images, symbols, icons, awards, celebrations, and other artifacts that are utilized in teaching children new knowledge, skills, and dispositions. Gay (2002) added, "Culturally responsive teachers are critically conscious of the power of the symbolic curriculum as an instrument of teaching and use it to help convey important information, values, and actions about ethnic and cultural diversity" (p. 108).

Very often, the symbolic curriculum is the mechanism to assimilate children into the mainstream American culture by emphasizing dispositions that are at the heart of white dominant culture. For example, values such as independence are admired and taught. In one child care center, parents of a toddler asked an educator to help their child feed himself because he does not eat well. The educator, who was from a culture different from the parents, objected because, she claimed, children need to learn to eat by themselves as part of the classroom goals and center's approach and philosophy. In fact, previous studies suggest that independence is a culturally loaded skill and value (Killen & Wainryb, 2000).

Teachers are culturally responsive, according to Ford and Kea (2009), when they "work proactively and assertively to understand, respect, and meet the needs of students from cultural backgrounds that are different from their own" (p. 1). Intentional educators incorporate culturally responsive practice in their instruction and plan classroom activities with the educational outcomes in mind, while keeping the child in the center. A thorough examination of classroom environments and how they reflect children's backgrounds, in addition to a careful examination of the curriculum and how it responds to children, are needed to increase educators' effectiveness (Gay, 2002) and improve student outcomes. Having a culturally responsive environment accounts for children's prior knowledge in planning instruction; this is a major tenant of how children (and adults) learn (Bransford, Brown, & Cocking, 2000).

That is, implementing culturally responsive practice not only improves the outcomes and academic achievement of diverse students but also benefits every child in the classroom (Gay, 2002). A model by Cartledge and Kourea (2008) suggested addressing the needs of culturally diverse students as part of a comprehensive plan to close the achievement gap and ensure the success of students in a culturally responsive classroom. Culturally responsive practice relies on planning targeted interventions that are structured around improving English language skills among English language learners (Cartledge & Kourea). What needs to be added to the model are the children and their voices, cultural assets, prior knowledge, and family knowledge.

There are important social and emotional gains from utilizing culturally responsive practice and pedagogy. According to the *Head Start Early Learning Outcomes Framework: Ages Birth to Five* (U.S. Department of Health and Human Services, 2015), creating a culturally responsive classroom will help children show, for example "engagement in prosocial behavior with adults and usually responding appropriately to adult requests and directions" (U.S. Department of Health and Human Services, 2015, p. 29). Children also better understand similarities and respect differences among people (e.g., gender, race, special needs, culture, language, family structure) when exposed to culturally responsive practice. Previous research consistently shows gains for all children in the classroom when each child feels secure, accepted, and respected in a culturally responsive classroom.

Strategies of Culturally Responsive Practice

Phuntsog (2001) suggested four "conditions" necessary for culturally responsive learning to occur in the classroom: "cultural literacy, self-reflections, respect for diversity, and a transformative curriculum" (p. 54). Self-reflections and critical reflections have been identified in the literature as major tools to promote responsive practice amongst educators (Chen, Nimmo, & Fraser, 2009; Maude et al., 2009). According to Chen et al., "As children begin to construct an understanding of human differences and similarities during their earliest years, early childhood teachers are challenged to be culturally responsive to the diversity of the children and families" (p. 101). Chen et al. suggested using self-study as a reflective tool of educators' attitudes, assumptions, and knowledge of what is culturally responsive. In their study, they piloted their reflective tool with 33 undergraduate preservice teachers. The preservice teachers responded to four entries, including their beliefs and biases, the classroom physical environment, pedagogical practices, and relationship with families. The reflections in the study increased preservice candidates' awareness of their biases and practices and allowed further intentionality in acting as culturally responsive educators.

In Maude et al. (2009), teachers used self-study to explore their own backgrounds and knowledge. As suggested by Kidd, Sanchez, and Thorp (2008), preservice teachers who engaged in self-reflection were able to bring the process of attitude shift and change into practice. What was unique about the Maude and colleagues study is that teachers explored representations of diverse families in popular cultures. They were able to reflect on stereotypical portrayals of families of their own students and their country of origin.

Culturally aware and responsive teachers reflect on the ways that harmful stereotypes, such as those influenced by media portrayal of different groups, have influenced their beliefs; they also work against these biased images and others that children are exposed to (Bonds-Raacke, 2008). Maude et al. (2009) stated, "By considering their own culture first, students [preservice teachers and others] discover how their values, beliefs, customs, and behaviors have developed" (p. 38). In cases when children come to class and mimic a stereotypical character in a new film, intentional teachers conduct research and provide alternative narratives based on various cultures and social contexts.

Culturally Responsive Classroom Strategies

As a leading scholar in culturally responsive practice, Mariana Souto-Manning argued that teachers' engagement in self-reflection and, particularly, in action research, wherein they examine their own practice and study it, may increase teachers' culturally responsive practice. She concluded in her study with Mitchell (Souto-Manning & Mitchell, 2010) that when engaged in culturally responsive practice, teachers become learners with the children; therefore, who the children are, including their prior knowledge, becomes part of the curriculum. Later, Souto-Manning (2013) suggested strategies to use in the classroom with young children as a way to increase culturally responsive instruction. These are child-directed and planned activities and strategies, which include interviews, critical inquiry, culture circles, community resources and home literacy/ies, technology and media, and storytelling and acting.

Interviews   In interviews, educators encourage children to ask questions and reach out to community members for new knowledge and various perspectives. In this activity, children come up with questions that interest them, similar to what Elsa did in the vignette when she and her children wanted to know more about Morocco. Educators then facilitate a discussion with community service people with children's questions and experiences in mind.

Critical Inquiry   To engage children in critical inquiry, educators use a problem-based and inquiry-based curriculum. This is an integrated and interdisciplinary approach. A teacher presents a problem or a question to children and they collaborate on finding answers for it. For example, children may wonder why they have green trees in their classroom during Christmas time. The teacher provides the children the opportunity to learn more about the significance of trees in many holidays and celebrations among many cultures around the world.

Culture Circles   To implement the culture circles strategy, the educator initiates conversations and dialogues about events in the classroom. The educator starts by listening to children's conversations and finding a book that addresses a common issue of inequity affecting the lives of children. Teachers in this activity need to be open to children's questions about authority and equity. For example, a group of boys refuse to let a girl play with them in outdoor play because "she can't run." The teacher calls for a meeting for the whole classroom and discusses the incident with the children as part of a cultural circle. Children learn to negotiate differences through a process that the teacher introduces to them; for example, the teacher may propose first stopping the action by leaving the space, second thinking about it, and third talking to an adult when there is a conflict. In the example of the girl who was excluded, the teacher used the cultural circle to highlight differences and the importance of respecting those and not using them against each other. In this case, the difference was gender; of course, in other situations, the difference will vary.

Community Resources and Home Literacy/ies   To tap community resources and master home literacy, educators develop funds of knowledge by reaching out to the community. This strategy recognizes and values the community knowledge as well as the individual knowledge of each child and includes it in the curriculum. This requires a deep understanding of children and families' multiple sources of cultural knowledge and wisdom. Home visits at various points during the school year can increase the knowledge of community resources and home literacy.

Technology and Media   Another strategy to increase culturally responsive instruction is to use social media and recent technologies to send a message of diversity. The teacher can work with her children to create content using technology. For example, a teacher could prepare an audio recording of cultural stories and family backgrounds or create a YouTube video with the children on the topic of culture.

Storytelling and Story Acting   Educators can provide room for oral storytelling and acting as a way to make the curriculum more inclusive and culturally responsive. This activity may involve parents and families who can write or record a story from their culture and send it to the teacher or come in and tell it to the students. Oral histories and storytelling are part of many cultures around the world. Another suggestion made by Haley & Austin (2014) is to allow children to express themselves by telling a child-generated story about their own cultures.

Elements of Culturally Responsive Teaching

When students are taught in a culturally responsive classroom, they are empowered both individually and collectively, which makes room for authentic participation. As a result, the students bring a wealth of knowledge and are able to respect and value each other's cultures. Schrodt, Fain, and Hasty (2015, p. 590) hypothesized that this call for culturally responsive teaching promotes five essential elements:

1. Developing a knowledge base about cultural diversity

2. Including ethnic and cultural diversity content in the curriculum, including symbolic curriculum

3. Demonstrating caring and building communities

4. Communicating respect for all students, especially those who are ethnically diverse and from marginalized communities

5. Responding to ethnic diversity in the delivery of instruction

Early childhood environments intentionally set up to support cultural responsiveness and respect will be evident immediately. Characteristics to look for in classroom environments are that the adults in the room have a positive perspective on parents and families in general, communicate high expectations, use child-centered instruction that is situated within the context of culture, and act as facilitators for learning that is mediated by culture. In the LEARN IT professional development program, educators are encouraged to examine their classroom environments and note changes needed to make the classroom more welcoming to families and children who are different, in order to meet every child's needs.

This, of course, does not mean giving up the practices that have been working well in early childhood, such as labeling learning centers in several languages, greeting children in several languages, providing diverse materials that represent the cultural diversity of the children, and providing multiple opportunities for children of all abilities to participate at their own pace. For examples, educators should continue to make sure the room flows well and does not include too many barriers if there are children with physical disabilities. Likewise, educators should provide various skin color crayons and dolls to represent all types and shades of people. The call by Lin, Lake, and Rice (2008) to strengthen the antibias agenda in early childhood classrooms provides many examples to increase teachers' sensitivity and awareness of biased practices that are often aligned with raising awareness of culturally responsive pedagogy. The authors advocate for the use of self-study as a vehicle to explore self-awareness and increase reflectivity of educators.

As children need educators to be more responsive to their cultures and their families' beliefs and practices, those planning and implementing professional development need to consider the importance of offering professional development content that is respectful of educators. In addition, identifying participants who are willing to engage in enactment, assessment, and reflection around this sensitive topic is also important. This includes a close examination of educators' values and belief systems, as well as a close examination of the environment of the classroom. For example, educators need to examine their classroom management practices and ask difficult questions, such as the following: What is the race and gender breakdown of the students I send to rest time or send outside the classroom? How often do I do that with the same students? Very often, educators discover that they send African American males to visit the director of the preschool or the principal of the school more often than other children. This discovery helps educators examine their expectations, values, and beliefs about "proper" behaviors and what is important for "these" kids to learn.

The Professional Development Activities section that follows describes two LEARN IT activities that are specifically planned to enhance educators' knowledge and skills about culturally responsive practice. The first activity focuses on understanding and implementing culturally responsive practice; the second explores culturally responsive practice.

Culturally Responsive Practice

Through LEARN IT professional development, the goal of promoting a culturally responsive practice in the classroom may be explored through connecting knowledge from research with best practice. This strand focuses on enabling educators to understand the meaning of culturally responsive practice and the connections between culturally responsive practice and intentional teaching. Educators engage in a facilitated institute, implementation and mentoring sessions, and the supportive learning community, which are all designed to emphasize that culturally responsive practice necessitates an in-depth exploration of individual children's culture and home environment and educators' own culture. Participants will explore ways to utilize individual children's cultural knowledge and prior knowledge in teaching and learning.

LEARN IT Institute

Prior to the LEARN IT institute, participants should read the Foundations section of this chapter along with the articles listed in the Culturally Responsive Practice Resources text box. These articles provide useful and usable information on practices that promote culturally responsive practice.

CULTURALLY RESPONSIVE PRACTICE RESOURCES

Kalyanpur, M. (2003). A challenge to professionals: Developing cultural reciprocity with culturally diverse families. *Focal Point: A National Bulletin on Family Support and Children's Mental Health, 17*(1), 1–5.

Montgomery, W. (2001). Creating culturally responsive, inclusive classrooms. *Teaching Exceptional Children, 33*(4,) 4–9. (This article also includes the Diversity Checklist used by participants. See Handout 5.2 for a modified version of the checklist.)

This LEARN IT institute focuses on understanding culturally responsive practice. It begins with an in-depth examination of participants' attitudes and perceptions about cultures and home environments different from their own. To begin, the large group gathers and educators share their responses to the assigned readings. Participants write, on an index card, a useful idea they gained from the articles. Then, participants form small groups to engage in deeper discussions on insights gained from the articles. In their small groups, participants discuss the ideas written on the index cards and provide new insights on culturally responsive practice. They exchange real examples of how these ideas translate into practices in their classrooms. To conclude the discussion, small-group members share with the large group their main discussion points on lessons learned from the readings.

In the activity that follows, educators will consider deeper levels of engagement in culturally responsive and sensitive practice and how they can be more intentional about taking a culturally responsive approach. Participants return to their same small groups and review Handout 5.1. The graphic organizer featured on that handout represents the intersection between intentional teaching and culturally responsive practices, and the areas of overlap. Those areas are conceptual as well as practical; they both support responsiveness to children and their families. Participants should identify and list the areas of overlap, working with their small groups. Likewise, they should discuss additional strategies for how they could extend culturally responsive instruction in their classrooms and be more intentional about it. Then, participants compare their own strategies and ways to incorporate more intentionality when they interact with children, especially English language learners, with the graphic. Returning to the large group, educators discuss the best ways to promote culturally responsive

Graphic Organizer

Identify the common themes and practices related to both culturally responsive practices (CRP) and intentional teaching (IT).

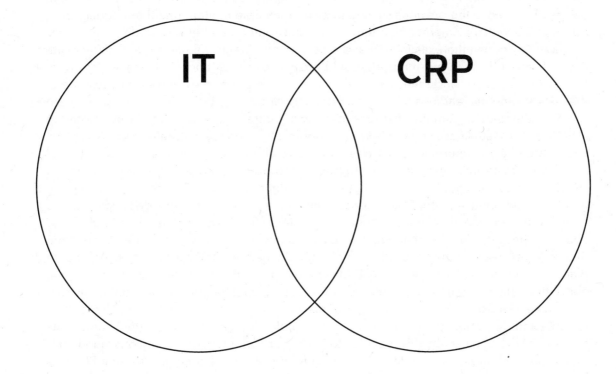

practice that is authentic, is purposeful, and relies on educators' knowledge of every child in their classrooms.

After the institute, to further extend their reflections on being intentionally responsive, educators complete Handout 5.2 when they are back in their classrooms. This handout is an environmental checklist for diversity that is a modified version of the work by de Melendez & Ostertag (1997). The checklist will be used in the implementation and mentoring session and in the supportive learning communities to discuss modifications needed in the educators' classrooms to promote culturally responsive practices.

Implementation and Mentoring

Prior to this implementation and mentoring session, educators fill out and share Handout 5.2, as discussed in the previous subsection, and the implementation and mentoring form, Handout 5.3, with their mentor. Handout 5.2, the environmental checklist for diversity, serves as a way to deepen the examination and discussion between the mentor and participant. After reviewing both forms, mentors should provide feedback and guidance as educators further enact, assess, and reflect upon the culturally responsive strategies they learned in the institute and the readings.

Elsa, the teacher from the chapter's opening vignette who unsuccessfully attempted to include a new Vietnamese student in her classroom, attended the culturally responsive practice institute. Upon returning to her classroom, Elsa conducted a thorough examination of her classroom environment using the checklist in Handout 5.2. As she reviewed her results, she decided to highlight her areas of need on the mentoring form. During the implementation and mentoring session, Elsa's mentor, Isabella, addressed various ideas, such as the need to label centers in languages spoken by children in the room other than English and Spanish. They also decided that Elsa would ask parents to bring books or oral stories from their cultures to use in the culture circles that she learned about through the readings. Elsa planned to use a book or story every Friday morning to initiate conversation and dialogue about the different cultures represented in the classroom. She also examined the environment in her classroom and made changes to make children and their families feel more comfortable and welcomed in the classroom. For example, Elsa decided to conduct home visits because of the opportunity this provides to learn more about cultural, religious, and family beliefs and practices that may affect or enrich their children's learning. Although Elsa was hesitant, Isabella emphasized that the home visit is not intrusive and that teachers should check with families, as many welcome teachers to their homes. See Chapter 7 for more information about home visits.

Supportive Learning Communities

Participants should bring their completed version of Handout 5.2, the environmental diversity checklist, to their next supportive learning community meeting. At the meeting, participants share insights on what aspects of their classroom needed modifications, such as ways to strengthen the parents' corner and make it more sensitive to the needs of the families. Next, participants pair off. In pairs, they should review Handout 5.4 and use the questions included as a guide for meaningful, reflective discussion. The opportunity to network while entertaining the LEARN questions in the handout enriches the educators' experiences and increases their rapport of activities and strategies.

Environmental Checklist for Diversity

Interactions in the Classroom

❐ Do you encourage children to talk to each other?

❐ Do you provide times when children can tell imaginative and true stories of their own experiences?

❐ Do you help children who do not speak English to participate in conversations?

❐ Do you respond to children's specific ideas and questions instead of making general comments like "good idea" or "we'll get to that later"?

Family Involvement

❐ Do you encourage family members to visit classrooms at any time?

❐ Do you solicit family participation?

❐ Do you make arrangements as necessary to accommodate all family members, including those with disabilities and extended family members?

❐ Do you consider children's home cultures in planning preschool events?

Physical Environment

❐ Do you demonstrate the world's variety of languages in your classroom?

❐ Do materials in the room reflect the cultural diversity of the children and the world?

❐ Do you provide "mailboxes" where children can leave private messages for each other and for teachers?

❐ Do you make a bulletin board available to the children as a work space for notes and plans and for works in progress?

Adapted from De Melendez, W. R., & Ostertag, V. (1997). *Teaching young children in multicultural classrooms: Issues, concepts, and strategies*. NY: Delmar.

Implementation and Mentoring Form

To be completed by early educators

Educator's name _____   Mentor _____

Site _____   Date _____

Identify the **intentional teaching strategy** you want to **enact**. Select one child to interact with during ☐ center time ☐ small group ☐ individually. Describe the support you would like from your mentor to help you implement the **intentional teaching strategy.**

Intentional teaching strategy of focus:

Culturally Responsive Practice

☐ Choose an area and set it up to reflect children's cultures

☐ Account for child's interest-background and use child's prior knowledge

☐ Inspire child to complete the idea/activity by connecting it to his/her home culture

☐ Provide specific feedback to extend child's play in that area

☐ Question to promote higher-level thinking

Interactional Reading

From *Bringing Words to Life*

☐ Choosing vocabulary words

From Dialogic Reading

☐ Prompt

    ○ Completion prompt

    ○ Recall prompt

    ○ Open-ended prompt

    ○ Wh- question prompt

    ○ Distancing prompt

☐ Evaluate the child's response

☐ Expand the child's response

☐ Repeat–child repeats the expanded response

Expanded Vocabulary

☐ Math vocabulary (5 words)

☐ Science vocabulary (5 words)

Assessment and Instruction

☐ Follow child's interest

☐ Observe and record child learning behaviors

☐ Initiate conversations and write plans with child

☐ Provide meaningful learning opportunities informed by assessment

Extending Play

☐ Redirect play to replace violent play

☐ Plan play

☐ Act out stories

☐ Dramatic use of the constructions child makes

Inclusion

☐ Adapt environment

☐ Adapt routines

☐ Adapt materials and activities

☐ Adapt requirements

☐ Adapt instruction

Continue on back if needed

Focus child _____

Elaborate on how you will implement the intentional teaching strategy. _____
_____
_____

What type of in-class support do you think will help you?

☐ Modeling while you take notes

☐ Assistance with co-teaching the child

☐ Feedback after observation

☐ Other _____

Use back if needed

Promoting Intentional Teaching: The LEARN Professional Development Model for Early Childhood Educators by Julie K. Kidd, M. Susan Burns, and Ilham Nasser.
Copyright © 2019 by Paul H. Brookes Publishing Co., Inc. All rights reserved.

LEARN Discussion Questions

Learning/knowledge: What do I know and how did I learn the information about children, their families, and cultures?

_____
_____
_____
_____
_____
_____
_____

Enact: How do I act upon this knowledge of children and families?

_____
_____
_____
_____
_____
_____

Assess: Did my enactment work and prove to be sufficient to meet the needs of culturally different children and families?

_____
_____
_____
_____
_____
_____
_____

Reflect: Were there other options and alternatives that I did not pursue, and did I choose the most appropriate methods to address cultural differences and misunderstandings?

_____
_____
_____
_____
_____
_____

Network: What do teachers in my supportive learning community do in similar situations?

_____
_____
_____
_____
_____
_____

For example, in her learning community, Elsa discussed her class activity where she expanded on the trip to Morocco based on the knowledge she gathered from one of the children. Others shared their own individual adaptations to make their interactions more culturally responsive and sensitive to the needs of every child, including English language learners.

Figure 5.1 is a checklist of this LEARN IT strand that the professional development team can use to assess whether they implemented all aspects of the LEARN framework. Facilitators can use this checklist as a guide as they work through each step of the LEARN IT strand on culturally responsive practice. If all aspects of the LEARN framework are utilized across this strand of LEARN IT, participants will engage in learning knowledge and skills specific to culturally responsive practice. They will have multiple opportunities to enact, assess, and reflect on specific aspects of LEARN within the context of their classroom and a supportive learning community that includes mentors and colleagues interested in culturally responsive practice.

Checklist for Culturally Responsive Practice

	LEARN IT institute	Implementation and mentoring	Supportive learning communities
Learn	❒ Facilitators presented research and best practices related to promoting culturally responsive practice in the classroom.	❒ Mentors explained the purpose of using the environmental checklist in their classrooms.	❒ Mentors reviewed culturally responsive intentional teaching practices and the purpose of the environmental checklist.
Enact	❒ Facilitators provided participants with an opportunity to identify the intersection of intentional teaching and culturally responsive practice.	❒ Mentors guided participants as they used the environmental checklist in their classrooms.	❒ Mentors provided participants with an opportunity to use the results of their environmental checklist to identify classroom modifications.
Assess	❒ Facilitators guided participants as they compared their instructional strategies with culturally responsive intentional teaching strategies.	❒ Mentors discussed the results of the environmental checklist with participants.	❒ Mentors gave participants an opportunity to share how their implementation of a culturally responsive intentional teaching strategy worked.
Reflect	❒ Facilitators encouraged participants to share and discuss ways they can incorporate culturally responsive intentional teaching strategies into their classrooms.	❒ Mentors helped participants use the results of the environmental checklist to identify culturally responsive practices that will work in their classrooms.	❒ Mentors guided participants as they explored how they will implement culturally responsive intentional teaching strategies.
Network	❒ Facilitators provided opportunities for participants to meet in large and small groups to learn, discuss, and reflect.	❒ Mentors provided opportunities to network with peers and follow up in supportive learning communities.	❒ Mentors provided opportunities for participants to learn together and encouraged discussion and reflection among participants.

Figure 5.1.   Checklist for Culturally Responsive Practice.

Personalizing Culturally Responsive Practice

In the second LEARN IT strand, participants are further exposed to what it means for them to be culturally responsive to young children and families. Specifically, the participants are challenged to experience what their English language learners do when they are exposed to English in their classrooms. This professional development session focuses on what culturally responsive practice means for individual educators. It is intentionally planned to challenge educators and their perceptions on the topic and enhance their awareness and understanding so they are more purposeful about it. Educators will learn to take individual children's perspectives and interests, in addition to family perspective, into considering when planning lessons. In particular, educators will better understand and respond to families that cannot communicate in the dominant language and have different cultural values from theirs. By participating in the following institute, implementation and mentoring session, and supportive learning community meeting, educators will further learn to intentionally enact culturally responsive practice in their classroom.

LEARN IT Institute

The LEARN IT institute starts with a demonstration of a lesson, given in a different language that is spoken by a LEARN IT facilitator. The goals are to illustrate 1) the difficulty of learning a new language and 2) ways to introduce a new language to young learners, such as use of gestures, pictures, and vocal clues. It can be conducted in any language available other than the dominant language in the group. A facilitator or mentor who is bilingual should review the directions in the following paragraph before the institute.

To begin the session, participants learn that they will be taught in a foreign language. Then, the bilingual facilitator or mentor teaches a simple song as a warm-up activity. That facilitator also teaches educators how to recognize and say familiar things in the environment, such as animal names, understanding the concept of big and small, and categorizing animals according to their size. Educators also become familiar with the concept of big and small through the use of visual cues, modeling, and imitation of gestures. Next, they categorize the animals of different sizes and use basic vocabulary that was learned. This type of activity is an important learning tool for adult learners, as it generates unexpected reactions and triggers authentic responses to the unfamiliar by the participants. It easily provokes emotional responses similar to those of children who are exposed to a new language and not given tools to cope with the situation.

In the large group, participants reflect on their momentary anxiety about learning to communicate in a foreign language. They relate those feelings to children who are speakers of other languages in their classrooms. Then, in small groups, participants assess their reactions and the kind of cultural clues and gestures that were helpful for them in learning a lesson in an unfamiliar language. When the discussion wraps up, participants complete Handout 5.5. This handout is the Diversity Self-Assessment, adapted from Bromley (1998).

Once they have filled out the assessment, participants engage in small-group discussions on the responses. They consider the following:

1. In what ways do they make their instructional program responsive to the needs of the diverse groups in the classroom?

2. What kinds of information, skills, and resources do they need to acquire to effectively teach from a multicultural perspective?

3. How can they collaborate with other educators, family members, and community groups to address the needs of all their students?

Diversity Self-Assessment

1. What is my definition of diversity?

2. Do the children in my classroom and school come from diverse cultural backgrounds?

3. What are my perceptions of students from different racial or ethnic groups? With languages or dialects different from mine? With special needs?

4. What are the sources of these perceptions (e.g., friends, relatives, television, movies)?

5. How do I respond to my students, based on these perceptions?

6. Have I experienced others' making assumptions about me based on my membership in a specific group? How did I feel?

7. What steps do I need to take to learn about the students from diverse backgrounds in my school and classroom?

8. How often do social relationships develop among students from different racial or ethnic backgrounds in my classroom and in the school? What is the nature of these relationships?

9. In what ways do I make my instructional program responsive to the needs of the diverse groups in my classroom?

10. What kinds of information, skills, and resources do I need to acquire to effectively teach from a multicultural perspective?

11. In what ways do I collaborate with other educators, family members, and community groups to address the needs of all my students?

_____

Reprinted with permission from *Language Arts: Exploring Connections, 3rd Edition* by Karen Bromley. Copyright 1996.

Participants share their reactions to the questions in the same small groups. They engage in in-depth discussions of personal views and share worries about diversity. The questions can generate honest conversations on a range of topics suggested in the self-assessment, such as attitudes about children and families that are different from them. Educators focus on their experiences and views. The conversations during the networking opportunities strengthen educators' awareness of what to do and what to avoid as culturally responsive educators.

Implementation and Mentoring

To enable their assessment and reflection in this implementation and mentoring session, educators videotape themselves enacting a culturally responsive activity in the classroom. If educators have children in their classroom who are English language learners, they should videotape their interactions with these children individually or in small groups. After videotaping, educators view their video and use it to inform the strategy they mark on the Implementation and Mentoring Form, Handout 5.3. Educators should share that form, along with the video, with their mentor. Elsa, for example, viewed the recorded lesson with her mentor, Isabella, to learn more about her own dispositions and behaviors with children who are English language learners. She noted her demeanor, gestures, and eye contact, among other techniques used to convey simple messages in English. Videotaping revealed behaviors and gestures that Elsa was not aware of, and Isabella was able to support her to make new discoveries about her practice. It was an inspiring step for Elsa to start the process of change to benefit children and families.

Supportive Learning Communities

To begin the supportive learning communities, the group reflects on the choices and judgments that people make when challenged with a situation of cultural misunderstandings, such as the one Elsa experienced with her student's Vietnamese family. Then, educators review the following real-life scenario, which presents cultural conflicts and misunderstandings:

> On Veterans Day, a teacher was teaching a lesson on heroes and ways to be thankful for the soldiers who protect our country. To illustrate, she brought in a backpack that is carried by soldiers in the U.S. Army and started taking contents out one by one and explaining to her children what soldiers do with them. When she got to a large green net, she said, "This net is for catching animals and bad people in far places like Iraq."

In small groups, educators use the questions on Handout 5.6 to discuss the scenario. In the scenario described, the educator conveys a stance on a political issue of a controversial nature. Furthermore, she is misleading children, as well as indoctrinating them into a certain way of thinking. In fact, she is strengthening the stereotype that there are only good guys (usually Americans) and bad guys (usually others such as Middle Eastern natives and Muslims). This scenario is a strong example to present when the participants have been previously exposed to this type of cultural stereotyping, as it provides the opportunity to have an in-depth conversation on a disputed topic that includes cultural as well as social and political beliefs. The facilitator can determine the depth the teachers can handle, based on knowledge of the participants and the previous LEARN IT strand focused on culturally responsive practices.

After the initial discussions in the small groups, educators engage in a large-group discussion using the reflective questions in Handout 5.6 as a guide. Participants should take time to answer the questions and examine their own beliefs and views about the various scenarios

Scenario Discussion Questions

1. What is your interpretation of the situation described in the vignette? _____

_____

_____

_____

_____

_____

_____

2. What is your analysis of the issue? _____

_____

_____

_____

_____

_____

_____

3. What are the personal and cultural values, beliefs, and assumptions present in this situation? _____

_____

_____

_____

_____

_____

_____

_____

4. What additional knowledge is needed and what are ways to obtain it? _____

_____

_____

_____

_____

_____

5. What are your next steps? Include instructional ideas and pedagogical steps. _____

_____

_____

_____

_____

_____

provided. The safe and supportive forum allows participants to share success stories. Nevertheless, some participants may be reluctant to further elaborate on their responses. The group leader should encourage all to share their responses on the reflective questions, as there is no one correct answer. One goal is to increase participants' repertoire of culturally responsive intentional teaching strategies that can be included in their daily lesson planning.

Educators should further engage in order to deepen the discussion on perceptions, beliefs, and fears of cultural diversity and differences by specifically addressing misunderstandings with families. Participants self-examine and reflect on where they can explore ways to be more intentional about respecting families and their needs and desires. Educators can use the following ideas to guide communication with families:

1. Send a survey, at the beginning of the school year, with questions about family habits, traditions, and practices. For example, many families have food restrictions, and sending a survey to ask is better than assuming.

2. Share information with families and ask them to share information that is pertinent to their backgrounds and family traditions or even current events that may affect the child. For example, it is valuable to know if a child is from a conflict area where things change constantly and the family may be affected.

3. Incorporate the knowledge gathered from families in planning and check with them when in doubt.

4. Attend community events and public gatherings of the communities represented in the classrooms.

5. Conduct research on the communities represented in the classroom. There are plenty of resources to learn some basic facts and some useful words to communicate.

6. Take a tour of the school neighborhood and learn about ways of living in the surrounding areas of the school. Explore grocery stores, services, playgrounds, and other features of the neighborhood.

After reviewing these ideas, participants generate additional ideas and select one that they would like to try out in their classroom. In pairs, they brainstorm ideas on strategies to meet that goal.

Figure 5.2 is a checklist of this LEARN IT strand that the professional development team can use to assess whether they implemented all aspects of the LEARN framework. If all aspects of LEARN are utilized across this strand of the professional development, participants will engage in learning knowledge and skills specific to personalizing culturally responsive practice. They will have multiple opportunities to enact, assess, and reflect on specific aspects of the LEARN framework within the context of their classroom and a supportive learning community that includes mentors and colleagues interested in personalizing culturally responsive practice.

Checklist for Personalizing Culturally Responsive Practice

	LEARN IT institute	Implementation and mentoring	Supportive learning communities
Learn	❐ Facilitators presented research and best practices related to what it means for individual educators to promote culturally responsive practice in the classroom.	❐ Mentors emphasized key ideas regarding culturally responsive intentional teaching strategies while working with participants.	❐ Mentors shared information on cultural conflicts and misunderstandings.
Enact	❐ Facilitators guided participants as they engaged in a mini lesson in a foreign language.	❐ Mentors guided participants as they video-recorded their interactions with children in their classroom.	❐ Mentors guided participants as they explored scenarios involving cultural dilemmas.
Assess	❐ Facilitators provided an opportunity for participants to assess what they learned during the mini-lesson that was taught in an unfamiliar language and how they felt throughout the lesson. Facilitators encouraged participants to respond to diversity self-assessment questions.	❐ Mentors worked with participants to identify what they do that supports cultural responsiveness and what they do in their interactions with children that could be changed.	❐ Mentors helped participants determine their knowledge of the cultural dilemmas presented in the scenarios.
Reflect	❐ Facilitators invited participants to share their reactions to the mini-lesson activity and the diversity self-assessment questions. Facilitators encouraged participants to consider how these learning experiences might inform their instructional practices.	❐ Mentors encouraged participants to identify culturally responsive intentional teaching strategies that will enhance their interactions with the children in their classroom.	❐ Mentors guided participants as they considered ways to use insights from the discussions about the scenarios with children and families in their class.
Network	❐ Facilitators provided opportunities for participants to meet in large and small groups to learn, discuss, and reflect.	❐ Mentors provided opportunities to network with peers and follow up in supportive learning communities.	❐ Mentors provided opportunities for participants to learn together and encouraged discussion and reflection among participants.

Figure 5.2.   Checklist for Personalizing Culturally Responsive Practice.

Promoting Intentional Teaching: The LEARN Professional Development Model for Early Childhood Educators
by Julie K. Kidd, M. Susan Burns, and Ilham Nasser.
Copyright © 2019 by Paul H. Brookes Publishing Co., Inc. All rights reserved.

SUMMARY

The LEARN IT activities in this chapter provide participants with much greater insights into and understanding of students who are experiencing challenging situations in their classrooms as English language learners or as part of a marginalized group. Educators need the opportunity to assess their experiences and practices that affect their cultural responsiveness. They also need to discuss the challenges they experience as well as their successes in safe spaces that begin with the daylong institute and continue with supportive learning communities and one-on-one with a mentor. They are supported to enact changes in their environment and instruction to improve their responsiveness to children.

To intentionally implement culturally responsive practice, educators must plan and adapt activities that are respectful of family-identified outcomes, preferences, interaction styles, and cultural norms. They must develop and reflect on various behavior management strategies for culturally, linguistically, and ability diverse young children that are aligned with family goals. They must also apply current research on effective developmentally appropriate practices to teaching young children from diverse backgrounds and of varying abilities.

Assessing Diverse Young Children

6

With Leslie La Croix and Sehyun Yun

James, the lead teacher in an inclusive Head Start classroom, looks down and smiles at the handmade book Desmond left at the reading center for his friends to read. Desmond joined the prekindergarten classroom in mid-October, just after his 5th birthday. James stopped to reflect on the experiences that led Desmond to author his book and share it with the class that afternoon. He realized that his own intentional focus on the connections between instruction and assessment opened creative and important learning spaces for Desmond to begin to explore a number of emergent literacy skills. James also recognized that Desmond had accomplished a great deal in a short amount of time.

A few days earlier, James had initiated a repeated interactive reading of *What Do You Do With a Tail Like This?* (Jenkins & Page, 2004). The children were immediately drawn into the text's structure, which invites readers to guess mystery animals by seeing just a part of the animals' body. Readers are then rewarded with rich illustrations of the mystery animal on the subsequent page and a brief description of how the animal uses the body part. Throughout the reading and rereading of different pieces of the texts, James focused on children's responses to his probing questions and guided them to consider how the body part helped each animal survive. James also focused on attending to children's phonological awareness skills. By segmenting animal names in the text into syllables, the children discovered that *hippopotamus* had more syllables in its name than any other animal in the book. Through his observations of the children's responses, James realized the children were most excited about the "guessing" structure of the book. So, James also used the text to orally segment animal names for the children to blend together as a way to discover the mystery animals on the next page. For example, to support the children's predictions to the text's question, "What do you do with ears like these?," James pointed to the bat ears at the top of the page and prompted, "Oh, I know what animal this is. I am going to stretch out the sounds of the letters in this animal's name for you. Then, we will put the sounds together to find the mystery animal. Ready? /B/.../a/.../t/... what animal's name did I sound out?" The children happily responded, "Bat!"

Continuing, James sprinkled the oral segmenting game sparingly throughout his read aloud; he recognized that prompting the children to blend more phonemically complex words like "scorpion" would not explicitly support the children's emerging metalinguistic understandings. Rather, James made strategic decisions about how to use the language throughout the text to enhance children's developing phonemic awareness skills.

James had not realized that Desmond would use *What Do You Do With a Tail Like This?* (Jenkins & Page, 2004) as a mentor text to create his own version of the story. Yet, the day before, on his play plan, Desmond told James he wanted to go to the writing center "to make a book." After all of the children had gone to their centers, James noticed Desmond flipping through the new magazines James had added to the center for the children to use in their own writing projects. James sat down next to Desmond to ask some questions about what he was thinking about writing; James expressed support for Desmond's ideas about creating another animal guessing book. Then, James watched Desmond carefully cut out pictures of animals, glue them into his book, and add labels to the pictures he selected. Periodically, James would check in with Desmond to ask guiding questions about what he was writing and to support Desmond's efforts to sound out words. James knows Desmond's book reveals a great deal about his emerging literacy skills. So, he decides to take pictures of it to include in Desmond's electronic portfolio as evidence of Desmond's fine motor, emergent writing, and emergent reading skills. In addition, James knows Desmond's book will be an important artifact to take with him to the next supportive learning community meeting because Samita, a kindergarten teacher in the same school, will also be there. Samita has been tapped as Desmond's teacher for the following year and is an invited member of the transition team put into place as part of Desmond's IEP. James is looking forward to sharing Desmond's achievements with Samita and knows that she will recognize the important emergent literacy skills revealed in Desmond's book.

James' focused attention on syllable segmentation was related to his recent implementation of the Assessment, Evaluation, and Programming System for Infants and Children®: Test (AEPS®; Bricker, Capt, & Pretti-Frontczak, 2002). He was glad that, after attending the LEARN IT institute on Exploring Formal Assessments for Diverse Young Learners, he had asked to pilot the use of AEPS® in his prekindergarten classroom. AEPS® is an observational assessment that presents educators with a developmental continuum of skills that children typically begin to master at certain ages. The AEPS® observational checklists are delineated across six developmental areas: fine motor, gross motor, adaptive, social, cognitive, and social-communication (Bricker et al., 2002). Accordingly, James frequently used embedded assessment moments to explicitly attend to children's emerging cognitive phonological awareness skills; he took quick anecdotal notes about what individual children are saying and doing in response to his questions. At the end of each day, James stopped to reflect on the children's comments and transfer the observational assessment information to the AEPS® data recording form. James liked how well the assessment fit into the rhythm of the children's daily routines, and the assessment criteria helped him to think strategically about how he engaged children. He also valued the curriculum-based approach that served as the philosophical foundation for the assessment and appreciated the clearly delineated goals, criterion, and objectives. More important, James thought the AEPS® assessment allowed him to confidently represent children's current understandings and next learning goals to students, families, and professional colleagues. James, like many of the other educators who attended the institute, realized the potential in formal assessment tools to enhance understanding of children's development across multiple domains and positively influence curricular decisions and daily interactions with children.

WHAT TO EXPECT IN THIS CHAPTER

Prior to engaging in the LEARN IT professional development program, James' understanding of assessment conformed to the prescribed assessment regimens of his school. His experiences administering a series of mandated assessments throughout the school year is commonplace across institutions as school administrators seek to respond to the varying demands of stakeholders at the national and local levels. In an effort to provide uniform data regarding children's performances and demonstrate growth, schools often systematically administer assessments at the beginning, middle, and end of the year. Educators, like James, often express frustration regarding the amount of time required to administer assessments that are not strategically aligned with their curricular goals or explicitly analyzed by the teachers to inform responsive decisions about curricular opportunities in the future. However, as James realized through the LEARN IT experiences, assessments, when appropriately selected and embedded, can yield rich insight into children's performances and enhance educators' responses to children's learning.

This chapter explores essential aspects of formal assessment practices in early childhood education contexts. This chapter

- Explores factors influencing school-based assessment practices

- Presents essential terminology used by formal assessments to document young children's performances

- Discusses the benefits and limitations of formal assessment practices in capturing culturally, linguistically, and ability diverse children's knowledge

- Identifies areas of potential bias inherent in the design and administration of formal assessment protocols

- Provides LEARN IT professional development activities that guide educators in becoming assessment literate

FOUNDATIONS: ASSESSING DIVERSE YOUNG CHILDREN

Assessment is a vital part of high-quality early childhood education programs. Given the impact of social interactions on children's development, particularly those between children and surrounding adults, teachers in early childhood education play a significant role in children's development and learning (Lightfoot, Cole, & Cole, 2013). Assessments provide valuable information to teachers and schools regarding how to support the development of children by understanding their interests, abilities, and needs. The position statement from the NAEYC and the National Association of Early Childhood Specialists in State Departments of Education (NAECS-SDE) (2003) emphasizes assessment as a process of collecting and interpreting information to 1) aid teachers in making sound instructional decisions, 2) identify children who might need focused intervention, and 3) help programs improve their educational processes.

Assessment for Learning, Assessment of Learning, and Assessment as Learning

When entering into conversations about specific assessment practices, educators should first determine the overall purpose of the assessment. Broadly, educators can classify assessment data into one of three categories: 1) assessment for learning, 2) assessment of learning, and 3) assessment as learning (Earl, 2003; DeLuca & Klinger, 2010).

Formative assessments are instrumental in assessment *for* learning because they reveal what children already know and understand about a given instructional focus; they inform educators' curricular progressions with children (Antoniou & James, 2014). Black and William (2010) defined formative assessment as "all those activities undertaken by teachers and by their students in assessing themselves that provide information to be used as feedback to modify teaching and learning activities" (p. 82). Thus, the main purpose of formative assessment is to provide information that guides teachers' instructional actions to meet children's interests, abilities, and needs.

Assessment-of-learning tools provide a summative evaluation of a child's performance. They typically occur at the end of a unit of study to "capture what a student has learned, or the quality of the learning, and judge performance against some standards" (National Research Council, 2001, p. 25). Results capturing assessment of learning may be used to consider an individual child's current understandings or to ascertain what a group of children has come to know and understand. In addition, assessment of learning data may be used to evaluate overall program effectiveness after children engage in focused instructional opportunities.

Finally, assessment *as* learning emphasizes children's active roles in assessment and learning (Earl, 2003). Assessment-as-learning tasks allow children to reflect on their own learning and identify their strengths and needs (Earl). In assessment as learning opportunities, educators in prekindergarten and kindergarten work to explicitly guide children in considering their own thinking and recognize their active role in learning.

These multiple purposes of assessment demonstrate the complexities of assessing children as well as its role in learning and teaching in early childhood education.

External Factors and Policies Influencing School-Based Assessment Practices

Since the early part of this century, the accountability and standards-based movement in education has influenced early childhood education. Two major pieces of legislation led to an increased emphasis on standards-based curricula and assessments in early childhood programs: 1) the George W. Bush administration's Good Start, Grow Smart Early Childhood Initiative and 2) the development of the Head Start National Reporting System (NRS; Roach, Wixson, & Talapatra, 2010). Announced in 2002, the Good Start, Grow Smart initiative compelled states to develop quality standards for early childhood education, including guidelines on early reading, language, and mathematics skills that align with state K–12 standards (Child Care Bureau, n.d.). Subsequently, the NRS was initiated in 2003 to evaluate the quality of Head Start programs. The NRS required Head Start programs to assess the literacy, mathematics, and language skills of 4- and 5-year-old children at the beginning and end of each year. The test results were used as quality indicators of programs, even though children's performance outcomes are not solely reliant on the experiences they engage in while attending a specific Head Start program (Meisels & Atkins-Burnett, 2004). In a critique of the assessment, Meisels and Atkins-Burnett censured the NRS for being "rife with class prejudice" and "developmentally inappropriate." Concerns surrounding the validity of the assessment and its negative effect on children, families, and educational programs increased. In 2007, the NRS was suspended (FairTest, 2008).

The Improving Head Start for School Readiness Act of 2007 (PL 110-134) removed the NRS-prescribed testing regimen. Instead, it prompted Head Start centers to use ongoing "research-based developmental screening tools that have been demonstrated to be standardized, reliable, valid and accurate for the child being assessed" (PL 110-134). The shift in assessment language was seen as a significant triumph for early childhood advocates. However, the concurrent demand for accountability and formal evidence in the K–12 educational system continued to highlight that high-quality early education programs were needed to increase children's academic success in later grades (Roach et al., 2010). Also, in order to provide evidence of program quality and effectiveness, many states required the implementation of large-scale assessments as measures of students' achievements and progress (Gilliam & Frede, 2015). The 2016 Head Start Performance Standards uses similar language and reaffirms assessment as a central aspect of all quality early childhood education programs. Specifically, the new rules state, "A program must conduct standardized and structured assessments, which may be observation-based or direct, for each child that provide ongoing information to evaluate the child's developmental level and progress in outcomes aligned to the goals described in the Head Start Early Learning Outcomes Framework: Ages Birth to Five" (Head Start Performance Standards, 2016, p. 61, 298).

The standards-based accountability pressures have noticeably affected young children's early learning experiences (Bassok, Latham, & Rorem, 2016; Gullo & Hughes, 2011). According to kindergarten teachers, approximately 70% of kindergarten children took standardized tests at least once or twice a year in 2010 (Bassok et al.). This is 2.6 times more often than first-grade students in 1998. This change in emphasis on testing influenced teachers' beliefs and their instructional time. For example, the results show that kindergarten teachers in 2010 were more likely than teachers surveyed in 1998 to believe that children needed to acquire some academic skills before kindergarten entry. Also, content standard requirements and instructional time in literacy and mathematics in kindergarten have increased since 1998 (Bassok et al.). This intensified focus on teaching literacy and mathematics is a pattern that emerges across the literature that examines the relationship between standardized testing and the amount of instructional time spent teaching discrete academic skills (e.g., Im, 2017; Miller & Almon, 2009).

In an environment where there is increased emphasis on testing, early childhood educators must be able to select and administer assessments that are valid, are reliable, and minimize bias. They need to be able to collaborate effectively with families and other professionals throughout the assessment process and interpret the results of these assessments for diverse stakeholders. Educators must incorporate assessments that provide insights into young children's prior experiences, interests, abilities, and needs. Ultimately, early educators need to be able to use what they learn from the assessments to plan and implement curricular experiences that result in positive learning outcomes for each child in the classroom.

Considering Formal and Formalized Assessment Practices

Early childhood educators will likely be exposed to numerous formalized assessment practices throughout their careers. Therefore, nurturing a thoughtful approach toward the incorporation of new assessment protocols is an essential professional attitude to develop. Formal or standardized tests are defined as test instruments that are administered, scored, and interpreted in the same manner for all children; this allows test outcomes to be compared (Shepard, Kagan, & Wurtz, 1998). In early childhood education, different types of formal assessments are designed and administered for various purposes. Screening tests identify children who may need further assessments to confirm developmental and health risks (NAEYC & NAECS-SDE, 2003). Diagnostic tests are used to decide whether children are eligible for special education services or are in need of other interventions (Gilliam & Frede, 2015). Readiness tests are used to document children's performances on prerequisite skill sets, identified as influential on children's success in the subsequent educational setting (Gilliam & Frede). Finally, program evaluations are formal assessments used to gauge a program's overall effectiveness and compare one program to another (Maxwell & Clifford, 2004).

The broader term, *formalized assessment practices*, recognizes that schools implement diverse sets of assessments to document children's performances across an academic year. Formalized assessment practices include commercially available standardized assessments as well as assessments developed internally by schools and school systems to monitor children's performances. In order to ensure formalized assessments equitably document the accomplishments of individual children, educators should critically examine each assessment utilized. Educators should ask, "Who developed this assessment and for what purpose?" The psychometric qualities for each standardized, commercially available assessment should be reviewed carefully. In particular, educators should review norming data that reveal important information about the sample population(s) demographics and size. This is important because an assessment that derives validity and reliability metrics from a subset of typically developing children may not be appropriate for children with learning exceptionalities. Similarly, although specific psychometric information may not be available for internally developed assessments, educators should scrutinize test items and protocols for mitigating factors. Mitigating factors that influence an assessment's reliability and validity include the following:

- Unfamiliar vocabulary that skews a child's response

- Administration of protocols that are not standardized

- A reliance on interpretations of a child's performance level without deriving common understandings among evaluators about the performances children should be able to do at specific levels

Internally developed assessments should be examined for ambiguous or confusing constructs embedded in the test directions and test items that may interfere with a child's response. When considering school-based formalized assessment practices, educators should consider the following questions:

- What specific assessments will be used to document children's performances?

- What does each assessment measure?

- When and how will each assessment be administered?

- Who will administer each assessment?

- Who will complete the assessments?

- Who will evaluate the assessment results?

- How will the assessment results affect future curricular decisions?

These initial questions encourage educators to consider the cycle of formalized assessment practices in place within a particular classroom, school, or school system. Once educators possess an understanding of the purpose and pattern of assessment practices used by their school, attention should shift toward developing an understanding of how the assessment results will influence children's educational experiences. Accordingly, subsequent reflections on formalized assessment practices should include collaborative grade-level and cross-grade-level explorations of assessment data. These reflections should intentionally focus on identifying areas for focused curricular and program development. Intentionally linking assessment data with curricular decisions for children underscores the imperative need for assessment practices that provide accurate and actionable insights into children's learning.

To enhance their own professional knowledge of young children's performances across cognitive, social-emotional, oral linguistic, and physical domains, educators must implement formal assessments that articulate a range of performance indicators. Both criterion-referenced and norm-referenced formal assessments can be used to inform educators' understandings of children's domain-specific performances. Criterion-referenced assessments are designed to show how an individual performs in relation to defined sets of learning goals, objectives, or standards. Such goals, objectives, or standards can be set, for example, in relation to writing, numeracy, or social play. Data for criterion-referenced assessments focus on articulating the child's performance level regarding a specific skill or behavior. The criteria are arranged by difficulty, and terms such as *not evidenced, emerging, developing, inconsistent, proficient,* and *mastered* are frequently used to communicate a child's current level of performance.

Alternatively, norm-referenced assessments are designed to show how an individual child's performance compares to other children's performances. Data for norm-referenced assessments are presented along a bell curve. This bell curve is broken into a nine-point scale, indicated by nine stanines, meaning nine divisions in the curve. The majority of children's performance scores will cluster in the middle of the curve, at stanines four, five, and six. A score in the middle of the curve suggests that a child's performance in this range is similar to the majority of other children who completed the assessment. By extension, performance scores that fall in stanines one, two, and three, on the left side of the curve, typically represent below-average performances. The scores that fall in stanines seven, eight, and nine, on the right side of the curve, typically represent above-average performances.

Many criterion-referenced assessments and norm-referenced assessments in early childhood education are focused on developmental milestones. Such developmental milestones allow educators to view learning along a progressive continuum, interpret children's performances as indicators of growth, and consider subsequent areas for instruction. Commercially available formal assessments also present psychometric properties with reliable and valid protocols for implementation with diverse groups of young children. Consequently, educators' confidences and perceived value of formal assessment tools increase when the assessment tools align with children's cultural and linguistic backgrounds.

There are a number of commercially available standardized formal assessments that rely on ongoing observational data collection methodologies for documenting young children's learning. AEPS® (Bricker et al., 2002), Battelle Developmental Inventory (Newborg, 2005), and GOLD (Teaching Strategies, 2010) are all examples of standardized formal assessments that use observation as the primary assessment method for gathering information about a child's performances across developmental domains.

AEPS® (Bricker et al.) and GOLD (Teaching Strategies) are criterion-referenced assessments. Battelle Developmental Inventory (Newborg) is a norm-referenced assessment. The developmental scales presented by these assessments inform an educator's understanding of a child's current level of performance. They also serve as a guide for educators seeking to develop curricular experiences that promote increasingly complex cognitive, social and emotional, linguistic, and physical skills and understandings. These assessments also underscore the reciprocal relationship between assessment and instruction; they encourage educators to flexibly embed ongoing assessment practices into the children's authentic learning environments.

Formal Assessment Practices and Considerations   There are a number of beneficial reasons for using formal assessments in early childhood education. For example, standardized assessments help educators to monitor children's progress, articulate areas for growth, and identify children with special education needs. However, there are also concerns about the validity and the reliability of standardized assessments for young children (Gilliam & Frede, 2015; Goldstein & Flake, 2016; McGoey, McCobin, & Lindsey, 2016). When formal assessments are used, care must be given to select measures with "good psychometric qualities," that have "evidence of predictive validity," appear "appropriate for the age and characteristics of the child," and "address referral or intervention questions" (Division of Early Childhood of the Council for Exceptional Children [DEC], 2007, p. 15). To successfully identify such measures, educators tasked with administering the assessment required by their schools must be well informed about the assessment's statistical reliability and validity.

Reliability, according to Field and Hole (2003), "is the ability of the measure to produce the same results under the same conditions" (p. 46). In other words, will the assessment consistently document a child's performance and accurately represent a child's ability (Brassard & Boehm, 2007)? Educators frequently work with colleagues to obtain inter-rater reliability; that way, if either teacher A or teacher B administers the assessment to the child, the results would be the same. However, as noted by Gilliam and Frede (2015), young children do not show their abilities consistently. Various factors may affect a child's performance, including internal test constructs such as the question format and unfamiliar assessment protocols. Other factors that may prevent children from representing their abilities during an assessment include being tired, hungry, or ill, as well as their overall temperament (Office of Superintendent of Public Instruction, 2008). Goldstein and Flake (2016) explain that assessment outcomes may reflect not only what children have gained from a particular learning experience but also their comfort level at a certain moment, familiarity with assessment practices, and knowledge gained thus far. Accordingly, educators must remember that standardized tests represent a snapshot of young children's abilities and provide limited information about what a child can do in a highly constrained situation.

Validity is defined as a characteristic that occurs when "the tool really measures what it claims to measure" (Maxwell & Clifford, 2004, p. 6). Formal assessments often include basic concepts that might impede children's understanding of what is expected of them. For example, children's misunderstanding of test directions can affect their test scores (Kaufman, 1978; Lakin, 2014). Specifically, educators need to be aware that sometimes an assessment instrument may include directional vocabulary that may be unfamiliar to children and therefore undermine their ability to select appropriate responses (Kaufman; Lakin). Before a child can provide a response to a specific test item as directed by the assessor, a child may need to be familiar with additional concepts such as row, below, beginning, different, whole, half, inside, or middle. For example, a child may have a working knowledge of the word "skipping" as it relates to playground play but not as it relates to passing over or moving forward to another test item. These instructional words are not directly associated with the test item being measured; however, children may perform poorly on the subsequent task because they fail to understand verbal concepts in the directions (Kaufman). Similarly, educators also need to be well versed in the assessment's administration protocol; this will preserve the assessment's validity and help the educator to avoid concerns regarding the ethical administration of the test (DEC, 2007, p. 15). If test administrators follow the assessment protocols for administering and interpreting children's performances, educators are more likely to trust the assessment results and to allow the data to inform their instructional decisions moving forward. Issues of assessment validity are particularly acute for children from culturally, linguistically, or ability diverse backgrounds, whose experiences responding to testing formats and directional language may be markedly different across home and school settings (Lakin). With this understanding, the NAEYC and NAECS-SDE recommended that educators ensure selected assessments "are designed for and validated for use with children whose ages, cultures, home languages, socioeconomic status, abilities and disabilities, and other characteristics are similar to those of the children with whom the assessments will be used" (NAEYC & NAECS-SDE, 2003, p. 11). Finally, educators need to remember that many formal assessments represent a child's performance at a specific moment in time and should not be the only measure used to make important educational decisions for individual children (DEC; NAEYC & NAECS-SDE).

Examining Assessment Practices
With Culturally and Linguistically Diverse Children

Recently, the Every Student Succeeds Act (ESSA; PL 114-95) was established as a new movement to create uniform criteria within a state and to provide English language proficiency assessments across states (Cimpian, Thompson, & Makowski, 2017). ESSA requires identifying English learners within 30 days of enrollment (Office of Superintendent of Public Instruction, 2015). English learners are defined as students who were born outside of the United States or whose home language is one other than English.

To fulfill the ESSA requirements, school districts use a home language survey to identify children who are exposed to a language other than English at home (Abedi, 2008; Massachusetts Department of Elementary and Secondary Education, 2016). The format and question items on the home language survey differ across states and seek only to identify children's home languages (Abedi). Successful identification of culturally and linguistically diverse students is essential in establishing effective educational environments for young children and nurturing meaningful relationships with families. However, the identification processes currently in place may mischaracterize children's language experiences. Abedi noted that the validity of the information from home language surveys may be low; he explained that parents might provide inconsistent information for various reasons, including 1) parents' concerns over equal opportunity for their children, 2) citizenship issues, and 3) poor understanding of interview or survey questions.

Issues with reliability and validity are a concern for all children but are especially of concern when using formal assessments with children with varying abilities and children with diverse cultural and linguistic backgrounds. Formal assessments are often not appropriate for diverse young children because they are constructed with a lack of sensitivity toward individual characteristics such as language skills, cultural background, and problem-solving approaches (Winter, Kopriva, Chen, & Emick, 2006). Because of language and cultural biases within the construction of the test, children with diverse cultural and linguistic backgrounds are often misidentified as needing special education or English for Speakers of Other Languages (ESOL) programs (Abedi, 2008; Brassard & Boehm, 2007; Schon, Shaftel, & Markham, 2008). Children's developing English language skills might be mislabeled as cognitive disabilities, academic delays, or language processing disorders; unfamiliar behavior patterns might be mislabeled as behavior problems (Office of Superintendent of Public Instruction, 2008; Schon et al.). Misidentification of children's specific learning needs may negatively affect those students' academic progress and self-esteem (Abedi).

There are ways educators can help to mediate the impact of testing bias for children. First, educators should ensure that testing for developmental delays or disabilities is administered in children's primary languages (Office of Superintendent of Public Instruction, 2008). However, the use of standardized tests that have been formally or informally translated into children's native languages may render the tests invalid. Translating instructions and items of standardized measures may not provide accurate test results because the translation may change the difficulty level of the items and the original psychometric properties (Espinosa, 2010; Ochoa, Powell, & Robles-Piiia, 1996). Currently, in the United States, existing English versions of assessments are often translated into Spanish. However, large national studies of children's development do not intentionally include Spanish-speaking children; this omission results in fewer relevant data points documenting children's developmental pathways within diverse Spanish-speaking populations (Espinosa). Therefore, norming performance results of tests against a population that is not representative of the population completing the test brings into question the validity of the assessment data.

Likewise, because large-scale tests are typically based on white, middle-class populations, cultural differences or cultural influences on the assessments are not considered (Notari-Syverson, Losardo, & Lim, 2003; Schon et al., 2008). Thus, students whose dominant languages are not English or whose cultural identities do not belong to mainstream norms might not be familiar with the content of most standardized tests (Notari-Syverson et al.). This unfamiliarity with assessment tasks and content has a negative impact on culturally diverse students' overall performance on the assessment (Enciso, 2001). Recognizing bias in formal assessment practices is an important advocacy stance for early childhood educators. As Kirova and Hennig (2013) reminded educators, "through a process of assessments, children's diverse knowledge has been marginalized and devalued as compared to the privileged knowledge associated with the norms promoted by the dominant discourse within the field" (p. 107). Therefore, it is important for early educators to use assessments that focus on children's strengths and that reveal the full spectrum of children's understandings and skills.

Nurturing a Strength-Based Perspective

To ensure children's skills and understandings are accurately represented, educators must select and implement formalized assessment practices designed to reveal and document children's performances across cognitive, social and emotional, linguistic, and physical domains. The assessment tools that educators use shape the conversations that educators, families, and colleagues engage in when interpreting and discussing children's accomplishments. Educators should practice analyzing assessment results with colleagues to gain experience describing the nuances of each assessment. Educators need to be able to confidently identify areas of strength for individual children as well as positively discuss areas of development where children would benefit from strategic instructional support in order to further support and enhance children's evolving skills and understandings. The DEC (2007) specifically recommended educators learn to "talk about strengths and emerging skills, and write narrative summaries that are objective and positive" (p. 35).

Learning to frame children's performances using a strengths-based approach means guarding against language that perpetuates a deficit perspective of the child's accomplishments. Deficit perspectives problematize children's learning and focus on what is wrong or of concern (Victoria, Australia, Department of Education and Early Childhood Development [DEECD], 2012). In an age of high-stakes, standards-based assessment practices, it may be easy to identify what children *do not* know. Similarly, the structure of some formalized assessment practices may inadvertently perpetuate deficit perspectives by identifying age-appropriate benchmarks that children must meet to be considered on grade level. Educators must focus on the specific information that individual assessments provide, while also seeking additional evidence to complement the data obtained, in order to ensure that a more holistic understanding of the child as a learner is presented. This practice also affords educators an opportunity to identify when and how children may be showing evidence of emerging skills that may not have been captured on a specific assessment at a specific moment in time. Standards and benchmarks provide educators and families with important guidelines regarding the specific skills and understandings that children should be engaged in exploring and demonstrating. In this way, standards help shape young children's curricular experiences.

Embracing a strengths-based approach requires educators to carefully consider the lens they use to identify children's progress as well as the language they use to discuss children's performances. This may require a paradigm shift. For example, an educator may use an assessment protocol that uses a checklist to document a kindergarten child's upper and lowercase letter knowledge at the end of the year. The child may accurately and consistently identify 12 lower case and 16 upper case letters. However, the standard states that kindergarten children will "recognize and name all upper- and lowercase letters of the alphabet" (CCSSO & NGA, 2010, p. 15). At this point, it would be easy for an educator to summarize the test results and report to either the child's family or other educators that the child does not know all of her letters. In this case, "the deficit-based model fails to provide sufficient information about strengths and strategies to support a child's learning and development" (DEECD, 2012, p. 6).

Conversely, a strengths-based approach would underscore the child's specific learning accomplishments and leverage the child's existing letter knowledge while focusing on how to continue to promote the child's emerging letter knowledge. The DEECD (2012) articulated the following principles to guide educators in embracing strengths-based approaches: "(a) understand that children's learning is dynamic, complex, and holistic, (b) understand that children demonstrate their learning in different ways, and (c) start with what's present—not what's absent—and write about what works for the child" (p. 6). Accordingly, an educator's characterization of the kindergarten child's progress may be that "she successfully identified 12 lower case and 16 upper case letters. With continued opportunity to participate in shared writing, read alouds, and guided letter play experiences, she is poised to consistently identify the remaining upper and lowercase letters."

It takes time to reframe and rephrase assessment data. To begin considering strengths-based approaches, educators should start by monitoring the language they use to characterize children's performances. Consider rephrasing sentences that include words and phrases like "don't," "can't," "doesn't," "won't," "knows nothing," and "if she would just." These words often lead to problematizing the child and act to shift the "blame" for current performance levels to the child. Alternatively, strengths-based approaches remain positive and neutrally focused on the strengths that the educator can leverage to enhance the child's development across domains. The goal of a strengths-based approach is to empower children to develop "enduring habits of mind and actions" that promote engaged learning and a growth mindset (DEECD, 2012, p. 26).

The Professional Development Activities section that follows describes two LEARN IT activities that are specifically planned to enhance educators' knowledge and skills on assessing diverse young children. In the first activity, educators will explore formal assessments for diverse learners; in the second, they will consider site-based formal assessment practices.

Exploring Formal Assessments for Diverse Young Learners

Learning to implement, interpret, and respond to holistic criterion-referenced assessment instruments may be a daunting proposition for educators, who are already immersed in orchestrating and enriching children's daily learning environments. This strand of LEARN IT encourages educators to reflect on current assessment practices, consider new assessment tools, and interpret assessment results with colleagues. Throughout the LEARN IT institute, implementation and mentoring, and supportive learning communities, educators will develop a working knowledge of how to strategically use diverse measurement instruments and effectively contextualize assessment results for peers and families.

LEARN IT Institute

The initial focus for this LEARN IT institute is to develop a common language for analyzing and discussing various aspects of formal assessments. The institute provides educators with a framework for considering formal assessments. The framework builds assessment literacy and encourages educators to use a critical lens when selecting, implementing, and interpreting assessment results for children and their families. In preparation for this institute, focused on examining formalized assessment practices, participants should read the Foundations section of this chapter and come prepared to explore the formal assessment instruments their school currently implements.

To begin the institute, the large group discusses the following questions:

- What are the current formalized assessment practices that my school uses to document children's learning?

- How does the information in the chapter related to the purposes of assessment and the impact of bias confirm or contradict my experiences as an educator administering assessments or interpreting assessments?

- How do the assessment practices influence my work with culturally and linguistically diverse children and families?

Educators initially consider their personal experiences with formal assessments and acknowledge that assessments are an important part of school cultures. Educators begin to consider how their assessments shape learning opportunities for children and how results are communicated to diverse stakeholders. Stopping to reflect on current practices empowers educators to recognize the valuable information that formal assessment instruments provide regarding young learners while also acknowledging potential assessment limitations.

Framework for Exploring Formal Assessment

Learning how to thoughtfully analyze the structure of formal assessments is a necessary skill for educators to develop in order to ensure that children are well represented by the assessment tools selected. For this activity, participants use Handout 6.1, which provides a framework to guide their explorations of commercially available formal assessments. The framework prompts educators to consider specific constructs that are essential components of valid and appropriate assessments for children.

In this activity, participants will examine a variety of preselected, commercially available standardized assessments. As the goal of this first activity is to develop participants' knowledge of essential formal assessment vocabulary, they should not examine a familiar assessment. Therefore, participants engage in an exploration of rich standardized,

Framework for Considering Formal Assessments

	Consider the developmental domains:	Identify the purpose of the assessment:	Provide a description of the assessment.	Describe how it is administered.	Consider the following constructs of the assessment:	Describe how bias is minimized.	Think about ensuring assessment results are accurate.
Standardized Assessment Provide the full name of the assessment. Identify the publisher.	Physical Social and emotional Cognitive Communication/language	Screening Diagnostic Readiness Monitor Progress and/or Inform Instruction	What type of standardized instrument does the assessment use?	Think about the materials, time, frequency, etc.	Validity Reliability Norming		How might leniency errors skew the data results reported? Administration errors? Scoring errors?

Results

How are the results reported?

Norm-referenced or criterion-referenced

Grade-equivalent or age-equivalent

How are the results interpreted?

How are the results used to make decisions?

Documentation

What does the evaluator collect as evidence of the child's performance?

observation-based assessments such as the following: Transdisciplinary Play-Based Assessment, Second Edition (Linder et al., 2008); GOLD (Teaching Strategies, 2010); AEPS® (Bricker et al., 2002); Ages and Stages Questionnaire®, Third Edition (ASQ®; Squires & Bricker, 2009), and Battelle Developmental Inventory (Newborg, 2005).

To begin this activity, educators gather in small groups; each group receives an assessment kit, markers, and a large piece of chart paper. On the chart paper, participants replicate Handout 6.1; this will be used for presentation purposes. Each group should review a brief description of their assigned assessment. As an introduction to the activity, educators review the framework, as described in Handout 6.1, for exploring formal assessments along with a brief description of key terms. Using the framework, participants consider the overall structure of the assessment and work to identify relevant assessment elements.

As participants collaborate to determine the nature of each assessment examined, they should first focus on the overall purpose of the assessment, including whether the assessment was developed for screening, diagnostic, readiness, program evaluation, monitoring progress, and/or informing instruction. They should likewise consider for whom the assessment is designed, which domains are emphasized, and how the assessment gathers the data. Facilitators should be available to support educators' interpretations of assessment constructs, including validity and reliability factors, norm-referenced versus criterion-referenced, and the probability of leniency errors (i.e., scoring and administration errors). Educators should also consider how the standardized instrument is used to capture evidence of the child's performances. Once each group has worked through the framework, they fill out the chart paper and prepare to share with the large group. The primary goal of this experience is for educators to begin to grapple with the academic language surrounding formal assessments (e.g., reliability, norm-referenced, criterion-referenced, and validity) and to gain confidence in analyzing and discussing the structure of formal assessments.

Stop, Jot, and Synthesize

Before the groups present, participants turn to Handout 6.2, the Stop, Jot, and Synthesize form. They should fill out the "positive connections" and the "wondering" boxes on the form as each group presents. Those boxes prompt educators to consider the benefits of using assessment instruments that allow them to see a continuum of progressively complex domain-specific understandings and skills. Each group presents, and educators and facilitators ask clarifying questions and give feedback as needed. After the presentations, educators discuss the specific assessment instruments that each presented assessment uses to document children's performances. Through the discussion, educators understand how, where, and when each assessment is administered.

Next, educators discuss the first synthesizing question on the Stop, Jot, and Synthesize form. The first question prompts educators to compare the assessments explored at the institute to other formal assessments they have experienced. Finally, educators move from table to table to get a closer look at some of the materials included in each assessment kit. By engaging in individual tours of the assessments, educators enhance their understandings of the assessment instruments and interpretation guides. Once educators examine the assessments they were interested in exploring further, they should synthesize the experience by responding individually to the final question: "Identify an assessment tool you would like to use in the future and explain why you think that assessment would enhance your work with children."

Stop, Jot, and Synthesize

Use the table to capture thoughts that pop into your head about the assessments you are learning about.

Assessment explored	Positive connections	Wonderings	Is this tool for me?
Transdisciplinary Play-Based Assessment, 2nd ed. (Linder et al., 2008)			Yes No Maybe
GOLD (Teaching Strategies, 2010)			Yes No Maybe
Assessment, Evaluation, and Programming System for Infants and Children (Bricker et al., 2002)			Yes No Maybe
Ages and Stages Questionnaire, 3rd ed. (Squires & Bricker, 2009)			Yes No Maybe

Stop and Synthesize: How are these assessments alike or different from the other formalized assessments you have experienced?

Identify an assessment tool you would like to use in the future, and explain why you think that assessment would enhance your work with children.

Implementation and Mentoring

This implementation and mentoring session will allow educators to implement an assessment tool in their classroom. To begin, educators share Handout 6.2, the Stop, Jot, and Synthesize form, with their mentor, along with the completed Implementation and Mentoring Form, Handout 6.3. Mentors should work closely with educators to further assess whether that is the best tool to implement in the classroom. Likewise, mentors should provide feedback and guidance as educators implement their chosen assessment.

Head Start educator James, introduced at the beginning of the chapter, attended the LEARN IT institute on exploring formal assessment for diverse young learners. Like many of the other educators who participated, James recognized that criterion-referenced assessments that clearly delineate a progression of skills across domains of learning could positively enhance his work with children. He learned that milestone-linked assessment tools could help him to align instructional experiences with children's emerging understandings. As a prekindergarten teacher who works in an inclusive classroom context, James also values assessment instruments, such as AEPS®, that encourage educators to flexibly arrange testing environments to account for children's specific needs while still remaining a valid and reliable assessment tool for IEP reporting purposes. He also appreciates formal assessment tools that allow him to clearly document a child's performances across multiple domains without removing the child from the learning environment. After engaging in an exploration of AEPS® at the institute, James was particularly interested in seeing how the assessment instrument would work in the context of his own classroom environment. However, learning how to implement new comprehensive, formalized assessment protocols into the daily classroom routine can be an overwhelming prospect. Therefore, James decided to ask his mentor, Janet, to work with him to pilot AEPS® with his prekindergarten students and their families.

Janet knew that the rich domain-specific assessment areas delineated in AEPS® would need to be strategically practiced over a period of time. As such, she suggested that James initiate the process by identifying a specific domain-related strand to focus on first. Having attended the dialogic reading institute, James decided to focus on the Phonological Awareness and Emergent Reading, Strand H, articulated in the Cognitive Area on AEPS®. James also requested that Janet implement the assessment with one of his students, allowing James to observe the process. He was particularly interested in seeing how Janet would document the child's performance using the AEPS® data recording form. Janet agreed that observing a data collection session was a good place to start. To support the modeling opportunity, she suggested James begin looking for the specific phonological awareness and emergent reading objectives and criterion, identified on the Child Observation Data Recording Form, prior to the implementation and mentoring session.

When Janet arrived for the implementation and mentoring session, she brought a collection of stories for sharing with a small group of children in the classroom reading nook. She also brought copies of the recording sheet provided in the AEPS® Administration Guide, Volume 1, for strand H (Bricker, Pretti-Frontczak, Johnson, & Straka, 2002). James and Janet met briefly in the morning, before the children arrived, to talk through how Janet anticipated working the children through this assessment opportunity. Janet showed James the prompts she had created to ask the children as they explored books together, as well as the spaces underneath the prompts for anecdotal notes. Janet explained that she prefers to create observational data collection sheets that can then be used to transfer to the AEPS® form at the end of the day. In this way, she was sure to remain focused on the individual learning moments that arise with children when exploring texts, while also being able to capture assessment data on the side.

Implementation and Mentoring Form

Educator's name _____   Mentor _____

Site _____   Date _____

Identify the **intentional teaching strategy** you want to **enact**. Select one child to interact with during ☐ center time ☐ small group ☐ individually. Describe the support you would like from your mentor to help you implement the **intentional teaching strategy.**

Intentional teaching strategy of focus:

Culturally Responsive Practice

☐ Choose an area and set it up to reflect children's cultures

☐ Account for child's interest-background and use child's prior knowledge

☐ Inspire child to complete the idea/activity by connecting it to his/her home culture

☐ Provide specific feedback to extend child's play in that area

☐ Question to promote higher-level thinking

Interactional Reading

From *Bringing Words to Life*

☐ Choosing vocabulary words

From Dialogic Reading

☐ Prompt
  ○ Completion prompt
  ○ Recall prompt
  ○ Open-ended prompt
  ○ Wh- question prompt
  ○ Distancing prompt

☐ Evaluate the child's response

☐ Expand the child's response

☐ Repeat–child repeats the expanded response

Expanded Vocabulary

☐ Math vocabulary (5 words)

☐ Science vocabulary (5 words)

Assessment and Instruction

☐ Follow child's interest

☐ Observe and record child learning behaviors

☐ Initiate conversations and write plans with child

☐ Provide meaningful learning opportunities informed by assessment

Extending Play

☐ Redirect play to replace violent play

☐ Plan play

☐ Act out stories

☐ Dramatic use of the constructions child makes

Inclusion

☐ Adapt environment

☐ Adapt routines

☐ Adapt materials and activities

☐ Adapt requirements

☐ Adapt instruction

Continue on back if needed

Focus child

Elaborate on how you will implement the intentional teaching strategy. _____

_____

_____

What type of in-class support do you think will help you?

☐ Modeling while you take notes

☐ Assistance with co-teaching the child

☐ Feedback after observation

☐ Other _____

_____

_____

Use back if needed

James watched Janet engage the children in an exploration of the books. He noticed how she balanced the assessment questions with comments and suggestions that encouraged the children to examine the text further or share more of their own connections with the text. Simultaneously, while the children shared and explored the stories, Janet would jot quick notes about individual children. At the end of the day, James and Janet analyzed the informal observational sheet Janet had used to capture evidence of the children's emerging literacy skills. Together, they worked to transfer the information to individual AEPS® recording sheets. As they did so, James noticed that not all of the data questions were answered for all children. This led to a discussion of ongoing assessment practices. Janet shared that James should plan alternate opportunities to engage children in explorations of the phonological awareness and emergent literacy objectives within their daily routines. At the end of the implementation and mentoring session, James had identified several opportunities throughout the day when he could embed assessment moments into the children's regular routines. James and Janet decided the next step would be to bring data sheets for Strand H to the next supportive learning community meeting. At that time, based on a collective analysis of the data presented, James would receive feedback from the group on possible next steps with his learners.

Supportive Learning Community

It is important for educators to feel safe in sharing assessments results with colleagues. Educators need to trust that information they share about children's performances will not be interpreted as negative indicators of their own teaching practices. Supportive learning communities provide an appropriate space for educators to openly question the results of assessment data and seek feedback that will enhance instructional opportunities for their students to support children's learning. When educators are implementing a new assessment instrument, providing frequent opportunities for colleagues to share their efforts to interpret and respond to the data is particularly beneficial. As members of a supportive learning community share their assessment experiences, educators deepen their understandings of how the assessments may inform their work with children.

Prior to the supportive learning community session, participants should try out a new assessment in their classroom and record the results of the assessment on individual student data sheets. Likewise, they should complete Handout 6.4, Leveraging Assessments to Enhance Children's Learning, to examine their efforts. Participants should bring this handout, along with student data sheets, to the session.

To begin the session, participants share their experiences with trying out a new assessment. The questions that follow can guide the discussion:

- What assessment did you enact and what was your purpose for using this assessment?

- What did you find easy about conducting the assessment?

- What did you find challenging about conducting the assessment?

- What would you do the same or differently the next time you conduct this assessment?

- Overall, what do you believe was valuable about using this particular assessment?

After participants share their experiences enacting the assessments in their classrooms, they gather in small groups of three or four to discuss what they learned about their students from the assessment. The participants will use Handout 6.4, the Leveraging Assessments to

Leveraging Assessments to Enhance Children's Learning

As you prepare to share your assessment experience with your supportive learning community, consider the following questions:

1. What assessment data will you be sharing? _____
_____
_____
_____
_____
_____

2. How were assessment data collected? _____
_____
_____
_____
_____
_____

3. What are your initial reactions about the assessment process? _____
_____
_____
_____
_____
_____

4. What are your initial reactions about the assessment results? _____
_____
_____
_____
_____

5. What would you like for the group to help you consider next? _____
_____
_____
_____
_____
_____

Enhance Children's Learning questions, to guide their conversation. They share their individual student data sheets with their colleagues and describe how they embedded the assessment into their instructional experiences. Then, participants discuss what they learned about the children. For example, as Head Start educator James walked his colleagues carefully through the individual student data sheets, Samita, a kindergarten teacher, noted she was glad to see that so many of the prekindergarten children were already comfortable creating rhymes and working on segmenting and blending sounds. This led to a discussion of what James' other colleagues noticed about the children and gave him greater insights into the wealth of information he had collected. As he listened to others share, he gained additional ideas on assessments to use and the types of information that might help him to better understand his students' abilities.

Once participants have shared their individual student data sheets, educators should return to the large group to discuss the implications of their data analyses on future instructional plans. Volunteers summarize how they embedded the assessment into an instructional experience and what they learned about the children. Then the group brainstorms ways to use this information to plan future instruction. To conclude the discussion, participants write down one instructional implication that they identified based on the data they collected and recorded on the individual student data sheet.

James found this final discussion to be a valuable synthesizing activity. After he finished describing how he embedded much of the phonological awareness assessment opportunities into the children's reading experiences, Samita wondered whether perhaps James could begin to intentionally capture the children's understandings of letter–sound relationships in their writing as well. Returning to the assessment tool, James and the rest of the supportive learning community members realized that by focusing on writing, the children would have the opportunity to demonstrate a slightly more complex literacy skill. The supportive learning community continued to brainstorm ways James could encourage children to think about letter–sound relationships while engaging them in writing. At the end of the session, James decided to infuse a few interactive writing moments into the morning message time and to review all of the centers to make sure that fresh writing materials were readily accessible.

Figure 6.1 is a checklist of this LEARN IT strand that the professional development team can use to assess whether they implemented all aspects of the LEARN framework. Facilitators can use the checklist to guide the process as they implement this professional development program on exploring assessment for diverse young children.

Checklist for Exploring Formal Assessments for Diverse Young Learners

	LEARN IT institute	Implementation and mentoring	Supportive learning communities
Learn	❐ Facilitators presented research and best practices related to formal assessment for diverse young learners.	❐ Mentors shared information about the specific formal assessments participants chose to implement in their classrooms.	❐ Mentors reviewed information on assessment for diverse young learners.
Enact	❐ Facilitators guided participants' review and critique of a specific formal assessment.	❐ Mentors supported participants as they implemented a specific formal assessment with a child in their classroom.	❐ Mentors engaged participants in analyzing the data collected from their implementation of a specific formal assessment.
Assess	❐ Facilitators provided an opportunity for participants to share their review and critique of a specific formal assessment.	❐ Mentors guided participants to discuss the effectiveness of their implementation of the specific formal assessment.	❐ Mentors provided an opportunity for participants to discuss what they learned about the children assessed using a formal assessment.
Reflect	❐ Facilitators encouraged participants to consider which formal assessments, reviewed and critiqued in the institute, they might explore in more depth and potentially use in their classrooms.	❐ Mentors promoted reflection on the information gathered about a child after implementing a specific formal assessment.	❐ Mentors supported participants' discussion of the implications of the data collected and analyzed.
Network	❐ Facilitators provided opportunities for participants to meet in large and small groups to learn, discuss, and reflect.	❐ Mentors provided opportunities to network with peers and follow up in supportive learning communities.	❐ Mentors provided opportunities for participants to learn together and encouraged discussion and reflection among participants.

Figure 6.1. Checklist for Exploring Formal Assessments for Diverse Young Learners.

Considering Site-Based Formal Assessment Practices

Learning about and infusing new assessment tools into practice can be an enriching experience for students, families, and educators. However, educators should guard against infusing too many formalized assessments into the early childhood classroom. Each assessment needs to have a clear purpose and yield meaningful insight into children's developing understandings and skills. Therefore, periodically, it is important to systematically consider the formalized assessment practices used within each school context. In this LEARN IT activity, the purpose of the review is to ensure that, collectively, the assessments provide all students with opportunities to demonstrate their understandings in diverse and meaningful ways and that all learning domains are thoughtfully represented in the data. Systematic reviews of school-based assessment practices also afford educators opportunities to consider data across grade levels and individual classrooms. Supportive analysis of data can encourage shifts in instructional practices to better serve the diverse needs of young learners. This stand of LEARN IT professional development encourages educators to engage in a thoughtful review of current assessment practices and honors the efforts educators are already engaged in to enhance young children's learning experiences. Educators will consider the existing formal assessment practices at their school.

LEARN IT Institute

This LEARN IT institute focuses on formal assessment practices that the educators are already using across the various school sites. Accordingly, participants should sit with their school-based colleagues. Before the session, educators and mentors should collaborate to compile a list of the formalized assessment practices currently used on site.

Taking a Closer Look

To begin the institute, educators acknowledge that many early childhood centers adopt at least one or two formal or commercially available assessment tools to help monitor and discern student knowledge. Taking time to periodically examine the parameters of the specific assessments used in a particular school ensures that educators are comfortable discussing, sharing, and interpreting common assessment results with colleagues, families, and other interested stakeholders. The goals of this institute are to analyze the common assessment tools used by the school to make curricular decisions about individual and groups of students. Educators will

- Consider the nature of the data each assessment provides

- Discuss how to interpret the results

- Think about appropriate ways to use the results to inform classroom practices

Strategic considerations of school-based assessment practices should also encourage educators to identify biases inherent in formal assessments and seek assessments that minimize bias.

After this introduction, educators break into small groups of four. The small groups explore and reflect on their current assessment practices using Handout 6.5 to guide their evaluation.

Following the small-group work, the groups share key points raised in their discussions with the whole group. Then the whole group discusses how the educators may effectively use the results of formal assessments in the future. This discussion should underscore the benefits of formalized assessment practices as well as the limitations.

Using Assessments

1. First, consider the overall purpose of the assessment.

   • Who is the assessment designed for?

   • What, specifically, does the assessment measure?

   • How do the authors of the assessment intend for the results to be used?

2. How does your educational context use the assessment results?

   • Is this use reasonably consistent with the assessment's original design?

3. To achieve reliable and valid results across test subjects, commercially available assessments establish strict administration procedures. As you examine the assessment protocol with your group, think about protocol restrictions that may contribute to underestimating a child's performance.

4. Identify other assessments in place at your site that supplement the information gained using this assessment tool.

5. Finally, reflect on what needs to be considered when selecting, administering, and interpreting formal assessments.

Critiquing Assessments for Bias

After participants consider the formalized assessment processes that they currently use across their school contexts, they should think critically about hidden biases that may underlie some of the assessment instruments currently in place. To facilitate this conversation, the groups should thoughtfully consider the questions in Handout 6.6 related to assessment validity and bias. These questions provide participants with an opportunity to learn about additional types of testing bias that may affect the validity of the results.

Subsequently, once educators identify areas with potential biases, they should engage in an open dialog across groups to share concerns about bias in testing practices and strategies for mediating the impact of bias in test results. Ultimately, the activity should heighten educators' sensitivities and encourage educators to seek ways to mediate the bias in testing practices so that all data collected present a more accurate picture of each child's knowledge and skills.

Assessment Action Plans

Periodically considering all of the formalized assessment practices that children and educators engage in is an essential task for promoting program development and enhancing intentional teaching practices. This activity is designed to help educators look across all of the formalized assessments currently used by their schools to document children's learning. Accordingly, educators should work together at the institute, in the same group as that of their supportive learning community. Educators use Handout 6.7, Considering Our Formalized Assessment Practices, to facilitate their considerations of the assessments already in place at their school. The handout provides space for educators to reflect on three assessments; additional handouts may be necessary if the school uses more than three different assessments across the school year to document children's performances.

Working in the supportive learning community groups, educators create a timeline of when each required assessment is administered. Once all of the assessments are represented on the timeline, educators engage in a careful evaluation of the purposes of each assessment. They can use the guiding questions in Handout 6.8 to examine rationales for each assessment and discuss how the test either directly or indirectly supports children's learning.

Personal Assessment Action Plan

Once the supportive learning communities analyze the formalized assessment practices currently used to document children's learning, educators are poised to develop personal assessment action plans. Personal assessment plans empower educators to leverage data results for the benefit of all learners in their classrooms. Facilitators should remind educators that, because assessment data are typically collected across time, attending to data and reflecting on curricular goals is a recursive process. Educators will need to think strategically about the relevancy of each data point at any given point in time and, if appropriate, intentionally modify curricular opportunities for learners. Participants review Handout 6.9, the Personal Assessment Action Plan. This action plan guides educators to consider the direct impact and relevance of each assessment administered. The activity affords educators an opportunity to take personal ownership of the formalized assessment practices and helps educators appropriately contextualize the assessment event by considering how well it informs specific educational opportunities for children.

Assessment Validity and Bias

Use the descriptions below to reflect on current testing procedures and instruments that may leave children vulnerable to bias in testing results.

- **Consider potential areas for construct bias.** Construct bias may exist if the assessment scenarios favor either the interests or probable background knowledge for specific groups of learners in your school (i.e., gender, socioeconomic, cultural, linguistic, or religious). Construct bias may be found in the language and topics presented in assessment texts. For example, consider word problems in math, data charts in science that compare one group to another, and reading passages that privilege some background experiences easily recognizable by most members of one group and not another.

- **Consider potential areas where administration bias may affect the data results.** Administration bias may occur when the person giving the test breaks administration protocol in some fashion, such as the following:

  - Reading directions multiple times when the protocol only allows for one reading

  - Extending the amount of time prescribed by a given test

  - Inadvertently providing clues about the appropriate responses with confirmatory smiles or questioning looks, subtle vocal inflections, or prompts that encourage students to think and take their time

- **Is there evidence that any of your current practices may hold predictive bias?** Predictive bias relates to the test's ability to "predict" a person's performance on a given task in the future. Are there groups of students (i.e., gender, linguistically, culturally, or ability diverse) who may be affected by the results of an assessment whose predictive validity may hold bias?

- **After examining your current assessments for areas of potential bias, stop to brainstorm solutions to mediate bias in testing practices.** For example, you may decide training is necessary to ensure all teachers administer the tests in the same way. Or you may decide that additional assessments need to be included for students who are culturally and linguistically diverse to ensure the formal assessments are not underrepresenting performances in particular domains.

Considering Formalized Assessment Practices

Use this graphic to consider the diverse sets of data you are already collecting. Consider the following questions as you reflect on each assessment:

- What kinds of curricular decisions can I make when I analyze these assessment results?

- Do I see any "gaps" in the assessment data? What other information do I need to collect to create a clear picture of children's performances?

- Are there any shifts in assessment practices we should consider?

- How do I share these assessment results with families?

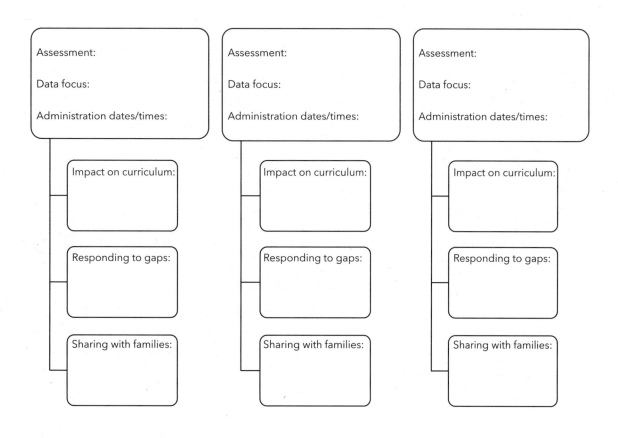

Considering How We Use Assessment Results

1. What kinds of curricular decisions can be made after an analysis of the assessment results? _____
   _____
   _____
   _____
   _____
   _____

2. Are there any "gaps" in the assessment data? _____
   _____
   _____
   _____
   _____
   _____

3. What other information should the school consider collecting to create a clear picture of children's
   performances? _____
   _____
   _____
   _____
   _____
   _____

4. Are there any shifts in assessment practices we should consider? For example, are all learning domains
   considered? Are we overassessing in any given domain? _____
   _____
   _____
   _____
   _____

5. How do we share these assessment results with families, and what impact will the results have on children and
   their families? _____
   _____
   _____
   _____
   _____
   _____

Personal Assessment Action Plan

After considering the assessment practices in which you already engage, you will be ready to develop a personal assessment plan. Personal assessment plans empower educators to leverage data results for the benefit of all learners. Your final step is to consider how the data will be shared with others. Assessment data are typically collected across time; therefore, attending to assessment data and its impact on curriculum is often a recursive process. Be sure to reflect on how you will use information gained through the assessment process to essentially "begin again."

Assessments I will use to inform my curriculum	Curricular decisions	Anticipated impact on student learning	Resources I may need to implement the assessment or respond to results	Sharing the data

For example, sometimes school districts may administer the same (or conceptually similar) assessment at the beginning and end of the year. The object of the assessment is to demonstrate a positive change in children's understandings in any given domain. This type of assessment follows a pretest-posttest protocol. Necessarily, the pretest will contain test items that are probably unfamiliar to children. This is because the test is capturing evidence for all of the domain-specific standards the children are expected to learn by the end of the year. In this particular case, how educators contextualize children's performance data on the pretest would be substantially different from how educators contextualize the posttest performance data. Educators may decide to use the pretest results to identify strategic learning groups for children or pinpoint specific foundational content knowledge children need to possess before moving forward with the year's curricular goals. However, the educator may not consider the preassessment data particularly relevant for families, and sharing the assessment results may actually cause families undue concern about their child's specific understandings. Conversely, the end-of-year performance data may have real implications for individual learners and their families, as well as for the enacted curriculum.

Implementation and Mentoring

This implementation and mentoring activity is designed to support individual educators' dialogues with families about specific assessment results. To begin, educators identify an opportunity to share assessment results with a family. They talk through the results of the assessment with their LEARN IT mentor. Educators and mentors will collaborate to systematically review children's artifacts and performance scores. Likewise, they should work together to facilitate conferences with families and prepare talking points, in order to ensure that educators are confident in discussing test scores.

For example, in preparing for Desmond's annual IEP review at the end of the year, James wanted to make sure that he articulated the results of the AEPS® appropriately. James realized that because Desmond's family and other professionals on the IEP team were not familiar with the AEPS® protocol, he would need to be confident in his interpretation and presentation of the data. James completed an Implementation and Mentoring Form and invited Janet, his mentor, to meet with him prior to his scheduled conference time with Desmond's parents and other members of the IEP committee.

When Janet arrived, James presented the little book Desmond created with the animal pictures and labels as a recent example of Desmond's emergent literacy skills. Pointing to the labels in Desmond's book, James explained that he was really excited about sharing Desmond's book because "it's so creative and shows that he is making some meaningful connections between letters and sounds." James went on to say, "But he is not consistently using letter sounds to sound out and write words." James explained that he sat next to Desmond when he started to write the labels in his book. James referred Janet to Desmond's labels for monkey /MK/, toucan /TK/, and snake /SK/. James said that Desmond did not sound out the words on his own, and even though James was guiding him, Desmond did not use any vowels. As Janet reviewed the artifact and listened to James' explanation, she paused to consider the language James used to describe Desmond's efforts. Janet knew that James was proud of Desmond's work and she recognized that James intentionally analyzed Desmond's writing to look for meaningful patterns. However, Janet also understood that because James focused on explaining what Desmond was not doing, James had missed opportunities to pinpoint the specific emergent literacy skills Desmond's efforts did reveal.

To help James reframe his emphasis from a deficit perspective to a strengths-based perspective, Janet asked him to practice "flipping his lens." More explicitly, Janet asked James to look at the AEPS® assessment tool and start by identifying the phonological awareness and emergent literacy skills Desmond already demonstrated consistently. Recalling the strengths-based language approach discussed in this chapter, James understood that articulating the skills a child already possessed provided a positive performance foundation upon which other emerging skills could be layered. Using the strengths-based assessment perspective, James analyzed again, saying, "Desmond is using his knowledge of key consonants like M and K to sound out and write words." James went on to explain, "As Desmond continues to experiment with writing, he will begin to consistently represent the consonants he hears within words and use vowels." Encouraged by James' revision, Janet prompted him to identify, for the parents and the other members of the IEP team, instructional strategies he believed would support Desmond's emergent literacy skills.

Drawing on his earlier experiences with his supportive learning community, James suggested that including more opportunities to explicitly model how to sound out and write words would support Desmond's evolving understandings of letter–sound relationships. James also thought that his own presence at the writing center, to scaffold children's work sounding out words, would become an important instructional routine that would benefit Desmond as well as other children. In this fashion, James and Janet talked through the data James presented and they worked together to articulate the strengths Desmond demonstrated and identify strategic areas for instructional support. After the meeting, James recognized that the artifacts and observational assessment data would serve as concrete conversational guides as he collaborated with the family and the other members of the IEP team to help Desmond make a successful transition into kindergarten the following year.

Figure 6.2 is a checklist of this LEARN IT strand that the professional development team can use to assess whether they implemented all aspects of the LEARN framework.

Supportive Learning Communities

The purpose of this supportive learning community session is to begin to establish a common language for analyzing, interpreting, and responding to trends in state- or local-level data. Assessments that articulate student performances in core academic areas such as math, reading, writing, science, and/or social studies work well for this activity. Frequently, this type of data is disaggregated to inform stakeholders, at various levels, about the overall performances of specific groups of learners. Several demographic groups are often presented, typically including gender, ethnicity, and socioeconomic status (as evidenced by a student qualifying for free or reduced lunch). For this supportive learning community, educators will analyze a set of data drawn from their own student population. The goal is to identify common trends in data for their specific student population. In particular, the supportive learning communities will identify areas where all students are performing well, as well as areas where students may need additional supports to obtain higher levels of proficiency. Local-level and state-level assessment results often use descriptive indicators such as "proficient" or "developing" to describe students' performances on any given aspect of a test. To support this analysis, the supportive learning community will use Handout 6.10, the Focused Analysis of Local-Level or State-Level Data Table. This handout may need to be modified to support the analysis of the specific school context. After filling out the table, participants complete the Analyzing Local-Level or State-Level Data questions that follow.

Collectively, the supportive learning community should be able to identify positive performance patterns and areas that may benefit from targeted interventions. When colleagues gather to discuss localized performance assessment data, perceptible patterns in student performances often emerge. These dialogs can lead to meaningful changes in the curricular opportunities and supports that children experience within their own classrooms.

Checklist for Considering Site-Based Formal Assessment Practices

	LEARN IT institute	Implementation and mentoring	Supportive learning communities
Learn	❒ Facilitators presented research and best practice on issues related to formal assessments, such as appropriate use, reliability, validity, and test bias.	❒ Mentors helped participants identify particular needs in discussing children's performances and using assessment results to inform instructional decisions.	❒ Mentors reviewed information on formal assessments and explained how to analyze and review data.
Enact	❒ Facilitators engaged participants in an evaluation of a formal assessment used at their site.	❒ Mentors supported participants as they articulated formal assessment results.	❒ Mentors engaged participants in analyzing data collected using the formal assessment.
Assess	❒ Facilitators provided participants with an opportunity to report what they learned from the activity.	❒ Mentors encouraged participants to consider how to take a strength-based approach when articulating formal assessment results.	❒ Mentors provided an opportunity for participants to identify positive performance patterns and areas that might benefit from targeted instruction.
Reflect	❒ Facilitators engaged participants in developing assessment action plans related to using formal assessment in their classrooms.	❒ Mentors promoted reflection on how to prepare to share formal assessment results with families and professional colleagues.	❒ Mentors provided an opportunity for participants to reflect on the patterns they saw in the data and how they will use the information to inform instruction.
Network	❒ Facilitators provided opportunities for participants to meet in large and small groups to learn, discuss, and reflect.	❒ Mentors provided opportunities to network with peers and follow up in supportive learning communities.	❒ Mentors provided opportunities for participants to learn together and encouraged discussion and reflection among participants.

Figure 6.2. Checklist for Considering Site-Based Formal Assessment Practices.

Focused Analysis of Local-Level or State-Level Data Table

Assessment				
Gender		Pass +	Pass	Developing
	Female			
	Male			
Ethnicity		Pass +	Pass	Developing
	Black			
	Asian			
	White			
	Hispanic			
	*			
	*			
Socioeconomic status		Pass +	Pass	Developing
	Free/reduced lunch			
	No free/reduced lunch			
Grade level		Pass +	Pass	Developing
	Pre-K			
	K			

Note. Table may be modified to support the analysis of the specific school context.

* Additional culturally, linguistically diverse groups should be included as relevant to the specific school context.

Analyzing Local-Level or State-Level Data Questions

1. Where do we see that our students are doing particularly well on this particular assessment?

2. Where do we see that our students are performing less well than we would anticipate?

3. Which groups of our children are outperforming other groups?

4. Which groups are underperforming other groups?

5. What is our plan moving forward to close any identified performance gaps between groups?

SUMMARY

The first part of this chapter introduced James as he thoughtfully evaluated Desmond's emerging literacy skills. We then explored factors influencing school-based assessment practices including school-based expectations and legislative policies. Throughout the chapter, we examined the specific language informing the structure of formal assessments. We considered the role that formalized assessment practices play in supporting an educator's intentionality and, in turn, enhancing curricular experiences that promote student learning. We then focused on opportunities for educators to develop a deeper understanding of current and prospective assessment practices that support the needs of diverse young children. The content provided in the chapter, combined with the guided experiences in the LEARN IT institute, implementation and mentoring session, and supportive learning communities, affords educators unique opportunities to enhance their conceptualizations of formalized assessment practices for children and their families.

Linking Assessment With Curriculum and Instruction

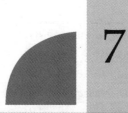

7

With Leslie La Croix

After the last of their kindergartners boarded the bus, Samita, the lead teacher, and Nadia, the assistant teacher, sat down to prepare for the next day's instruction on patterning that they would provide for Crystal, Fahed, and Wayne. All three children were eager learners and enjoyed working with other children in the class. Samita and Nadia had noticed that Crystal required a higher level of scaffolding than many children in the classroom. However, with repetition and Samita's and Nadia's support, she learned new skills and applied them independently once she had learned them. Fahed was a dual language learner who spoke Arabic and English at home. He learned new skills quickly, and Samita and Nadia continually looked for ways to challenge him. Samita and Nadia had come to know Wayne as a curious child and found that they needed to help direct his attention to the task at hand. When engaged, he learned quickly; however, he was often more interested in what was going on around him than in the activity in front of him.

When planning the lesson, Samita and Nadia used anecdotal notes recorded during previous instructional interactions; these notes indicated that Crystal, Fahed, and Wayne could identify and describe repeating *ABAB* patterns with colors (e.g., *red, black, red, black*), objects (e.g., *rabbit, horse, rabbit, horse)*, and shapes (e.g., *circle, square, circle, square*). In their previous assessments, they also noted that the children could extend the pattern by adding additional colors, objects, or shapes to the end of the sequence (e.g., *blue, green, blue, green*). As they planned, they jotted down notes on the lesson planning template and referred to the notebook that contained the local curriculum and the state and national standards that guided their instruction. According to state and national standards of learning, kindergarten children are expected to identify, describe, and extend simple patterns that repeat (National Council of Teachers of Mathematics, 2000; Virginia Department of Education, 2009). Samita and Nadia knew from previous professional development that research suggests that understanding and being able to manipulate patterns is the foundation of algebra (e.g., McGarvey, 2012; Papic, Mulligan, & Mitchelmore, 2011) and can influence mathematics and reading achievement (e.g., Kidd et al., 2014). Using what they knew about the three children, the state and national standards, and current research, they identified 1) learning outcomes, 2) materials, and 3) plans for collaborating with families and other professionals. They then developed an instructional plan that included deciding on 1) the context or setting for the instruction, 2) intentional teaching strategies to implement, 3) adaptations and

Small Group Instructional Focus: *Students will show they understand how to complete a pattern when an item is missing. Use rainbow bears.*	
Student	Anecdotal notes
Fahed	*Fahed easily responded to the missing item prompts.*
Crystal	*Crystal is still developing her understanding. First, she extended the pattern. I drew her attention to the beginning of the pattern and prompted her to orally fill in the missing item.*
Wayne	*Wayne used the colored bears to make outlines of shapes, including circles and squares. He needs additional opportunities to explore patterns.*
Reflection: *I supported Crystal's experience, but I am worried that Fahed is ready to show me more and I missed the opportunity to extend his learning. Also, I need to find out what will motivate Wayne to engage in pattern play. I'll talk to Nadia.*	

Figure 7.1. Anecdotal notes.

accommodations that may be needed, and 4) how to bring closure to the instruction. By the end of the planning session, Nadia had a clear sense of how she would approach instruction with the children.

When Nadia began the lesson the next day, she knew that the lesson would focus on completing a pattern when a middle item was missing (e.g., *AB?BAB*). While teaching, Nadia used her notepad to make anecdotal notes about each child's interactions with the task. See Figure 7.1 for a sample of her notes. She noted that Crystal and Fahed showed an interest in the activity but Wayne did not. She also noticed that Fahed identified the missing piece of the pattern with ease, but Crystal experienced some difficulty. In addition, she wrote down that because Wayne did not fully participate, she could not get a clear sense of what he was able to do. As Nadia modified instruction to provide Crystal with additional scaffolding, she noted the strategies that worked and which strategies fell short of the support Crystal needed to succeed. She wondered what else she could do to help Crystal to identify the missing piece of the pattern. She also considered whether she had adequately challenged Fahed and what she could do to more effectively engage Wayne in the learning activity.

WHAT TO EXPECT
IN THIS CHAPTER

Prior to engaging in LEARN IT, Samita and Nadia, like many other early educators, thought of assessment as a list of skills that need to be checked off by the end of the school year. Their school reinforced this idea by providing a long checklist of discrete skills that kindergartners needed to master. Their belief was further reinforced by the state's approach to testing the standards of learning that relied heavily on recall of information. For educators like Samita and Nadia, professional development is necessary to develop their knowledge of interactive, embedded assessment of young children; such assessment takes place within the context of intentional teaching and involves meaningful interactions among children and between children and adults. In addition, educators benefit from professional development that focuses on how to use the information gathered to make informed instructional decisions for individual children.

Assessing diverse young children was addressed in Chapter 6 and set the stage for using assessment to make informed instructional decisions. This chapter examines intentionally linking assessment with curriculum and instruction. This chapter

- Highlights the importance of linking assessment to curriculum and instruction

- Explores the nature and context of intentional assessment that is interactive and embedded in instruction

- Presents strategies for assessing young learners within the context of intentional teaching

- Provides professional development activities that promote educators' understandings of ways to intentionally link assessment with curriculum and instruction.

FOUNDATIONS: INTENTIONALLY LINKING ASSESSMENT WITH CURRICULUM AND INSTRUCTION

An important aspect of intentional teaching is purposefully linking assessment with curriculum and instruction. Although decisions about what to teach are influenced by local curriculum and state and national standards, instruction must take into account the myriad pathways that children's learning and development take. As emphasized in previous chapters, children possess varying abilities and come to school with a variety of cultural and linguistic experiences that influence their interests, abilities, and prior knowledge. Purposeful and intentional assessment embedded in everyday instructional activities, and focused on individual children, provides educators with information about the prior knowledge, interests, abilities, and needs of the children in their classroom. This information can then be used to intentionally plan and implement curriculum and effective instruction for each individual child. This type of intentional assessment informs instruction that includes each child and is differentiated to enhance individual children's learning and development.

When educators intentionally gather information about children's prior knowledge, interests, abilities, and linguistic and cultural backgrounds, they engage in assessment designed to support intentional teaching interactions. Intentional assessment takes place within the context of educators' interactions with children and families. Intentional assessment is also continuous, multidimensional, and guided by knowledge of the curriculum (DEC, 2007; Gullo & Hughes, 2011; NAEYC & NAECS-SDE, 2003; Pyle & DeLuca, 2013). When educators link assessment to curriculum and instruction, they plan and implement instruction guided by their knowledge of 1) the ways children develop and learn; 2) the curriculum and expected learning outcomes; and 3) individual children's prior knowledge, interests, abilities, and cultural and linguistic backgrounds. In this way, educators integrate what they know about children and expected curricular learning outcomes to plan and implement instructional experiences focused on children as well as curriculum (Gullo & Hughes; Pyle & DeLuca). This approach enables educators to provide instruction that meets individual children's educational needs and aligns with local curricular learning outcomes and state and national standards.

Within these contexts, educators take a multidimensional approach to assessment, relying on a variety of ways to gather data about young learners, including observing and conversing with children, noting children's responses to instruction, and engaging children in activities that require them to apply and transfer learning (DEC, 2007; Gullo & Hughes, 2011; NAEYC & NAECS/SDE, 2003; Pyle & DeLuca, 2013). Intentional educators recognize that children's developmental and learning pathways vary and, therefore, use varied sources of information to understand what children know and can do (Gullo & Hughes). In addition, they not only are concerned about whether children learn specific knowledge and skills, but also are interested in how young learners apply their knowledge and skills in other contexts (Gullo & Hughes; Shepard, 2000). Therefore, intentional educators use their interactions with children to gather information that provides a well-rounded account of children's knowledge and abilities. This dynamic, interactive approach enables educators to determine what children are "able to do independently as well as what can be done with adult guidance" and provides "valuable insights about how understanding might be extended" (Shepard, 2000, p. 10). This interactive, embedded approach to assessment is used to purposefully inform future instruction that addresses curricular outcomes as well as individual children's educational needs (Pyle & DeLuca).

Intentional assessment is linked to standards and expected learning outcomes (Grisham-Brown, Hallam, & Brookshire, 2006). It also takes place while children are involved in learning experiences (Gullo & Hughes, 2011), and it informs instruction (Grisham-Brown et al., 2006). Therefore, assessment becomes a tool to create and modify curriculum as well as to determine the effectiveness of the curriculum (Gullo & Hughes). Assessment of this nature occurs within the context of rich curricular content, such as fine arts, language arts, mathematics, science, and social studies, and is guided by expected learning outcomes. Educators' intimate knowledge of the curriculum and learning outcomes enables them to intentionally assess children's learning and use knowledge of the curriculum, as well as of the children, to inform their instructional decisions. Through assessment embedded within high-quality interactions, educators have opportunities to use information gathered to plan and implement instructional experiences based on the individual children in their classrooms (Grisham-Brown et al.). They also use the information to judge the effectiveness of the instruction and monitor children's progress. As instructional decisions are implemented and evaluated within the context of intentional interactions, educators make curricular and instructional decisions influenced by what they learn about individual children's progress toward expected learning outcomes.

Assessment Opportunities

Intentional assessment makes use of a variety of informal assessment approaches and tools. These assessments are embedded within the curriculum and are conducted in the context of educator–child interactions within the classroom (Grisham-Brown et al., 2006). They include observations, conversations and interactions with children, and formative and summative assessment. Intentional assessment is embedded in naturally occurring activities during play and individual or small-group experiences. It involves "systematic observation and documentation of each child's unique qualities, strengths, and needs" (NAEYC, 2009, p. 13). Fisher and Frey (2010) described assessments as "the hallmark of the learning process because they can describe a student's present understanding and provide useful feedback to the teacher on what's working and what's not" (p. 94). Accordingly, educators need to be comfortable using a variety of assessment tools to understand how young learners are progressing socially, emotionally, and cognitively within the context of their early learning classroom environment (DeLuca & Hughes, 2014). By blending a variety of assessment methods across time, educators can compile rich descriptions of children's preferences, understandings, and goals across the social, emotional, cognitive, and physical learning domains. Intentional assessment practices include anecdotal records, checklists, frequency counts, informal activity protocols, rubrics, and technological applications, and should be embedded into instructional interactions with children. Embedding such practices allows educators to make informed decisions about later curricular experiences.

Learning From Families   One valuable source of information about children is their families (Birbili & Tzioga, 2014; DEC, 2007; Grisham-Brown et al., 2006; Gullo & Hughes, 2011; NAEYC, 2009; NAEYC & NAECS-SDE, 2003; Pyle & DeLuca, 2013). Parents and other caregivers possess a wealth of information about their children; as such, intentional assessment involves building partnerships with and learning from families. Partnerships with families develop when educators take time to visit with families in their homes, in school settings, and in the community. Sharing of information is bidirectional; families should share information about their children with educators and educators should likewise share what they know about children with the children's families. These relationships are important because families possess vast information about children's prior knowledge and interests and have first-hand information about children's development and learning. In their report on how people learn, Bransford, Brown, and Cocking (2000) explain that children come to school with a range of experiences and knowledge that influences how they organize and view the world and ultimately "affects their abilities to remember, reason, solve problems, and acquire new knowledge" (p. 10). Children use these prior experiences and their preexisting knowledge to construct new knowledge and understandings as they interact with the world around them (Bransford et al.). Educators who listen to families and engage them in the assessment process gain insights into cultural and family practices that influence what children know and can do (Kidd, 2011). These interactions also help educators develop understandings of family priorities and what children can do in other contexts that may not be evident within the classroom (DEC; Kidd, Sanchez, & Thorp, 2008). The information families share gives educators opportunities to link children's new learning to familiar information and experiences. Moreover, identifying family concerns and strategically monitoring experiences that support children's progress toward these goals "increases the likelihood that expected outcomes will be achieved and that the child's development and learning within the family and community will be facilitated" (Banerjee & Luckner, 2013, p. 232).

Developing relationships with families and including them in the assessment of their children often takes place in the context of the family's home. Gullo and Hughes (2011) asserted that "home visits conducted early in the school year lay a foundation of understanding for, and appreciation of the diversity and strengths that each student brings to the kindergarten classroom" (p. 325). Information gathered during home visits helps educators address the strengths and needs of the individual children in their classrooms; home visits are opportunities to get to know the child and family in their own environment (Kidd, 2011; Kidd et al., 2008). To that end, educators should approach the home visit, not as an opportunity to ask a long list of questions, but rather as a time to get to know the family through observation and conversation. Figure 7.2, the Home Visit Guide, provides guiding questions for the home visitor to consider

Home Visit Guide

Child's name: _____   Home visitors: _____

Family members' names: _____   Date and time of visit: _____

_____

Planning for the Home Visit

What is the purpose of this visit? _____

_____

What assumptions do I hold about the family? _____

_____

What do I hope to learn about the child and family? _____

_____

Context and Participants

Who was at the meeting and what is each participant's relationship to the child? _____

_____

What was the purpose of the meeting? _____

_____

When was the meeting? _____

_____

Where was the meeting held? _____

_____

How would I describe the behaviors and interactions among those at the meeting? _____

_____

Family Background

What did the family share with you about their cultural and linguistic background? _____

_____

What significant events in the child's and/or family's life did they share? _____

_____

Daily Routines

What is the child's typical daily routine? _____

_____

(continued)

Figure 7.2.   Home visit guide.

Figure 7.2. *(continued)*

What are some activities that the child and family enjoy? _____
_____

What are some activities with which the child/family has difficulty? _____
_____

What materials and toys are available and accessible to the child? _____
_____

What other individuals does the child interact with and where? _____
_____

Family's Views on the Child's Development

How is the child viewed in the family? _____
_____

What are the family's views on the child's development (e.g., how the child learns and grows)? _____
_____

What are the family's goals, hopes, and dreams for their child? _____
_____

Reactions

What is my impression of the child's role in the family? _____
_____

What were my initial assumptions about and reactions to the family and the child? _____
_____

How did my assumptions about the family change as a result of this visit? _____
_____

What are some dilemmas I faced in listening to the family? _____
_____

What information from this home visit will I use to develop culturally responsive instruction and why? _____
_____

Based on the home visit, what are my expectations for this child and what are potential learning
outcomes for the child? _____
_____

Other

What other thoughts do I wish to note? _____
_____

while interacting with the family. It is designed to guide educators' thinking as they prepare for and conduct the home visit with families. As can be seen, some guiding questions (e.g., What did the family share with you about their cultural and linguistic background?) include information gathered from conversations with the family rather than direct questions. Other information (e.g., What are some activities that the child and family enjoy?) might be gathered using questions that directly ask about the information. After the home visit, it is important for educators to reflect on their reactions to the family and what they learned about the child and family during the visit. Reflecting on initial impressions and assumptions provides educators with an opportunity to explicitly acknowledge the assumptions they brought to the meeting and any changes in assumptions that occurred based on spending time with the family.

Engaging families in assessment is not limited to home visits. Educators can also seek help from family members in documenting development and learning at home. In a study of families from preschools in Greece, Birbili and Tzioga (2014) asked parents to complete an observation sheet focused on their child's development, a questionnaire that prompted parents to reflect on their child's development, and a sheet to record what their child said that was of interest to them. They concluded that parents from these preschools "were not only capable of providing informed perspectives on their children but also willing to do so" (Dirbili & Tzioga, 2014, p. 170). In addition, educators can learn valuable information about the children in their classrooms when families are invited into classrooms to share their experiences and stories (Bardige & Segal, 2005; Kidd et al., 2008). These stories are vehicles for learning more about children's prior knowledge and experience. The information families share can be used to plan and implement curriculum and instruction that is culturally responsive and takes into account individual children's unique experiences (Kidd, 2011; Kidd et al.).

Kindergarten educators Samita and Nadia recognize the value of engaging families in the assessment of their children and using the information gathered to inform instruction. In addition to the anecdotal notes mentioned in the opening vignette, Samita and Nadia also draw upon what they learn from families to plan and implement culturally and individually responsive instruction. For example, when Samita and Nadia were discussing how to provide Fahed with more challenging patterning learning experiences, they recalled Fahed's father sharing with them how fascinated Fahed is with geometric art in their home and place of worship. They contacted Fahed's father and talked with him about ways they could engage Fahed in a project that would build on this interest and further develop his understanding of complex patterns. Fahed's father offered to e-mail them photos of some of the geometric designs. They used these examples to develop a project in which Fahed could decorate cardboard picture frames using familiar geometric designs. This enabled Fahed to create complex patterns that were then used to frame photos displayed in their classroom.

Observation   One approach to gathering information about children is through observation (DeLuca & Hughes, 2014). When educators observe children engaged in learning experiences, activities, play, and daily routines, they gain insight into children's development and learning and see how they respond to successes and challenges within their environment (NAEYC, 2009). These observations take place in a variety of contexts within the classroom, including during indoor and outdoor play, individual and small-group instruction, and interactions with peers and other adults in the room, as well as in children's homes and communities. Through observation, educators "develop a broad sense of who children are—as individuals, as group members, as family members, as members of cultural and linguistic communities" (NAEYC, 2009, p. 13).

Intentional assessment practices rely on mastering the art of observing young children actively engaged in problem-solving, interacting with peers and adults, and learning across the school day. Observational records are one tool educators use to capture evidence of children's performances. They take on a variety of forms and, when analyzed across time, may be used to illuminate patterns in young children's experiences socially, emotionally, cognitively, and physically. Observational records typically include anecdotal vignettes, scribed by educators with as much detail and accuracy as possible, to capture exactly what a young child is saying and doing at a particular point in time. Depending upon the specific questions educators have about particular children, anecdotal notes may be used in conjunction with time sampling or event sampling, which are described later in the chapter, to ensure that children's experiences within the classroom environment are well observed and documented (Read, Gardner, & Mahler, 1993).

Use of observational records was evident in the vignette at the beginning of the chapter, in which Samita and Nadia kept anecdotal records on Crystal's, Fahed's, and Wayne's attempts at identifying and extending patterns. Based on their notes, they knew that all three had previously been successful with identifying, describing, and extending repeating *ABAB* patterns. Using this information, they determined that the children should be ready to learn how to identify a missing element in the middle of a repeating *ABAB* pattern. As Nadia worked with the three of them, she made notes about their interest and engagement in the activity as well as their ability to complete the pattern by identifying the missing piece. As she reviewed and reflected on the notes, she realized that her attention had focused on Crystal, which raised additional questions about Fahed and Wayne. She noted that she will need to observe Fahed and Wayne further to gain a clearer sense of next steps in their instruction.

Play-Based Assessment   Intentional assessment also occurs when educators interact and converse with children during play and informal interactions. Assessment in these contexts affords educators opportunities to learn about children's prior knowledge, interests, abilities, and linguistic and cultural backgrounds in more child-directed contexts. When educators engage in play-based assessment, they may use some of the tools described later in the chapter, such as checklists, frequency counts, time and event sampling, and activity protocols. They may also use formal assessments like the Transdisciplinary Play-Based Assessment, Second Edition (Linder et al., 2008), which was described in Chapter 6. DeLuca and Hughes (2014) found in their study of 12 primary-grade teachers that teachers view "play-based pedagogies as a key opportunity to observe students' growth and development, and as an opportunity to develop learning relationships with students" (p. 457). As they interact with children in informal ways, educators see firsthand how children apply knowledge and skills independently. Assessment in this context also provides insights into ways educators can facilitate learning through play.

For example, after implementing the patterning lesson discussed in the vignette, Nadia mentioned to Samita that Wayne had not appeared as engaged in the activity as Crystal and Fahed. Samita suggested that Nadia consider how she might use play as a way to assess what Wayne knows about patterns. Nadia knew that Wayne enjoys playing with LEGOs and building with blocks. She decided that she would observe him during their play-based center time the next day and determine how she could introduce some patterning activities into the play. For example, she thought that, in the kitchen area, she might be able to suggest that they make a trivet out of LEGOs to put the pot on after they are done pretend-cooking. Or if he goes to the construction area, she might encourage him to build something with a pattern. With a couple of ideas in mind, Nadia was confident that she would find a way to engage Wayne in building patterns in the context of his play.

Instructional and Conversational Interactions   Assessment during instructional interactions and conversations is also critical. As educators implement curriculum and instruction, they gain valuable insights into children's prior knowledge, interests, abilities, and linguistic and cultural backgrounds. They can also come to understand what and how children are learning. By attending to children's responses to learning experiences, educators gain a more nuanced understanding of children's learning and development that enables them to provide appropriate scaffolds to enhance academic learning (DeLuca & Hughes, 2014). For instance, focused observations documenting how children modify their approaches when engaged in mathematical problem solving provide information about their reasoning (Snow & Van Hemel, 2008). Educators use what they learn during these observations to modify levels of adult support and make informed instructional decisions.

This use of observations was noticeable as Nadia considered her notes about Fahed. She realized that she needed to take time to talk with him and not only see what he could do, but also what he was thinking. She suspected that the patterning activities that she provided had been too easy for him. If she could prompt him to talk about how he thought about patterns, she might be able to determine next steps for his instruction. She decided that instead of holding a small-group lesson with him the next day, she would sit down with Fahed and talk with him as he creates patterns of his own making. She planned to have a variety of items available, including bead stringing materials, parquet tiles, and paper and markers. Knowing that he is especially fond of cars, she might have the bin of vehicles of different types and colors readily accessible. As he creates, she will be ready to ask probing questions and make note of how he is thinking about patterns. This insight into his thinking will help her to identify how complex to make the photo frame activity previously discussed. She wants to develop an activity complex enough to challenge him but not so complex that he is unable to be successful.

Observational Assessment Tools

As Samita and Nadia contemplated future assessments of Crystal's, Fahed's, and Wayne's patterning abilities, they realized that they needed tools to efficiently document what the children could do and the children's next points of growth. The anecdotal records were helpful for capturing details in the moment but did not always provide the focus they wanted. They knew from their participation in LEARN IT that there are complementary forms of observational assessments tools that include checklists, frequency counts, and activity protocols. They knew that these assessment tools may be flexibly included as part of the observational records accumulated over the course of the year for particular children. Alternatively, they may be used as separate assessment tools to capture specific evidence of children's social, emotional, cognitive, or physical development. Similarly, they had learned that these assessment tools provide opportunities for educators to consider the effectiveness of specific curricular experiences and make strategic changes to match the interests and instructional needs of the children. With the help of their mentor, Janet, they decided to further explore their options. Janet reminded them of the assessment tools discussed at the LEARN IT institute and described in the next part of the chapter. Janet also found information on some additional tools that could be useful to Samita and Nadia and added them as possible resources.

Checklists   Checklists, whether educator-constructed or commercially developed, support educators' efforts to capture meaningful information about children's domain performances (Isenberg & Jalongo, 2001). Checklists prompt educators to attend to specific performances by particular children at any given point in time. For example, Samita and Nadia could identify or develop a checklist of various types of patterns, like the one shown in Figure 7.3, and check off the patterns that Crystal, Fahed, and Wayne consistently identified, created, and explained.

Educators, like Samita and Nadia, might also use a checklist for documenting what children can do in other areas of instruction. For instance, if interested in assessing children's phonological awareness strengths, Samita and Nadia might decide to engage small groups of children in singing *Down by the Bay* (Raffi, 1988). During the literacy experience, they might use an informal checklist to identify which children appear comfortable identifying the rhyming words presented in the song. Using the same checklist, they could follow children into an extended play center that encourages children to match the rhyming words, using felt pieces with pictures of the silly rhymes used throughout the song. For example, they could include a felt-backed picture of a fly and one of a tie that children could match. Extending the observation period into children's extended play period affords educators the opportunity to continue to monitor children's abilities in identifying and manipulating the rhyming words in the song. Allocating time to observe children across learning environments also allows educators to consider how children may be flexibly applying their knowledge in new contexts. As a result, the checklist data capturing children's phonological awareness across learning environments and time allow educators to make an informed decision about the types of experiences they will embed in the future. For example, knowing that their students can match pictures of rhyming words like *moose* and *goose*, *whale* and *tail*, and *tie* and *fly*, Samita and Nadia might decide to introduce an activity in which the children generate their own rhyming words. This might take place during play-based instruction in the kitchen area. A pot on the stove might be used to encourage children to call out words that rhyme with *pot*.

Name	Identify	Extend	Make/generate	Fill in missing	Explain

Figure 7.3.   Simple patterning checklist *(ABAB).*

Frequency Counts   Similarly, frequency counts provide insight into how often children engage in a particular activity of interest. See Figure 7.4 for an example template of a frequency count. For instance, Samita and Nadia may be interested in documenting how often children self-select the writing center as a place for engaging in opportunities intended to promote early writing skills. After monitoring children's preferences over the course of a week, they might determine that the writing center is not attracting as many children as desired. As a result, they might decide to renew children's interests in writing by introducing a new post office play-based thematic unit. The new unit will extend writing into the dramatic play center and provide opportunities to conduct read alouds that highlight letter writing and post office adventures, like *Never Mail an Elephant* (Thaler & Lee, 1997) and *The Post Office Book* (Gibbons, 1986). Their knowledge of children's interests opens opportunities for children to playfully engage in writing across the play-based centers.

Time Sampling and Event Sampling   Time sampling and event sampling are observational techniques that also reveal patterns in children's experiential preferences. Time sampling is an observational strategy used to document a child's performance across predetermined intervals of time. Time sampling may be used to strengthen educators' understandings of a child's level of engagement across the school day as the child encounters different learning opportunities. Taking time to carefully document a child's play and social interactions across a day or a week further informs educators' knowledge of the child's learning preferences and development and allows educators to make intentional modifications in the learning environment. Figure 7.5 is an example chart that can be used for time sampling.

For example, after time sampling captured where one child self-selected to play during center time across a week's time, Samita noticed that the child continued to navigate to the art table and demonstrated an indifference for engaging in explorations in the large block area. She noted that the arts center frequently promotes children's

Center	Monday	Tuesday	Wednesday	Thursday	Friday
Book nook					
Dramatic play					
Writing					
Blocks					
Science					
Math					
Art					

Figure 7.4. Monitoring children's self-selected explorations of centers (frequency count).

Name:					
Center	Monday	Tuesday	Wednesday	Thursday	Friday
Book nook					
Dramatic play					
Writing					
Blocks					
Science					
Math					
Art					
Reflection:					

Figure 7.5. Time sampling children's selection of play centers.

fine motor development through explorations with scissors, playdough, glue sticks, and markers, whereas the large block area promotes children's understandings of math and science concepts, including weight, balance, height, and cause and effect. As such, Samita intentionally modified the materials available at the art table by including smaller blocks along with photographs of modern sculptures. The small enhancement to the arts center expanded the child's hands-on explorations to include some of the principles children learn while building.

Similarly, event sampling may also be used to carefully monitor a child's performances or social preferences. Event-sampling observational records may be gathered frequently across a school day, such as during times of transition. Event sampling may also be used to focus on a child's interactions at a given point in time, such as during snack time, to reveal conversational patterns. It can also be used when a child prepares to go home for the day to ascertain the child's capacity for carrying out multistep processes such as putting on a coat and readying their school bag. Carefully documenting a child's activities during a specific event further contributes to educators' knowledge of each child's learning and development, allowing educators to make informed decisions about instructional or routinized prompts to guide children through the day.

Sociograms   Sociograms are another form of observational records (Gropper, Hinitz, Sprung, & Froschl, 2011) that work to reveal preferences in children's social practices. In particular, sociograms are used to graphically represent children's patterns of interactions with one another. When educators observe children's social behaviors and peer interactions, they gain a sense of children's patterns of interactions (Martinsen, Nærland, & Vereijken, 2010). Martinsen et al. suggested documenting 1) "Social Activity," children's time engaged in social interactions with other children;

2) "Social Centrality," the number of children involved in the interactions; and 3) "Social Focus, the number of times they are positively or neutrally addressed by other children minus the number of times they are negatively addressed by children, per minute" (p. 1,235). This documentation can be accomplished through observing children as they engage in activities in the classroom or by video-recording and analyzing the interactions at a later time. Data collected are then graphed, which enables educators to gain a sense of each child's social interactions within the classroom. Wohlwend (2009) suggested a similar approach that involves observing with whom children choose to play. She notes that although playmates may be fluid on any given day, over time "consistent patterns of favorite content themes and preferred activities" emerge (Wohlwend, 2009, p. 235). This type of analysis provides insights into with whom children play as well as reveals common activities or thematic play narratives that unify or separate young children into learning and play groups (Wohlwend).

Another approach Wohlwend (2009) found to be effective with 5- and 6-year-olds is to ask children to share three names of children with whom they usually play during a particular time of the day (e.g., center time, choice time, outdoor play). These interactions are mapped using one-way arrows from the child to the three children mentioned, two-way arrows if the two children mentioned each other, and no arrow if the child did not name other children or if no other children selected the child (Wohlwend). Figure 7.6 provides an example of how mapping out children's interactions across time may bring to light emerging friendships and preferences in play partners.

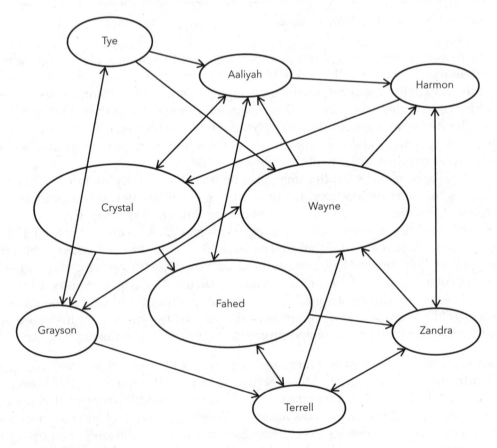

Figure 7.6. Mapping interactions.

Activity Protocols   Activity protocols are also effective play-based assessment tools that strategically link children's observable behaviors in the classroom environment to curriculum-based standards. As ongoing assessment is a necessary part of early childhood educators' practice, Grisham-Brown et al. (2006) preferred to use activity protocols over checklists or formal developmental assessments because the format counteracts educators' "tendency to pull children from preferred activities and assess them in an item-by-item fashion" (p. 48). Activity protocols ensure children remain meaningfully engaged in the curricular experiences while educators intentionally engage them in relevant conversation about the experiences at hand.

Accordingly, activity protocols prompt educators to observe and assess children in activities that occur naturally within the early learning classroom environment, including snack time, working with playdough, book making, structured play, dramatic play, and story time (Grisham-Brown et al., 2006). Each activity protocol emphasizes the learning standards expressed by children engaged in the particular activity. For example, as children work with playdough, educators naturally query children's concepts of physical attributes (i.e., color, size, and number) (Grisham-Brown et al.). Gathered systematically over time, activity protocols allow early childhood educators to make informed decisions about curricular experiences in response to areas of young children's observed performances across developmental domains.

Rating Scales and Rubrics   Rating scales and rubrics are designed to provide information beyond what can be obtained from checklists and frequency counts. Rather than documenting whether a behavior has been exhibited or how many times a behavior has been observed, rating scales and rubrics enable educators to evaluate the quality of the skill or behavior (Kostelnik, Soderman, Whiren, & Rupiper, 2015). Rating scales often contain a number scale and use anchor points that range from 1 to 5. A 1 indicates that a behavior was rarely observed, a 3 that it was sometimes observed, and a 5 that it was frequently observed. Rating scales might also contain a graphic scale that covers a continuum ranging, for example, from never to always (Wortham, 2008). Because rating scales tend to be rather subjective, some educators prefer to use or develop rubrics that include criteria that clearly evaluate the quality of children's performance (Kostelnik et al.). These scoring guides provide clear guidance for the evaluator. However, if they are written in a child-friendly manner, rubrics can assist children in knowing what they are expected to do and also serve as a guide for self-assessment.

Digital Technologies   The use of digital technologies, including video recorders, cameras, and voice recorders, complement the assessment tools previously described. Digital technologies expand educators' capacities for documenting children's development and learning, for providing opportunities for children's self-assessment, and for engaging in assessment of and reflection on instruction. A study by Boardman (2007) concluded that kindergarten teachers who used digital cameras and audio recordings believed the use of digital technologies enhanced their ability to document and assess children's learning. The teachers reported that digital cameras and voice recorders provided opportunities to capture what children were doing and then reflect on what they saw and heard. They also indicated that sharing photographs and audio recordings enabled families to gain greater understandings of what their children were doing and learning. Other digital technologies include computer games and simulations and web-based activities that keep track of children's performances.

Using Assessment Data

As educators use assessment data to gain insights into children's development and learning, they also use information collected to evaluate the effectiveness of the instruction and make informed instructional decisions. The information gathered enables them to adapt their lessons as they work with children and plan future lessons informed by their evaluation of the effectiveness of the instructional approaches and strategies (Shepard, 2000). For example, when children experience success in learning, educators identify not only what they are able to do but also what it is about the instruction that enhanced children's learning. Likewise, when children experience challenges in meeting the learning outcomes, educators adapt instruction to increase the likelihood of success. When children have accomplished learning outcomes, educators are prepared to extend their learning.

This interactive, embedded approach to assessment enables educators to examine their instruction and make adjustments to enhance children's learning outcomes (Shepard, 2000). This means that educators use what they know about children to select appropriate materials and instructional strategies as well as adapt instruction to meet children's needs (Grisham-Brown et al., 2006; Gullo & Hughes, 2011). They promote learning by assessing prior knowledge and providing appropriate levels of scaffolding and feedback (Shepard). In addition, educators adapt instruction by asking questions that promote thinking and extend learning; by capitalizing on teachable moments; and by responding to children's prior knowledge, interests, abilities, and cultural and linguistic backgrounds (Gullo & Hughes). Intentional assessment that is embedded in classroom interactions is also used to monitor children's progress in relation to the curriculum as well as to communicate progress to families and other professionals (Feldman, 2010; Pyle & DeLuca, 2013). Educators use notes from anecdotal records, checklists, activity protocols, work samples, portfolios, and other assessments to document children's development and learning. As educators gain expertise in monitoring children's learning using a variety of intentional assessment strategies, they are more readily positioned to make curricular shifts in response to individual learner's understandings.

The Professional Development Activities section that follows describes two LEARN IT activities that are planned to link assessment with curriculum and instruction. The first activity engages educators in intentional assessment, and the second helps educators to understand assessment strategies and tools. Each activity allocates time to discuss the knowledge and literature on assessment and guides educators through a series of tasks to expand upon their ability to successfully implement assessment in their own classrooms.

Engaging in Intentional Assessment

Educators gain greater understandings of children when they gather information in a variety of ways. Although formal assessments may provide some useful information about children's learning and development, they are often limited by the nature of the assessment and the focus on one snapshot in time. Families, on the other hand, possess valuable information and insights developed over time that can help educators to build on children's past experiences, prior knowledge, family culture, interests, and abilities. Likewise, educators' daily interactions with children during everyday routines and instruction enable them to gain clear understandings of what each child knows and is able to do. Through the LEARN IT institute, implementation and mentoring, and supportive learning communities, educators will learn about, practice, assess, and reflect on intentional assessment embedded in instructional interactions.

LEARN IT Institute

The goal for this institute is to develop educators' knowledge of effective assessment strategies and tools and provide opportunities to practice select strategies and tools. This will help educators to understand the link among assessment, curriculum, and instruction and to recognize the importance of using assessment to make informed instructional decisions. In preparation for the institute, participants read the Foundations section of this chapter along with the position statements listed in the Engaging in Intentional Assessment Resources text box.

ENGAGING IN INTENTIONAL ASSESSMENT RESOURCES

Division for Early Childhood of the Council for Exceptional Children. (2007). *Promoting positive outcomes for children with disabilities: Recommendations for curriculum, assessment, and program evaluation.* Retrieved from https://www.naeyc.org/sites/default/files/globally-shared/downloads/PDFs/resources/position-statements/PrmtgPositiveOutcomes.pdf

National Association for the Education of Young Children & National Association of Early Childhood Specialists in State Departments of Education. (2003). *Early childhood curriculum, assessment, and program evaluation: Building an effective, accountable system in programs for children birth through age 8.* Retrieved from https://www.naeyc.org/sites/default/files/globally-shared/downloads/PDFs/resources/position-statements/pscape.pdf

---

Intentional Assessment Background Knowledge and Experiences

To begin this LEARN IT institute, participants activate their prior knowledge and set the stage to connect their new learning to what they already know. After a brief introduction that emphasizes that participants bring a wealth of information about intentional assessment to their professional development experiences, participants break into pairs or small groups to discuss their current assessment practices. They begin talking about their goals or next steps related to intentional assessment, using the questions on Handout 7.1 to guide the discussion. Next, in a large-group discussion, participants share key ideas discussed in their small groups; facilitators reinforce connections made to the readings or that highlight learning experiences to come.

Snapshots in Time

The next activity, Snapshots in Time, encourages educators to consider the limitations of relying on one assessment, administered at one point in time, when making instructional decisions for children. To begin, the large group reviews the information on formal assessment

195

Assessment Practices

1. How do I currently use information from families, formal assessments, and intentional assessment within my interactions with children to inform my instruction? _____
   _____
   _____
   _____
   _____

2. What tools help me to assess children? _____
   _____
   _____
   _____
   _____

3. What challenges do I experience as I assess children? _____
   _____
   _____
   _____
   _____

4. What assessment strategies have I used that have been helpful? _____
   _____
   _____
   _____
   _____

5. What assessment strategies do I use that I might want to refine? _____
   _____
   _____
   _____
   _____

6. What types of assessment strategies and tools do I want to learn to use and try with my students? _____
   _____
   _____
   _____
   _____

addressed in the previous institute, from Chapter 6. The group reviews the uses and types of formal assessments, ways to minimize bias, and what can be learned from quality formal assessments like the ones presented in the last chapter.

Educators should then form small groups and review Handout 7.2. Each group is assigned one of the four photographs shown on the handout, which represent a snapshot in time in a young child's life. Participants examine the photo and discuss what conclusions they might draw about the child pictured. The questions in Handout 7.2 can be used to prompt their thinking and discussion. Following the small-group discussions, the large group discusses the key points that emerged from looking at the photos.

Linking Assessment, Curriculum, and Instruction

Before the next activity, the large group shares what they noticed in the vignette with Samita and Nadia that opened this chapter. The following questions guide the discussion:

1. What was the instructional context?

2. How did Nadia interact with the children?

3. How did Samita and Nadia document the children's learning prior to this lesson and during this lesson?

4. How did they use the documentation to make informed instructional decisions?

By discussing the vignette and the Foundations section, educators explore how intentional assessment is embedded in instructional interactions with children. Intentional assessment links assessment, curriculum, and instruction. It takes place through observations, play-based assessments, and interactions with children and families. The information learned is used to plan and implement instruction, taking into account children's diverse linguistic and cultural backgrounds, interests, abilities, and needs.

Following the discussion, participants gather in small groups. Each small group should choose either the NAEYC and NAECS-SDE position statement (2003) or the DEC position statement (2007), which they read prior to attending the institute. Participants should review the chosen position statement, paying particular attention to the language used by these organizations to characterize recommended assessment practices in early childhood. Next, group members work together to make a list of key elements of assessment detailed in the position statement as it relates to 1) the unique qualities of individual children, 2) the value of families as members of the assessment team, and 3) assessment as an embedded practice within the classroom routine.

After the groups finish their work, the large group convenes to share key ideas noted. To ensure that each group has a chance to share new information, the first group shares two ideas, and the following groups share two ideas on their list that were not already shared by a previous group. After all groups have had an opportunity to share, the group members share any additional ideas on their lists that were not already shared. The information generated should foster discussion, reinforcing key information discussed earlier in the chapter and emphasizing important points brought to light in the position statements.

Following the whole-group discussion, participants form pairs and discuss the recommended assessment practices that are readily observable within the context of their own classroom. They consider ways that they could enhance their own assessment practices to incorporate the assessment recommendations articulated in the position statements. The large group then discusses the assessment opportunities available, including observation, play-based assessment, instructional and conversational interactions, and interactions with families.

Snapshots in Time

(continued)

1. What conclusions do you draw about the child based on this snapshot? _____
_____
_____
_____
_____
_____
_____

2. How do your own or others' biases and perceptions influence what you might conclude based on a single photograph? _____
_____
_____
_____
_____
_____
_____

3. How is your discussion of the child limited because the photograph represents a one-dimensional view of the child in one moment in time? _____
_____
_____
_____
_____
_____
_____

4. What else you would like to know about the child? _____
_____
_____
_____
_____
_____
_____

5. How might you go about collecting the additional details and how might you use the information to inform instruction? _____
_____
_____
_____
_____
_____
_____

Learning From Children and Families

To begin the next activity, facilitators provide a brief presentation on how much educators can learn about children and families by actively listening to what children and families share about their lives. The skill of active listening takes practice and requires suspending interruptions, thoughts about what to say next, and questions until the person telling the story or sharing information is finished. Listening to people share personal stories is an excellent way to practice active listening. After a brief discussion of the information presented, participants form groups of three and follow the directions on Handout 7.3, Artifact Sharing.

After each participant shares his or her story, the other participants ask the questions that they refrained from asking as their peers' narrative unfolded. When everyone is finished sharing and asking questions, the small groups should consider the Sharing Stories Questions, also found on Handout 7.3.

After the small-group discussions, the large group reconvenes to extend understanding about what can be learned from interacting with and listening to children and families. After sharing key points from their small-group discussions, the participants talk about ways to learn from families and engage them in their children's development and learning. This is a good time to talk about the value of home visits and to review the information in this chapter about learning from families. It is important to stress that the purpose of home visits is not to ask a long list of questions but rather to open up authentic conversations that lead to learning more about the children and their families. Home visits are also an opportunity to observe children in their home environments and learn more about their prior experiences, interests, and abilities.

For the next activity, the group reviews Figure 7.2, the Home Visit Guide, which was described earlier in the chapter. Then, participants get back into their groups of three that were established for the previous activity. This time, one participant volunteers to be a family member and the other two to be home visitors. Participants use the directions at the top of Handout 7.4 to direct their role play. After the role play, participants debrief, first in small groups and later with the whole group. The questions on the bottom of Handout 7.4, the Home Visit Role Play Debriefing, guide the discussion.

To conclude this activity, participants write down the name of a family they would like to visit to try out the strategies discussed and practiced. They then make notes about how they plan to approach the visit, how they will engage the family, what they hope to learn, and how they might use the information and insights gained to inform instruction. To wrap up the session, several participants share their plans. As they share, other participants link what they hear to the content and strategies learned. They should note connections of specific components of the plans shared to key information addressed in the activities and content discussed in the chapter.

Implementation and Mentoring

This implementation and mentoring session focuses on learning from children and their families through interactions and conversations. Before the session, educators fill out and submit Handout 7.5, the Implementation and Mentoring Form, to their mentor. Mentors should provide feedback and guidance as educators enact, assess, and reflect upon intentional assessment strategies. In particular, mentors should enable educators to gain valuable information by actively listening as families talk about their children and their lives. Families can help educators to better understand children's strengths, interests, prior knowledge, and needs

Artifact Sharing

Directions:

- Identify a specific object or artifact you have on you or that is in the room nearby that you can use to tell a personal story about yourself. Be creative in your selection of the artifact and the personal story you wish to share. For example, you might pull out car keys and tell a story about teaching your child to drive or you might share a photo and use it to tell a story.

- When it is your turn to share, tell a story prompted by the artifact.

- When it is your turn to be a listener, your goal is to listen and learn more about your colleagues. During the story, refrain from asking questions or making comments. Your job is to listen and think about what your colleague is sharing.

- At the end of the story, ask questions and comment on your colleague's story.

Sharing Stories Questions

1. What did you learn about each other as you listened to the personal stories you shared? _____
   _____
   _____

2. What domains of learning happened to peek through the surface of the stories (i.e., social, emotional, physical, cognitive)? _____
   _____
   _____

3. What does this brief opportunity to share your own stories show you about the value of providing similar opportunities for children and families to share personal stories with you about their experiences? _____
   _____
   _____

4. What do you think you can learn from children and families by orchestrating ways to interact with and hear what they have to share? _____
   _____
   _____

5. Brainstorm with your group ways you might encourage children and families to share stories. _____
   _____
   _____

6. Consider carefully how you will demonstrate to children and families that their stories are respected and that families' voices are valuable in helping you to best develop curricular experiences for their children. _____
   _____
   _____

Home Visit Role Play

Directions:

- Identify who will be the family member and who will be the home visitors.

- If you are the family member, jot down a significant event in your life that you think would have been important for educators to know about you as a child (e.g., you immigrated to the United States when you were 2 years old, you had a major illness, you lost a close relative, the birth of a sibling). Pretend you are your parent or other family member and think about what you would want educators to know about the event.

- If you are the home visitors, talk about how you would engage family members in a conversation that would prompt them to talk about significant events in the child's life. Write down some questions or prompts you might use to encourage conversation. Be sure to avoid sounding like you are asking a list of questions. The questions or prompts should support your conversation, not drive your conversation.

- Role-play a home visit that focuses on getting to know the family's background and significant events in the child's life.

Home Visit Role Play Debriefing:

1. How did it feel to be the family member? _____
_____

2. How did it feel to be the home visitors? _____
_____

3. What went well in the conversation? _____
_____

4. What was challenging about the conversation? _____
_____

5. As home visitors, what did you learn about the child and family through the conversation? _____
_____

6. As the family member, how do you think what you shared will be valuable to educators? _____
_____

7. How can the information gathered in the home visit be used to inform intentional classroom interactions and instruction? _____
_____

To be completed by early educators

Implementation and Mentoring Form

Educator's name _____   Mentor _____

Site _____   Date _____

Identify the **intentional teaching strategy** you want to **enact.** Select one child to interact with during ☐ center time ☐ small group ☐ individually. Describe the support you would like from your mentor to help you implement the **intentional teaching strategy.**

Intentional teaching strategy of focus:

Culturally Responsive Practice

☐ Choose an area and set it up to reflect children's cultures

☐ Account for child's interest-background and use child's prior knowledge

☐ Inspire child to complete the idea/activity by connecting it to his/her home culture

☐ Provide specific feedback to extend child's play in that area

☐ Question to promote higher-level thinking

Interactional Reading

From *Bringing Words to Life*

☐ Choosing vocabulary words

From Dialogic Reading

☐ Prompt

   o Completion prompt

   o Recall prompt

   o Open-ended prompt

   o Wh- question prompt

   o Distancing prompt

☐ Evaluate the child's response

☐ Expand the child's response

☐ Repeat—child repeats the expanded response

Expanded Vocabulary

☐ Math vocabulary (5 words)

☐ Science vocabulary (5 words)

Assessment and Instruction

☐ Follow child's interest

☐ Observe and record child learning behaviors

☐ Initiate conversations and write plans with child

☐ Provide meaningful learning opportunities informed by assessment

Extending Play

☐ Redirect play to replace violent play

☐ Plan play

☐ Act out stories

☐ Dramatic use of the constructions child makes

Inclusion

☐ Adapt environment

☐ Adapt routines

☐ Adapt materials and activities

☐ Adapt requirements

☐ Adapt instruction

Continue on back if needed

Focus child _____

Elaborate on how you will implement the intentional teaching strategy. _____

_____

_____

What type of in-class support do you think will help you?

☐ Modeling while you take notes

☐ Assistance with co-teaching the child

☐ Feedback after observation

☐ Other _____

Use back if needed

The kindergarten educators discussed in the opening vignette, Samita and Nadia, participated in the LEARN IT institute on engaging in intentional assessment. They wondered how they might better understand their students by making connections between home and school. They decided to bring up this issue with Janet, their LEARN IT mentor. Samita placed a call to Janet because she did not want to wait until the next implementation and mentoring session to begin connecting with families. Janet suggested that she ask her kindergartners to bring in a photo of their family for a family photo board. Samita and Nadia could begin learning about the children and their families by listening to the children as they share their photos. Janet noted that the photos could be used to prompt stories that would provide additional insights into the richness of the children's lives. Janet also suggested that Samita and Nadia select one child's family to visit, as a way to get started. She reminded them that they should try out the strategies they learned about actively listening to families and using the information collected to inform instruction.

When Janet came for the implementation and mentoring session, family photos were posted on one of the bulletin boards in the classroom. As Janet stepped into the room, one of the children standing nearby took her hand and showed her the board. He proceeded to tell her not only about his own family but also what he knew about his classmates' families. Janet could tell that Samita and Nadia had embraced the family photo board idea and had been actively using the photos to create a closer community. For this day's session, Samita had asked for support in using the photos and children's stories to more intentionally learn information that could help her to make more informed instructional decisions. Samita had selected Crystal as her focus child for this implementation and mentoring session and had asked Janet to co-teach with her. Samita began by asking Crystal to tell her who was in the photo and then asked pointed questions like the following: "What are their favorite colors?" "What do they like to eat?" "Are all the children in elementary school?" Recognizing that Samita was getting frustrated by Crystal's limited one-word responses, Janet provided a more open-ended prompt: "Crystal, this is a wonderful photo of your family. I would love to know more about each of your family members." Janet then began talking with Crystal about the picture and asked her to elaborate on a story she mentioned about a family outing to the park. As Crystal began sharing her adventure, Janet actively listened and provided additional prompts as needed to encourage Crystal to share details of her story.

When Samita and Janet debriefed, they reviewed what was discussed about active listening at the institute, along with earlier institute discussions about asking open-ended questions to prompt elaborated responses. As they talked, Samita realized that she had learned quite a bit about Crystal from the conversation, including that her family enjoys going to the park for picnics and that Crystal and her sister like to look at the flowers with their father. It was apparent that Crystal's father had taught her some of the names of flowers and had talked about the role that bees and butterflies play in pollenating flowers. Samita decided that she would get some books from the library about flowers to have available in the classroom. She also considered how she would build on Crystal's knowledge in their study of what plants need to grow and survive. They concluded their session by discussing Samita's next steps in engaging families in relevant assessment that informs curriculum and instruction, including planning for her home visit with Crystal's family.

Supportive Learning Communities

The next supportive learning community session continues to focus on learning from conversations and interactions with families; it elaborates on gathering information about children through observation and play-based assessment. To begin, participants share their experiences learning from children and families and engaging families in the assessment of their children. The group discusses the successes and challenges that they encountered as they held conversations with children and conducted home visits with families. They share ideas for ways to modify what they did to increase their likelihood of gathering relevant information that can inform their instructional decisions.

Next, the participants discuss the importance of taking time to observe children to learn about their interests, abilities, and needs. The group views one or more of the videos in the Videos for Practicing Observation text box. Participants select a specific child to watch in the video and write down notes as they observe that child. After the observation, participants share what they learned about the child across developmental domains and how they can use this information to plan instruction. The activity concludes with a discussion of the value of observing children.

VIDEOS FOR PRACTICING OBSERVATION

- *Nelcy Takes a Walk:* http://www.draccess.org/videolibrary/Nelcy_takes_a_walk.html
- *Vanessa and Proloquo2Go—Blossoming as a Child:* http://www.youtube.com/watch?v=r0adFdlbYZE
- *Time for Oliver:* http://www.draccess.org/videolibrary/timeforoliver.html
- *Ari at Lunch:* http://www.draccess.org/videolibrary/ariatlunch.html
- *Carmen at Lunch:* http://www.draccess.org/videolibrary/carmenatlunch.html
- *Gina at the Sand Table:* http://www.draccess.org/videolibrary/ginasandtable.html
- *Sam Makes a Spider:* http://www.draccess.org/videolibrary/sammakesaspider.html
- *Isaac at Play:* http://www.draccess.org/videolibrary/isaac-at-play.html
- *Sean Playing With Flubber:* http://www.draccess.org/videolibrary/seanplayingwithflubber.html
- *Cameron Talking With Others:* http://www.draccess.org/videolibrary/cameron-talking-with-others.html
- *Five-Year-Olds Pilot Their Own Project Learning:* http://www.youtube.com/watch?v=_eyucHMifto

After the discussion on observation, the group reviews what was discussed previously about play-based assessment. Educators reflect on what they can learn about children as they interact with them during play. Then, participants pair off and select several objects typically available for play, such as small balls, blocks, vehicles, food, or dress-up clothes. The pairs discuss ways they can use the toys to assess children's learning and to provide instruction. For example, a toy car can be used to gather information on a child's understanding of up, down, forward, and backward in the context of playing with the car. The toy car can also be used to provide instruction that reinforces and teaches these concepts. Following the exploration, the group discusses how assessment links to curriculum and instruction when play-based assessment and instruction take place.

Figure 7.7 is a checklist of this LEARN IT strand that the professional development team can use to assess whether they implemented all aspects of intentional teaching across LEARN. Facilitators can use the checklist as a tool to guide the planning and implementation process of their LEARN IT professional development program about engaging in intentional assessment.

Checklist for Engaging in Intentional Assessment

	LEARN IT institute	Implementation and mentoring	Supportive learning communities
Learn	❑ Facilitators presented research and best practices related to intentional assessment with a focus on observation, play-based assessment, and learning from interactions and conversations with children and families.	❑ Mentors helped participants to identify particular needs they have in implementing intentional assessment that includes observation, play-based assessment, and learning from interactions and conversations with children and families.	❑ Mentors reviewed information on intentional assessment and provided additional information on observations, play-based assessment, and learning from interactions and conversations with children and families.
Enact	❑ Facilitators provided an opportunity for participants to apply learned information through the snapshots in time, artifact sharing, and home visit activities.	❑ Mentors supported participants as they implemented intentional assessment through observation, play-based assessment, and learning from interactions and conversations with children and families.	❑ Mentors engaged participants in observation of a child in a video scenario and in planning play-based assessment and instruction.
Assess	❑ Facilitators gave participants time to report what they learned from each activity.	❑ Mentors guided participants to discuss the effectiveness of their intentional assessment and provided feedback.	❑ Mentors provided feedback during role-play activities.
Reflect	❑ Facilitators encouraged participants to consider how this practice could be used in their classrooms.	❑ Mentors promoted reflection on why intentional assessment can inform instruction.	❑ Mentors supported discussion of intentional assessment.
Network	❑ Facilitators gave participants opportunities to meet in large and small groups to learn, discuss, and reflect.	❑ Mentors provided opportunities to network with peers and follow up in supportive learning communities.	❑ Mentors provided opportunities for participants to learn together and encouraged discussion and reflection among participants.

Figure 7.7. Checklist for Engaging in Intentional Assessment.

Assessment Strategies and Tools

This strand of LEARN IT professional development develops educators' practical knowledge of assessment strategies and tools. Prior to attending the institute, participants review the assessment strategies and tools information in the Foundations section of this chapter. They should reflect on their own assessment strategies as they look back at this section. In this part of LEARN IT, educators set personal goals for embedding new assessment practices into their existing assessment routines.

LEARN IT Institute

Collectively, educators rely on varied assessment tools to capture student performances in the classroom. Over time, individual educators develop preferences for specific assessment tools and often hone personalized documentation techniques to understand how a child is performing at any given point in time. This institute session begins with a brief overview of assessment strategies and tools based on the information shared earlier in the chapter.

Assessment Word Sort

To activate participants' prior knowledge, they break into groups of four to five to discuss the range of assessment practices available to early childhood educators. To initiate the exploration of common assessment practices, participants should review Handout 7.6; facilitators should provide sticky notes and pens or markers for this activity. Participants engage in an assessment word sort by following the directions on the handout.

After the activity, the large group reconvenes and participants share their categories or themes and examples within each. The ideas generated can serve as a starting point for a more in-depth discussion about the assessment strategies and tools discussed earlier in the chapter.

Assessment Role Play

To practice enacting assessment strategies and tools, participants split into groups of six. The focus of this experience is to consider a child's performance while exploring concepts of patterning in the blocks center. To begin, participants review Handout 7.7. To complete this role-play experience, the groups first decide which three group members will be the *educators* conducting the assessment and which three will be the 5-year-old *children* demonstrating knowledge of patterning concepts. Then the three educators meet and the three children meet to brainstorm their characters' intentions and possible responses when they meet with their educator or child counterpart to complete the role play. The educators should read the Educator's Role-Play Scenarios information on Handout 7.7 and use that as a guide for their brainstorm. The children should read the Child's Role-Play Scenarios. They should use the guiding questions for their educator and child roles, respectively, to decide how they will act their part during the role play.

After briefly considering the guiding questions for each role, the children and educators pair off and complete the role-play experience. The children initiate the role play by beginning to build a simple *ABAB* pattern with a set of blocks or Unifix cubes. The educators practice documenting the performance as well as guide the children into sharing what they understand about simple and complex pattern formation. The educators also practice engaging the children in supportive dialogue to promote the children's continued learning and development across the social, emotional, cognitive, and physical domains.

Assessment Word Sort

Materials: sticky notes and pens or markers

Directions:

- Use the sticky notes to record assessment strategies and tools that are familiar to you. Write out one idea per sticky note.

- Post your sticky notes on the wall or whiteboard that the facilitator assigned to your group.

- Take a few minutes to read your group members' notes.

- Talk with others in your group as you sort or group your sticky notes by common categories or themes. (For example, sticky notes that include digital cameras, digital recordings, and iPad assessment apps might be grouped together.)

- Decide on a category or theme for each grouping of ideas. (For example, the theme for the ideas in the previous bullet point might be digital technologies that support assessment.)

- Be prepared to share with the whole group.

Assessment Role Play

Directions: In your groups of six, designate three group members to be the *educators* conducting the assessment and three to be the 5-year-old *children* demonstrating knowledge of patterning concepts. The educators should read the Educator's Role-Play Scenarios information below. The children should read the Child's Role-Play Scenarios.

Educator's Role-Play Scenario

You will be documenting the child's current understanding of patterns. As you work with the child, listen for the child's capacity for identifying, creating, and extending patterns. Attend to opportunities for helping the child to transition into the creation of more complex pattern structures.

Guiding Questions for the Educators

- What is my purpose?

- What skills and strategies are to be developed?

- Develop an assessment strategy for documenting the child's understanding of the concepts of patterning. Assessment should be accurate, be complete, and inform the educator's next instructional steps.

- Once you understand the child's working knowledge of patterns, how will you encourage the child to consider more complex patterns?

Child's Role-Play Scenario

You will be a 5-year-old child demonstrating your knowledge of a simple *ABAB* repeating pattern. Creatively explore patterns with the Unifix cubes or blocks. Before you begin, think about the social, emotional, cognitive, and physical learning domains that may contribute to your response to the educator.

Guiding Questions for the Child

- What is my purpose?

- What skills and strategies does a child already understand and use to successfully create a simple *ABAB* repeating block pattern?

(continued)

- What knowledge would the child need to understand to demonstrate a more complex conceptualization of patterns?

- How will you respond when observed or asked to share your exploration with blocks with the teacher?

Reflection Questions

1. As the educator, share the aspects of learning and development you were able to capture with the assessment tool you elected to use.

   - How comfortable did you feel in conducting the assessment as the child continued to explore building patterns through play?

   - Based on your assessment, how do you think you would shape the child's next instructional opportunities?

2. As the child, what elements of learning and development were you seeking to demonstrate for the educator?

   - How easily were you able to respond to the educator's discussion prompts?

   - Did the conversation feel like a natural part of your exploration time?

3. Based on your shared experience, consider elements of the child's learning or development that were not readily captured during this brief exchange.

4. Identify aspects of intentional assessment strategies that warrant further examination or practice.

After completing the role-play scenario, the groups of six reconvene to debrief the experience. They consider and discuss the Reflection Questions on Handout 7.7.

Returning to the large group, participants share key ideas discussed in the small groups. The discussion should emphasize the importance of engaging in intentional assessment that is embedded in classroom instruction and includes interactions with individual children as they are engaged in learning.

Implementation and Mentoring

To develop professional knowledge and skills, educators must practice enacting their new or refined knowledge and skills in their own work with children. Based on their experience, readings, discussions, and the select activities intended to promote learning and reflection on their practices as an educator, their next step is to identify opportunities to enact what they learned in their own classroom. Educators fill out the Implementation and Mentoring Form, Handout 7.5, identifying the assessment strategy that they want to implement and share it with their mentor. Mentors should guide educators, providing feedback and corrections, as educators implement a new assessment tool.

During the implementation and mentoring session, assistant teacher Nadia decided she wanted to try using a new assessment tool with Wayne. Wayne was discussed in the opening vignette; he's a curious child who often needs help directing his attention to the task at hand. When engaged, he learns quickly; however, he is often more interested in what is going on around him than in the activity in front of him. In considering how she would implement the new assessment tool with Wayne, Nadia realized she had never heard of an activity protocol before. She was curious about how it worked and what she would learn if she developed one to use with Wayne. Nadia shared with her mentor, Janet, that she planned on intentionally engaging her students in an exploration of shapes over the next few weeks. Nadia thought that this would be a good time to continue to observe Wayne's knowledge of shapes and patterns.

Typically, Nadia examined and supported children's knowledge of a variety of math concepts in small math groups using a variety of manipulatives. Figure 7.8 provides an example of the checklists and anecdotal notes Nadia and her colleagues frequently utilized to capture student learning. With Janet's help, she developed an activity protocol to capture children's experiences working with shapes and patterns. See Figure 7.9 for the activity protocol that they developed. As Nadia worked with Janet, she realized that activity protocols encourage her to strategically expand children's opportunities to explore content knowledge across a variety of learning environments. Accordingly, Nadia worked to enrich the blocks area, the art center, and the playground to enrich children's explorations of shapes. Nadia also decided to use the activity protocol to continue to engage children in conversations about patterns.

After Nadia prepared the learning environments, she asked Janet to observe and take notes while she implemented it. After Nadia used the activity protocol with Wayne while he was in the block area, Janet began the debriefing by asking Nadia what she thought went well. Nadia responded that she thought she had used the protocol more effectively this time than her earlier attempt to use it. She acknowledged that she had captured some good information about Wayne's patterning skills the first time she used the protocol activity at the art table. She had noted shapes Wayne named as he created patterns using paper circles, triangles, and squares that he glued to his paper. However, she had not thought to name other shapes he could include in his patterns to see if he could recognize them and use those in his patterns as well. This time, in the blocks area, she again confirmed that he could identify circles, triangles, and squares by name; she also documented that he could identify

Name: *Wayne*		Observation dates: *3/21* *3/27* *3/31*		
Recognizing geometric shapes	Small blocks	Art table • Paper shapes	Playground • Chalk shapes	Play dough • Cookie cutters
Circle	N-3/27	N-3/21		
Triangle	N-3/27	N-3/21	N-3/31	
Square	N-3/27	N-3/21		
Trapezoid	R-3/27			
Rhombus			R-3/31	
Hexagon				
Rectangle	N-3/27		N-3/31	

R = Recognizes (e.g., points, picks up, identifies with another attribute like "it's the blue one")
N = Names the shape (e.g., circle, triangle, square).
Notes:
• At the art table, Wayne created ABCABC pattern with circle, triangle, square. He glued the paper shape pattern onto one of the dinosaur outlines available after our reading of *Shape by Shape* by Suse MacDonald. (3/21)
• In small block play, Wayne created ABAB pattern with circle and triangle. (3/27)
• On the playground, Wayne created a hopping pattern between the triangle and rhombus ABAB. (3/31)

Figure 7.8. Activity protocol.

rectangles by name and could pick up a trapezoid when she asked him to include trapezoids in his patterns. Realizing that he could recognize a trapezoid, even though he could not name it, gave Nadia an opportunity to help Wayne become familiar with trapezoids. Nadia supported Wayne in using the term *trapezoid* to name the shape as he created a variety of patterns.

Janet agreed that Nadia had used the activity protocol successfully and suggested that she also make note of the types of patterns Wayne created with the blocks. Nadia shared with Janet that next time she plans to implement the activity protocol on the playground when engaging in a hopscotch activity that will reinforce shapes and patterns. She noted that she plans to draw a triangle, rhombus, and rectangle on the playground blacktop using chalk. She will ask Wayne to create specific patterns (e.g., *ABAB*, *ABCABC*) by hopping among the shapes. At first, she will ask him to hop to a specific shape to see if he can match the shape and its name. Then she will ask him to name the shape as he hops to it. Janet thought her plan made sense and indicated that she looks forward to hearing how it worked.

Supportive Learning Communities

Educators must continue to learn about and practice using assessment tools throughout and after their professional development experience. Therefore, in this supportive learning community session, participants will share the assessment tools they used, assess their effectiveness, and reflect on the instructional implications. In addition, participants will also assess their own strengths and needs regarding the use of formal and informal assessments and will develop a plan for enhancing their use of a variety of assessment tools and strategies.

Participants should bring to this supportive learning community meeting examples of the assessment tools and strategies they implemented in their classrooms after the institute. To begin the session, participants share the assessment strategies and tools they enacted

Shapes and Color Assessment

Please visit the book's web site to obtain a full-color version of this activity that can be used with students.

- Print a copy of the cards and cut them apart.
- Lay them out in front of the child in a random order.
- Ask the child to point to or pick up the triangle, square, and so on.
- Point to or pick up a shape and ask the child to name the shape.
- Ask the child to point to or pick up the shape that is green, purple, and so on.
- Point to or pick up a shape and ask what color it is.

Shapes and Color Checklist

	Recognize shapes *Point to or pick up the [shape].*	**Name shapes** *What is the name of this shape?*	**Recognize colors** *Point to or pick up the [color] shape.*	**Name colors** *What color is the [shape]?*
Green triangle				
Purple square				
Red circle				
Blue pentagon				
Yellow hexagon				
Orange rectangle				
Total				

Notes:

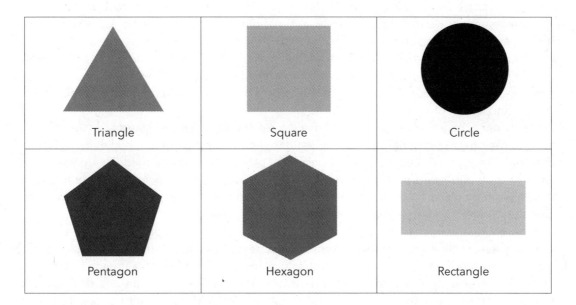

Triangle   Square   Circle

Pentagon   Hexagon   Rectangle

_____
Created by Christopher Kidd (2017).

Figure 7.9. Shapes and color assessment.

in their classrooms after the previous institute. They show their colleagues the assessment strategy or tool and how they captured information about the child using the strategy or tool. As educators share, their fellow participants reinforce the information discussed in the institutes and mentoring sessions and suggest additional strategies and tools that may be valuable.

After the opportunity to share, assess, and reflect on their assessment tools, participants focus to their own self-assessment, which will lead to setting goals for their use of formal and informal assessment tools. To get started, participants select a networking partner. They will work with this partner to develop a networking plan to help them meet their goals related to using effective assessment tools and strategies. As they select their networking partner, they should consider their personal needs as a professional educator. Educators should consider the following questions before selecting:

- Do you need to collaborate with a partner who has honed an effective assessment technique you would like to begin to refine in your own practice? Would you like a partner to demonstrate a specific assessment strategy and work with you to refine your implementation of the assessment?

- Or do you need a networking partner to serve as a reflective partner as you think through and monitor your own practice implementing and refining assessment practices within your classroom?

Participants meet with their networking partner and identify and articulate the assessment tools and strategies they want to implement with a specific child. Educators should keep in mind their goals for the child and how the assessment tools and strategies will inform their curricular and instructional decisions. They will work with their partner to decide how they will support one another to achieve their assessment goals. Networking relationships take a variety of forms. Networking partners can demonstrate an assessment technique, implement the assessment with the educator, or observe him or her enacting the assessment with the focus child. Most important, though, the networking partner will provide a safe space for the educator to critically reflect on the effectiveness of his or her assessment practice. Networking partners will also help the educator to consider how the assessment practice may be enhanced in the future in order to better inform his or her understanding of the child's learning and development.

Participants review Handout 7.8 and use the reflection questions listed to foster discussion with their networking partner. The questions should support their initial thinking about how they will enact and reflect on their assessment plan for their focus child. This initial brainstorming is an important part of the networking dialog before participants move to enact their assessment plans. It could take several conversations between partners as they work to refine their understanding of the assessment plans they would ultimately enact.

Figure 7.10 is a checklist of this LEARN IT strand that the professional development team can use to assess whether they implemented all aspects of assessment tools and strategies across LEARN. Facilitators use the checklist as tool to help them fully enact each step of the LEARN IT professional development strand on assessment tools and strategies. If all aspects of the LEARN framework are utilized across these strands of LEARN IT, participants will engage in learning knowledge and skills specific to assessment tools and strategies. They will have multiple opportunities to enact, assess, and reflect on specific aspects of assessment tools and strategies within the context of their classroom and a supportive learning community that includes mentors and colleagues interested in assessment tools and strategies.

Establishing a Networking Partnership

1. Guiding Questions Before You Enact

Educator's Prior Knowledge:

- Knowledge of Child
    - ❑ What does the child already know?
    - ❑ What are the child's interests?
    - ❑ What is the child's personality?
    - ❑ What are the child's skills, abilities, and talents?
    - ❑ What are the child's language skills?
    - ❑ What are the child's most effective ways to learn?
    - ❑ What are the child's individual needs?
    - ❑ What works and does not work with this child?
- Knowledge of Teaching and Learning
    - ❑ What do I know about the child's family?
    - ❑ What do I know about child development and learning?
    - ❑ What do I know about the content (e.g., language, literacy, mathematics, science)?
    - ❑ What do I know about teaching the content, skills, and strategies?
- Connecting to Child's Prior Knowledge
    - ❑ New Information
        - What new information does the child need?
        - What new information do I need? How will I obtain the information I need?
        - What have I recently learned that will help me teach the child?
    - ❑ Making Connections
        - How can I connect to the child's prior knowledge?
        - How can I connect to the child's family and real-life experiences?
        - How can I build on the child's cultural knowledge?
- Planning Instruction and Assessment
    - ❑ Environment
        - What do I need in the environment to support the child's learning?

(continued)

    – What can I use in the environment to support the child's learning?

☐ Instruction

    – How do I engage the child?

    – What strategies do I employ in my interactions with the child?

    – What balance of child-initiated and teacher-directed activity is needed?

    – How do I meet the child's interests, abilities, and styles of learning?

☐ Collecting Information

    – How will I know if the child meets the curricular goals?

    – How will I know if the child meets the desired outcomes?

2. Guiding Questions Following Your Implementation of the Assessment

- Child's Learning and Development

  – What has the child learned?

  – What can the child do?

  – What knowledge does the child still need to learn?

  – What skills and strategies does the child still need to learn?

- Assessment of and Reflection on My Instruction

  – How effective was my instruction?

  – What worked?

  – What did not work?

  – What might work more effectively with modifications?

- Assessment to Inform Instructional and Curricular Decisions

  – What did I learn about the child's learning and development that affects my curricular and instructional decisions?

  – What are my next steps with the child?

- Assessment to Inform Instructional Strategies

  – What strategies will I continue to use when interacting with this child?

  – What strategies do I need to modify when interacting with this child?

  – What strategies do I need to employ when interacting with this child?

Checklist for Assessment Tools and Strategies

	LEARN IT institute	Implementation and mentoring	Supportive learning communities
Learn	❐ Facilitators presented research and best practice related to assessment tools and strategies.	❐ Mentors helped participants to identify particular needs they have in implementing assessment tools and strategies.	❐ Mentors asked participants to share examples of the assessment tools and strategies they used since the institute as a way to review information on assessment tools and strategies.
Enact	❐ Facilitators provided opportunities for participants to apply learned information through role playing an intentional assessment scenario.	❐ Mentors supported participants as they implemented assessment tools and strategies.	❐ Mentors engaged participants in planning to work with a networking partner to enhance their use of assessment strategies and tools.
Assess	❐ Facilitators provided an opportunity for participants to report information they learned from the activity.	❐ Mentors guided participants to discuss the effectiveness of their use of new assessment tools and strategies and provided feedback.	❐ Mentors provided an opportunity for participants to work with a networking partner to consider what they know about a particular child.
Reflect	❐ Facilitators had participants consider the intentional assessment strategies and tools they can use in their classrooms.	❐ Mentors promoted reflection on how to use assessment tools and strategies to collect information about individual children.	❐ Mentors provided an opportunity for participants to reflect on what they know about individual children to plan future assessment and instruction.
Network	❐ Facilitators provided an opportunity for participants to meet in large and small groups to learn, discuss, and reflect.	❐ Mentors provided opportunities to network with peers and follow up in supportive learning communities.	❐ Mentors provided opportunities for participants to learn together and encouraged discussion and reflection among participants.

Figure 7.10. Checklist for Assessment Tools and Strategies.

SUMMARY

In the first part of this chapter, we introduced educators Samita and Nadia and their three kindergartners, Crystal, Fahed, and Wayne. We then explored connecting assessment with curriculum and instruction and examined approaches to assessment used to support intentional teaching in early education classrooms. We described ways to assess young learners within the context of intentional teaching and discussed tools and strategies to support the collection and analysis of information. We then discussed opportunities for educators to reflect on their current assessment practices, work with mentors to enact new assessments, and establish trusted networking partners to ensure a continued focus on developing intentional assessment strategies. Collectively, this provides the foundation for what educators need to know to engage in intentional assessment with diverse young learners that is embedded in instruction and includes interactions with individual children and their families.

Conclusion

Lillie, the educator from Chapter 1, reflected on her participation in the LEARN IT professional development. She realized that she appreciated having this opportunity to enhance her teaching by learning and enacting intentional teaching strategies with the support of mentors and professional colleagues. She acknowledged the benefit of taking time to assess the effectiveness of her instruction and to reflect on how to use what she learned about her children to inform future instructional experiences. In addition, she noted how the institutes had helped her to gain new knowledge and strategies and she recognized the value of the mentoring that took place as she enacted strategies with her own students and their families. She also especially enjoyed and benefited from the networking that took place during the supportive learning communities. Like the educators in the Nasser, Kidd, Burns, and Campbell (2015) study, Lillie was highly satisfied with LEARN IT and believed she had learned information and strategies she could use in her classroom.

UNIQUE ASPECTS OF LEARN IT

The LEARN IT professional development model brings together the evidence base about adult learning and teacher professional development. It uses the LEARN framework as the foundation for educators to learn the content and strategies developed across the LEARN IT institutes, implementation and mentoring, and supportive learning communities. Across all aspects of LEARN IT, educators learn new knowledge, enact what they learn, assess the effectiveness of what they enact, reflect on future implications, and network with colleagues and knowledgeable mentors (Nasser et al., 2015; Snow, Griffin, & Burns, 2005). As discussed in Chapter 1, LEARN serves as a framework for educators that helps them to use the information and strategies they learn by applying them in their work with children and families. The reflective aspect of the framework encourages educators to assess their implementation of strategies to make informed instructional decisions and refine their enactment of evidence-based strategies. Learning, enacting, assessing, and reflecting within a network of peers and mentors provides further support for educators' professional growth.

Educators' experience is enhanced by enacting the LEARN framework across institutes, implementation and mentoring, and supportive learning communities. The institutes provide opportunities for educators to learn new information and strategies and engage in guided practice. As educators implement a new strategy, they consider research that supports the strategy and the procedures for each aspect of the strategy they enact. The activities also encourage educators to note what they did well and what they need to continue to practice as they reflect on how they might enact the strategy in their own classrooms. Educators try out new ideas and strategies with their peers, which provides them with additional support and opportunities to learn with and from each other.

The site-based implementation and mentoring combined with supportive learning communities provide opportunities for educators to learn about strategies in greater depth and try them out with their own students in mind. Mentors are available to scaffold the planning and implementation of new strategies. Educators choose the strategies they wish to implement and also select the type of support they believe will best support their learning. They may ask the mentor to model the strategy, co-teach as they implement the strategy collaboratively, or observe while the educator implements the strategy. Time for feedback and debriefing is included as part of this process. In addition, further development of knowledge and ways to implement effective strategies occurs during the supportive learning communities. In small groups, educators have a chance to share their experiences with the colleagues and mentors, practice strategies, and engage in discussion.

Although the LEARN framework and institutes, implementation and mentoring, and supportive learning communities can be implemented to develop a variety of content areas, LEARN IT is unique in that it focuses on developing educators' intentional teaching strategies. In Chapter 2, we defined intentional teaching as follows (Burns, Kidd, Nasser, Aier, & Stechuk, 2012):

- Designing learning opportunities to meet the individual needs, interests, and prior knowledge of all children

- Using ongoing assessment practices to make informed curricular decisions and plan instructional strategies and activities

- Involving children in curricular explorations grounded in rich content (e.g., in science, creative arts, and social studies)

- Engaging in high-quality, high-quantity, reciprocal, codirected conversations with each child, rather than a select few, in learning centers, small groups, and individual teaching moments

- Establishing a positive classroom climate

Each aspect of intentional teaching was further developed in Chapters 3 through 7 as we examined learning through play, including each child, culturally responsive practice, assessing diverse young children, and connecting assessment with curriculum and instruction. Across these topics, LEARN IT engages educators in reflective practices that help them to become more intentional in their teaching of diverse young children and in their interactions with families.

LEARN IT RESEARCH BASE

In the Appendix, we present the findings from our research on our implementation of the LEARN IT professional development model with Head Start educators. Overall, participants were highly satisfied with LEARN IT and expressed their belief that the institutes, implementation and mentoring, and supportive learning communities were beneficial to their learning as well as to their enactment of intentional teaching strategies in their teaching (Nasser et al., 2015). Participants shared that they especially valued the support of the LEARN IT mentor and were appreciative of the mentors' willingness to share ideas and resources and of their involvement in the classroom (Nasser et al.). In addition, they indicated that networking with peers throughout LEARN IT enhanced their professional growth (Nasser et al.).

In a study comparing LEARN IT participants with educators engaged in their sites' typical professional development, differences in the use of intentional teaching strategies were evident, with the LEARN IT participants' utilization of intentional teaching strategies more prevalent than those in the control group (see Appendix). This was evident in educators' engagement of each individual child and in their interactions that promoted positive learning outcomes, creativity, and reasoning through intentional conversations and activities. Educators engaged in intentional interactions designed to develop children's knowledge and skills and to help children connect what they are learning to their own experiences. As they did, educators encouraged children to respond to questions, elaborate on their responses, and share ideas with their peers. In doing so, they intentionally used strategies that would enhance children's cognitive abilities and develop their understanding of curricular concepts and topics.

MOVING FORWARD

Because of LEARN IT's focus on intentional teaching, the processes and activities shared in this book are relevant to a wide audience of professionals and educators across content areas and curriculum models. It is our hope that professional developers, administrators, coaches, trainers, and teacher educators will use the information and activities shared as a model for professional development that develops educators' intentional teaching strategies across instructional contexts.

After reading and implementing the content addressed in this book, we hope professional developers, administrators, teacher educators, and early childhood educators will continue to use LEARN as a framework for guiding professional development. Learning, enacting, assessing, and reflecting with a network of supportive peers and expert mentors is essential to sustainable professional development. Though our focus here is on teachers of prekindergarten- and kindergarten-age children, the model had implications for teachers of children younger than that and also for those teaching upper elementary, middle, and high school.

It is our hope that, as a result of engaging in LEARN IT, educators will be more intentional in their teaching and will engage young children in play-based, culturally responsive assessment, curriculum, and instruction that includes each individual child. These intentional teachers implement a higher quality program for young children and their families. It is highly recommended to implement the LEARN IT model in its entirety to ensure that multiple opportunities are provided for teachers to deepen their knowledge, reflections, and networking in spaces that are supportive and safe.

Approach and Efficacy of the Model

The appendix shares findings from research on the LEARN (learn, enact, reflect, assess, and network) professional development model, which provides a systematic way to promote intentional teaching in early childhood education classrooms. First, we review the model (see Figure A.1) that we implemented with Head Start educators, and then we present data on the efficacy of the model. Next, we present information regarding the intradynamics of the model. The presentation on the model is a summary of information presented in Chapter 1. Please refer to that chapter for more detail.

THE LEARN PROFESSIONAL DEVELOPMENT MODEL

We developed the model with the goal of promoting Head Start teachers' and assistant teachers' use of intentional teaching practices. We drew upon adult learning theories to develop the model (Bransford, Brown, & Cocking, 2000; Darling-Hammond & Bransford, 2005; Snow, Griffin, & Burns, 2005). It included the following:

- 5 full group days throughout the year that involved meetings of teachers and assistant teachers across all sites in a large-group setting

- Monthly visits from the mentor to provide in-class mentoring

- Monthly small-group, on-site community meetings facilitated by a mentor

- Online support from the mentor on an as-needed basis

We organized the professional development using the LEARN framework, which encourages teachers to learn new content, enact it in the classrooms, assess the effectiveness, reflect, and network with peers (Nasser, Kidd, Burns, & Campbell 2015; Snow et al., 2005). The content focused on intentional teaching practices, including 1) culturally responsive practices, 2) including all children, 3) using assessment to inform curriculum and instruction, and 4) implementing intentional teaching strategies within the context of mandated curriculum.

We delivered the professional development through a process that involved teachers and assistant teachers learning together. Classroom instruction takes place within a context that includes, at a minimum, a teacher and assistant teacher working together. It makes sense to engage both in the learning process. This learning took place during the LEARN institute and the site-based community meetings in a variety of formats, including independent readings, small-group discussions and exercises, and observations of videos, including commercially produced videos and video recordings of participants' teaching. Participants received a practical, research-based set of reading materials related to effective teaching practices and instructional

LEARN *in Action*

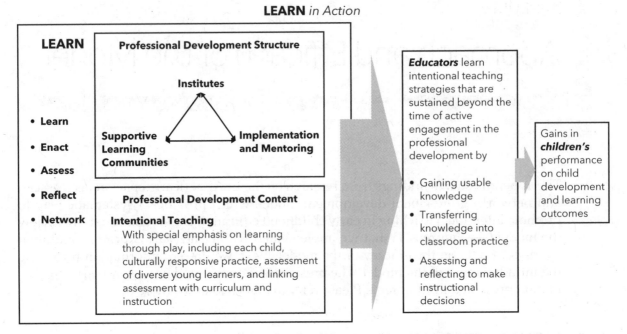

Figure A.1.   LEARN in action.

strategies. Each reading contained self-reflection questions to help teachers understand what they read. These articles were discussed in depth during the LEARN institute as well as at the community meetings. In addition, reviews and discussions of videos of children's early academic skills were incorporated into the sessions.

While learning each area of content, participants engaged in interactive activities that focused on practicing specific strategies to implement in their classroom. In addition, they learned assessment procedures designed to help them evaluate children's learning as well as the effectiveness of their teaching and the instructional strategies employed. Reflections on the outcomes of their teaching, changes they needed to make, and plans for future instruction were completed individually and in collaboration with other participants and the mentor. In short, the goal was to provide them with experiences that promoted deep understanding and application of the content.

As part of the incentive for participating in the study, participants were given the option to receive course credit. Ten of the participants elected to receive course credit. All participants, whether receiving course credit or not, were expected to participate in the face-to-face activities and complete all of the outside readings, activities, and assignments. The difference was that the mentor graded the written activities and participation of those participants receiving course credit. She provided feedback to all participants regardless of whether they were enrolled in the course.

The Role of the Mentor

In the first year of the project, a mentor with a Ph.D. in early childhood education and a background in speech and language was hired by the project to work with the researchers, research associates, and doctoral students to plan and implement the professional development. She worked with the research team to facilitate the activities during the LEARN institute. Then she followed up with the participants to provide in-class mentoring and to moderate the community meetings. She visited the classrooms each month to observe and provide support and mentoring. During the community meetings, she introduced key content through readings, videos, activities, and/or discussion prompts. She also provided teachers and assistant teachers with opportunities to present and discuss documentation of their work with children (e.g., digital pictures and student work samples), share their questions and ideas, and provide feedback to each other on what they have learned. In subsequent years of the project, multiple mentors participated, all with advanced experience with early childhood education or early childhood special education.

The mentor served as the course instructor and, therefore, took time to present and explain activities and assignments that took place outside of the face-to-face interactions, to support participants as they were completing these outside experiences, and to provide feedback on written assignments and video-recorded lessons of their implementation of intentional teaching strategies. Outside experiences included several activities designed to enact changes in participants' classroom environments and teaching practices. The mentor provided feedback as teachers and assistant teachers conducted an environmental analysis of the classroom and used the information shared in the LEARN institute to make changes to the classroom environment. She also supported them as they analyzed and reflected on video recordings of their implementation of intentional teaching strategies as well as their peers' implementation. In this activity, the teachers and assistant teachers videotaped themselves teaching two lessons that incorporated a strategy or strategies emphasized in the professional development. One lesson was a large-group lesson; the other was a small-group lesson. They then viewed the video recordings and used an observation/reflection guide to focus their attention on their teaching. The third type of assignment was the development of a series of lesson plans related to a curriculum unit. The mentor guided the participants as they worked in collaboration with peers to ensure they were incorporating intentional teaching practices emphasized in the professional development into the implementation of their curriculum. Throughout the text, we provide many examples of the mentors' roles, especially in the activities when addressing in-class mentoring and supportive learning communities.

LEARN Institute

We designed the 5 LEARN institute days to introduce participants to the LEARN process and help them to recognize the importance of taking ownership of their own professional development. Because learning new knowledge is an important aspect of professional development (Diamond, Justice, Siegler, & Snyder, 2013), the LEARN institute focused on developing knowledge as well as on specific teaching strategies. The researchers, research associate, graduate students, and mentor collaboratively planned and implemented the learning experiences using a variety of large-group and small-group interactive activities to enable participants to learn the content and practice ways to implement the strategies in their classrooms. In the first year of the project, we defined the content areas as 1) culturally responsive practices, 2) including all children, 3) using assessment to inform curriculum and instruction, and 4) implementing intentional teaching strategies within the context of mandated curriculum. In subsequent years, these areas were expanded and incorporated all content included in Chapters 1 through 7 of this text.

In-Class Mentoring and Community Meetings

We designed the monthly in-class mentoring and community meetings to develop teachers' intentional teaching practices, including the areas noted previously. Because individualized mentoring is an effective component of professional development (Diamond et al., 2013; Powell, Diamond, Burchinal, & Koehler, 2010), we employed a mentor who worked in the classroom once a month to observe, model, support, and provide feedback on intentional teaching strategies. The mentor followed up the in-class mentoring by meeting with teachers and assistant teachers during their on-site community meetings. These types of community-of-practice groups can have positive effects on instruction (Buysse, Castro, & Peisner-Feinber, 2010; Diamond et al., 2013; Vescio, Ross, & Adams, 2008). These meetings provided a less formal context for gaining and applying new knowledge, while providing teachers and assistant teachers time to assess and reflect on their application of what they learned in their classrooms. The community meetings brought the teachers and assistant teachers in different classrooms together as a community of practice where they could share "experiences and knowledge in free-flowing creative ways that foster new approaches to problems" (Wenger & Snyder, 2000, p.140). These community meetings allowed teachers to share with one another the data they collected, examine individual cases and trends in data from multiple children, and determine how the instructional strategies can be modified to enhance effectiveness. The focus of the community meetings was linked to the intentional teaching content areas described previously.

Online Mentoring

To ensure continuous professional development, we also included the opportunity for the teachers and assistant teachers to seek online mentoring from the mentor using Blackboard learning management software and e-mail communication. In this context, the availability of online mentoring enabled the mentor and the mentees to be in different locations and still allowed mentoring and learning to occur (Mashburn, Downer, Hamre, Justice, & Pianta, 2010; Pianta, Mashburn, Downer, Hamre, & Justice, 2008; Saltzberg & Polyson, 1995; Snyder, Hemmeter, & McLaughlin, 2011). In this project, the mentor used online technologies to share content and facilitate networking among teachers and across sites. She posted readings, handouts, and directions for assignments on Blackboard, making it easy for participants to obtain information. She also used the discussion board component of Blackboard to facilitate discussion. For example, a discussion focused on setting goals enabled the teachers and assistant teachers to share an instructional goal for the year and receive feedback and ideas from other teachers on ways to reach the goal. In addition, the mentor used e-mail correspondence to respond to individual questions and needs. We found, however, that not all schools were comfortable with the complexities of Blackboard, so in some cases e-mail, faxes, and phone calls were used more often. Still, mentors made themselves available to mentees to the best of everyone's ability.

Engagement in Developing the Professional Development

One other component of our model involved engaging teachers and assistant teachers in the building of the professional development itself. During each LEARN institute, we asked for written feedback or oral comments on the learning experiences, or both, and encouraged suggestions for ways to refine the activities to enhance learning. At the final LEARN institute, we engaged the teachers and assistant teachers in a reconstruction activity in which we asked them to review key learning experiences and share what they had learned as well as make suggestions for changes to the activity for future professional development.

In summary, we developed a professional development model focused on developing teacher and assistant teachers' intentional teaching practices. Intentional teaching requires teachers to move beyond procedural knowledge needed to teach in simple instructional contexts to the expert, adaptive knowledge needed to assess complex situations in ways that enable teachers to recognize difficulties, evaluate the situation, seek out new information, and incorporate new knowledge into their existing context (Snow et al., 2005). However, there is limited research about intentional teaching, what it entails, and how to promote intentional teaching. Therefore, to ascertain valid knowledge about intentional teaching, as presented in Chapter 2, our first research study focused on its definition (Burns, Kidd, Nasser, Aier, & Stechuk, 2012).

The study reported in Burns et al. (2012) was the first of numerous research studies we performed as we developed the model. After summarizing that study in the following section, we present findings from our study of teacher satisfaction of the model (Nasser et al., 2015). These first two studies have been previously published. We summarize those articles here and suggest those articles be reviewed if they are of greater interest. The third study on the implementation of the model is described next, and we end with an examination of variables related to positive outcomes.

DEFINING INTENTIONAL TEACHING

Our work on defining intentional teaching was influenced by and converged with previous seminal works in this area (Copple & Bredekamp, 2009; Epstein, 2007). In addition, it provided the necessary definition we required for this project, given the broad definition of intentional teaching in previous publications. Our findings helped us to determine and prioritize information to include in professional development and to assess the fidelity of the implementation of that professional development that provides specific and relevant guidance for all early childhood professionals.

Thirteen prekindergarten teachers in a community-based Head Start program participated in the study and were observed during large-group and centers or small-group activities by four early childhood experts. Two studies using qualitative methods are presented. In both studies, experts together observed focus teachers with attention to coding all instances of intentional teaching. They then discussed their observations. Discussions were recorded and analyzed with grounded theory analyses. Features of intentional teaching were specified.

Our findings indicated that intentional teachers give clear indicators that teachers need to address each child as an individual with particular needs and interests. Our findings integrated into our definition of intentional teaching and confirm previous authors' assertions; for example, Espinosa (2010) in her writing on intentional teaching stressed teachers' clear learning goals for students as well as inclusion of core content. Our findings specify that in intentional teaching "children's ideas are developed and thinking is demanded using rich curriculum content (e.g., in science, creative arts, and social studies)" (Burns et al., 2012, p. 284). Thompson and Twibell (2010) addressed teacher modeling of friendly, respectful interactions and strategies to promote a positive classroom environment and provide children with opportunities to make choices about their activities throughout the day. Our findings confirm their assertions; note the wording in our definition: "This takes place through reciprocal, codirected conversation between teachers and children in learning centers/small groups.... Planned instructional strategies/activities take place within a positive classroom climate" (Burns et al., 2012, p. 284). There are components of intentional teaching identified in the current research that were not explicitly stated by previous authors and there were points stated by previous authors that were not explicitly identified in the research, though in both cases one could argue that the components are implied. In our research, we found that it is important that "conversation happens with all children, rather than a selected few, and takes place on a consistent basis (high quantity as well as high quality)" (Burns et al., 2012, p. 284). This was not an explicit component of intentional teaching identified by previous authors. Our findings indicated that intentional teaching demands that both children and teachers play active roles in the processes that lead to children's learning and development (Burns et al., 2012).

TEACHER SATISFACTION

These data included two focus group interviews, one focus group with the teachers and one with the assistant teachers, that revealed a high level of satisfaction from both the teachers and assistant teachers (Nasser et al., 2015). We studied their perceptions of the professional development. (See the Nasser et al., 2015, study for details about data analyses and findings.) Overall satisfaction was high: "They believed all three elements [LEARN institute, in-class mentoring, and community meetings] gave them access to usable knowledge that could be enacted in their classrooms and that their learning was enhanced by networking with colleagues during the LEARN institute and community meetings" (Nasser et al., 2015, p. 10). They were less enthusiastic about the online facet of the professional development and cited reasons that included lack of time to get on the computer, limited computer skills and understanding of using online software, and discomfort with writing to rather than talking with peers. The participants in this study valued the support they received from the mentor (Nasser et al.). They appreciated the activities and resources she provided as well as how she became involved and knew their classrooms and children.

The main barriers discussed were missing the professional development provided by the Head Start administrators to those in the control group on the LEARN institute days and the challenges of the schedule for the community meetings. The community meetings were scheduled to begin right after the children were dismissed and lasted for 2 hours, which went beyond participants' contract hours and made it difficult for some to attend and meet family obligations. However, as is evident by their attendance, noted in the text to follow, they remained committed to the project despite these challenges.

IMPLEMENTATION OF THE MODEL

We investigated the effects of the professional development model on intentional teaching beliefs and practices. We examined its effects on teachers' and assistant teachers' beliefs, including multicultural efficacy and attitudes. We also examined differences between teachers who participated in our model and those who did not, regarding their implementation of intentional teaching strategies. Specifically, we investigated the following research questions:

1. Did participating in our professional development have an effect on Head Start teachers' and assistant teachers' beliefs?

2. Did participating have an effect on Head Start teachers' intentional teaching practices?

3. What aspects of intentional teaching were affected and not affected by participation?

Our study participants included 10 teachers and 13 assistant teachers from a community-based Head Start program in a large metropolitan area in the mid-Atlantic region. There were 15 classrooms at eight sites, with each site ranging from one to four classrooms. At the beginning of the study, each classroom had one teacher and one assistant teacher. After attrition, we had 23 who participated in the study. Twenty of the 23 participants were Black, two were Hispanic, and one was Asian/Indian. Sixteen indicated they spoke English only, four spoke English and Arabic, two spoke English and Spanish, and one spoke English and Urdu or Hindi. In terms of education, five held a bachelor's degree, four held an associate's degree, and 14 held a high school diploma. Six had more than 20 years of teaching experience, three had 10–20 years, five had 6–9 years, five had 3–5 years, and three had 2 years or less. The number of years of experience for one participant is unknown. Table A.1 shows the demographic information by experimental and control groups.

The average classroom size was 17 children. Classrooms had, on average, two children with identified disabilities, with a range of zero to five children with disabilities in each class. The average number of dual language learners reported was eight, with a range of zero to 18 per class. The number of languages spoken in classrooms by the multilingual children ranged from two to nine, with an average of four languages per classroom.

We randomly assigned participants to experimental and control groups by site. Sites were matched by size and then randomly assigned to either the experimental group or the control group. Random assignment was conducted at the site level to reduce the likelihood of cross-group contamination that can occur when teachers receiving professional development talk with teachers not receiving the professional development. The experimental group participated in the professional development described throughout this book. The control group participated in the regularly scheduled professional development provided by the Head Start administrators. The Head Start professional development met on the same days and at the same times as the LEARN institute days. The Head Start professional development sessions focused on various program-related topics. Specifically, there was a focus on the new curriculum model, the *DLM Early Childhood Express* (McGraw-Hill Education, 2010). Those in the control group participated in professional development specifically focused on the curricular units and materials needed to carry out *DLM* lessons and curriculum

Table A.1. Demographic information for teachers

Characteristic	Number	
	Experimental	Control
Race/ethnicity		
White	0	0
African American	8	12
Asian Indian	0	1
Hispanic/Latin/Spanish	1	1
Languages spoken fluently		
English only	6	10
English and Spanish	1	1
English and Arabic	2	2
English and Urdu/Hindi/Punjabi	0	1
Highest degree		
High school diploma	5	9
A.A. degree	1	3
B.A. degree	3	2
Teaching experience		
2 years or fewer	2	1
3–5 years	2	3
6–9 years	2	3
10–20 years	0	3
More than 20 years	3	3

as outlined. Separate from the 5 professional development days, all participants in the experimental and control groups participated in required Head Start professional development, such as to address Head Start policy changes.

Measures

Data sources included the Teacher Multicultural Attitude Scale (TMAS; Ponterotito, Baluch, Greig, & Rivera, 1998), the Teacher Multicultural Efficacy Scale (TMES; Guyton & Wesche, 2005), and the Teachers Demographic, Education, and Professional Development Activities survey. Data were also collected through two observational tools, the Early Childhood Classroom Observation Measure (ECCOM; Stypek & Byler, 2004) and the Classroom Assessment Scoring System (CLASS; Pianta, La Paro, & Hamre, 2008).

Teacher Multicultural Attitude Scale   The TMAS, developed by Ponterotito et al. (1998), is a teacher self-report measure with a five-point Likert scale in which teachers respond to items (strongly disagree to strongly agree) that represent different aspects of culturally responsive practice. Ponterotito et al. (1998) reported the coefficient alpha as .82. Within the scale, a score of 5 reflects a highly positive attitude toward multicultural curriculum and educational practices.

Teacher Multicultural Efficacy Scale   The TMES, developed by Guyton and Wesche (2005), is a four-point Likert scale that measures teachers' responses to items related to culturally responsive practice. The scale choices are as follows: A = I do not believe I could do this very well; B = I could probably do this if I had to, but it would be difficult for me; C = I believe that I could do this reasonably well if I had time to prepare; or D = I am quite confident that this would be easy for me to do. According to Guyton and Wesche, "These findings suggest that a score of 1 or 2 on an item is a low score, that a score of 3 is average, and that 4 is a high score" (p. 25). This scale asks questions related to culturally responsive practice and the teacher's attitudes and ability to integrate such methods of teaching into his or her practice. In addition, it measures attitudes and understanding of the larger sociocultural issues surrounding the integration of culturally responsive practices in classrooms. The Cronbach's alpha for this survey was reported as .83 (Guyton & Wesche).

Early Childhood Classroom Observation Measure   Stipek and Byler (2004) reported that "the ECCOM was designed to use in research as a tool for studying the effects of teacher training and other interventions on classroom practices, and the effect of classroom practices on child outcomes" (p. 391). The ECCOM measures the extent to which teachers of 4- to 7-year-olds use didactic, teacher-centered practices; provide little or no direction to children; or promote an environment of shared responsibility for learning between the teacher and children on the subscales of instruction, management, and social climate (Stipek & Byler). As in a study by Hauser-Cram, Sirin, and Stipek (2003), we used the ECCOM as a classroom observation measure. Those authors selected two sets of items: one set to examine classroom instructional environment and the other focused on teachers' rigidity in implementing classroom curriculum. In our study, we also used two sets of items. We examined support for learning and focused learning.

For each subtest, classrooms were rated in three areas labeled A, T, and C. The A column lists indicators of classrooms where there is a shared responsibility between teacher and children. The T column lists indicators of a teacher-controlled classroom. The C column lists indicators of a child-dominated classroom. The rating scale ranges are based on the percentage of time the indicators were observed: 1 (practices rarely seen), 2 (practices not seen very much), 3 (practices sometimes seen), 4 (practices are prominent), or 5 (practices predominate). Stipek and Byler (2004) established validity and reliability for this measure in kindergarten and first grade. Two researchers used a modified form of the ECCOM to collect data on the type of instruction that occurred, the quality of the instruction, and the classroom climate. The two researchers achieved reliability in Head Start classrooms with an overall interrater reliability of .82.

Classroom Assessment Scoring System   The CLASS is an observational tool that measures teaching within three domains: emotional support, classroom organization, and instructional support (Pianta, La Paro et al., 2008). Within each domain, classrooms are rated from 1 (minimally characteristic) to 7 (highly characteristic). The measure is used to assess the overall quality of teachers' instructional practices in the areas of concept development; quality of student feedback; language modeling and literacy focus; classroom organization such as behavior management; productivity and instructional learning formats; and emotional support such as positive climate, teacher sensitivity, and regard for students. Reliability and validity are established for the instrument (La Paro, Pianta, & Stuhlman, 2004). One researcher conducted all of the postintervention CLASS observations. This researcher attended the CLASS reliability training and was certified as a reliable assessor at the time of the CLASS observations. A CLASS training team at University of Virginia delivered the training on use of CLASS and achieving reliability. Our researcher passed a series of reliability tests. She watched segments of classroom interactions based on the domains and then scored the segments. These scores were compared with scores of "master trainers" to achieve reliability.

Intensity and Duration Data   Using a mentoring monitor form, the mentor recorded data about the amount of time spent at the LEARN institute, engaged in mentoring in the classroom, and at community meetings. She also noted the modes of communication (e.g., e-mail, phone, Blackboard) utilized in distance mentoring. These data were collected monthly.

Results

Our professional development took place over 9 months from late August, the week before children were expected to return, through late May, less than a month before school concluded for the children. Overall, the teachers and assistant teachers attended, on average, for 53 hours and 29 minutes, including LEARN institute days, in-class mentoring, community meetings, and online support. (See Table A.2 for average amount of time engaged in each facet of the professional development.) One teacher missed 30 minutes of a community meeting. Two assistant teachers were absent for one 2-hour session each. Use of online communication began in the second month of the professional development and included two types of online written communications each month: e-mail and Blackboard. The mentor also communicated with teachers and assistant teachers by telephone.

Teacher Multicultural Attitude Scale and Teacher Multicultural Efficacy Scale   On the multicultural efficacy and attitude scales, we were interested in whether there were any meaningful differences between participants in the experimental group and those in the control groups at the conclusion of the professional development. We first examined the TMES and TMAS results to ascertain whether the professional development had an effect on participants' perceived multicultural efficacy and attitudes. By conducting a one-way between-subjects ANOVA to compare the effects, we found there were no significant differences at posttest on the TMES, $F(1, 21) = .420$, $p = .524$, and on the TMAS, $F(1, 21) = .261$, $p = 1.336$.

Table A.2.   Professional development duration

Type of professional development activity	Average duration, all participants	Average duration, teachers	Average duration, assistant teachers
Institutes	31 hours, 30 minutes	–	–
In-classroom mentoring	4 hours, 29 minutes	3 hours, 55 minutes	4 hours, 56 minutes
Community meetings	17 hours, 30 minutes	17 hours, 53 minutes	17 hours, 12 minutes
Combined professional development	53 hours, 29 minutes	–	–

Observational Measures   When conducting one-way between-subjects ANOVAs using the ECCOM and CLASS scores, we found meaningful differences between the experimental and control groups in several subdomains. Because data for the ECCOM and CLASS were collected by classroom with a focus on the teacher, the following results are based on the data collected in the 10 classrooms.

Early Childhood Classroom Observation Measure   On the ECCOM, we examined support for learning and focused learning. Due to the low sample size, we created scatterplots to present the results in a meaningful way. (See Table A.3 for means and standard deviations for each scatterplot.)

     We first examined support for learning and found significant differences between the experimental and control groups, with the experimental group scoring higher, on average, on Support A (a balance of teacher- and child-guided practices), $F(1, 8) = 10.595$, $p = .012$, and the control group scoring higher, on average, on Support T (teacher-controlled practices), $F(1, 8) = 5.196$, $p = .05$. We found no significant differences on Support C (child-dominated practices), $F(1, 8) = 4.818$, $p = .059$. The effect sizes were large, with $d = 1.324$ for Support T, $d = 1.549$ for Support C, and $d = 2.234$ for Support A.

Table A.3.   Means and standard deviations for observational data in figures

Observational instrument	Observational items	Posttest score	
		Experimental group *M(SD)*	Control group *M(SD)*
Early Childhood Classroom Observation Measure	Student engagement		
	A: Teacher and child share responsibility—more intentional higher score	4.00 (.97)	1.70 (.97)
	T: Teacher controlled and directed—more intentional lower score	1.75 (.96)	2.70 (.44)
	C: Child dominated with little teacher direction or control—more intentional lower score	1.37 (.48)	2.60 (1.29)
	Support for communication skills		
	A: Teacher and child share responsibility—more intentional higher score	3.87 (.63)	2.10 (1.14)
	T: Teacher controlled and directed—more intentional lower score	1.87 (.85)	2.60 (.65)
	C: Child dominated with little teacher direction or control—more intentional lower score	1.37 (.48)	3.20 (1.44)
	Instructional conversations		
	A: Teacher and child share responsibility—more intentional higher score	4.00 (1.35)	1.70 (.84)
	T: Teacher controlled and directed—more intentional lower score	1.50 (1.00)	2.80 (.57)
	C: Child dominated with little teacher direction or control—more intentional lower score	1.75 (.87)	3.20 (1.35)
	Literacy instruction		
	A: Teacher and child share responsibility—more intentional higher score	4.00 (1.41)	2.10 (1.52)
	T: Teacher controlled and directed—more intentional lower score	1.50 (1.00)	2.90 (.96)
	C: Child dominated with little teacher direction or control—more intentional lower score	1.25 (.50)	2.50 (1.87)
Classroom Assessment Scoring System	Concept development		
	Higher score indicates more intentional teaching	4.00 (.82)	2.20 (1.30)

Finding significant differences for Support A (a balance of teacher- and child-guided practices), we explored the components of support for learning: choice of activities, student engagement, and support for communication skills. Upon analysis, we found significant differences in student engagement A (a balance of teacher- and child-guided practices), $F(1, 8) = 11.561$, $p = .009$, with the experimental teachers scoring, on average, higher than the control teachers, and student engagement T (teacher-controlled practices), $F(1, 8) = 5.297$, $p = .050$, with the control teachers scoring, on average, higher than the experimental teachers. The experimental teachers showed a clear difference between their score on student engagement A (a balance of teacher- and child-guided practices) and their scores on student engagement T (teacher-controlled practices) and C (child-dominated practices). There is no clear pattern within the teachers in the control group.

We also found significant differences on support for communication, with the teachers in the experimental group scoring higher, on average, on communication A (a balance of teacher- and child-guided practices), $F(1, 8) = 9.636$, $p = .015$, and on communication C (child-dominated practices), $F(1, 8) = 7.734$, $p = .024$.

For focused learning, we found significant differences between the two groups, with the experimental group scoring higher, on average, on learning A (a balance of teacher- and child-guided practices), $F(1, 6) = 13.016$, $p = .011$. We also found significant differences on learning T (teacher-controlled practices), $F(1, 6) = 18.856$, $p = .005$, with the control group scoring, on average, higher than the experimental group. There were no significant differences on learning C (child-dominated practices), $F(1, 6) = 2.070$, $p = .200$. The effect sizes for learning A and T were large, with $d = 2.913$ and $d = 3.544$, respectively. The effect size for learning C was medium, $d = .684$.

Finding significant differences on focused learning, we examined the components: instructional conversation, literacy instruction, and mathematics instruction. We found significant differences on instructional conversation A (a balance of teacher- and child-guided practices), $F(1, 8) = 12.877$, $p = .007$, with the experimental teachers scoring higher, and on instructional conversation T (teacher-controlled practices), $F(1, 8) = 7.877$, $p = .023$, with the control teachers scoring higher.

We also found significant differences on literacy instruction T (teacher-controlled practices), $F(1, 8) = 6.244$, $p = .037$, with the control teachers scoring higher, on average, than the experimental teachers. There were no significant differences in mathematics instruction.

Classroom Assessment Scoring System   On the CLASS, we examined the emotional support, classroom organization, and instructional support domains. There were significant differences in the instructional support domain, $F(1, 8) = 5.215$, $p = .05$, but no significant differences in the emotional support domain, $F(1, 8) = .014$, $p = .908$, and the classroom organization domain, $F(1, 8) = 3.694$, $p = .091$.

Because there were overall differences in the instructional support domain, we analyzed subscales within that domain. These analyses within the instructional support domain found significant differences in concept development, $F(1, 8) = 6.206$, $p = .037$, with a large effect size, $d = 1.515$, but no significant differences in quality of feedback, $F(1, 8) = 2.526$, $p = .151$, and language modeling, $F(1,8) = 3.328$, $p = .106$, with a medium effect size, $d = .673$. Given the significant findings and effect sizes for concept development, we expand on that finding. The experimental group scored, on average, 3.02 on the concept development component, placing them in the mid-range on the scale, whereas the control group scored, on average, 2.04 on the concept development component, placing them in the low range on the scale.

Limitations

Although the results of this study are promising, some limitations exist due to the nature of the sample and methodology. First, our study involved a small group of teachers and assistant teachers from one Head Start program in a large metropolitan area. The reliance on data from participants from a single program affects the ability to generalize the results. Also, the small sample size means that there may not be enough power to detect significant differences between the two groups if they exist. Second, the study is limited by the reliance on observation measures designed to observe overall classrooms rather than specific adults in the classroom. Because of the nature of the ECCOM and CLASS, we focused our attention on the teacher in the classroom and, therefore, do not have data that reflect assistant teachers' teaching practices. Finally, because all participants engaged in all facets (i.e., LEARN institute days, in-class mentoring, community meetings, and online support) of the professional development with similar intensity and duration, we are not able to determine which facets, if any, have more impact on the implementation of intentional teaching practices. Likewise, we cannot ascertain whether more or less time devoted to any one or combination of facets would have an effect on the results.

VARIABLES RELATED TO POSITIVE OUTCOMES

In our last study, presented here, we examined processes and factors associated with effective professional development. These are processes and factors that enhanced or impeded the impact of the professional development on teacher outcomes. Data examined included those in the previously discussed study as well as the implementation of the model with a new cohort of teachers and teacher assistants. The model in Figure A.2 depicts how the processes and factors function with teacher outcomes.

We believe that our professional development, as described throughout this book, affects outcomes for teachers, but that additional factors such as fidelity of implementation, especially fidelity of mentoring implementation, and teacher's characteristics upon entry into the project are associated with positive outcomes. Griffin (2009), in his introduction to a special issue of *Early Education and Development*, reported on a number of studies addressing processes and factors of professional development that are related to implementation fidelity and teacher outcomes with the goal of identifying those processes and factors that mask the impact of a particular intervention (see Domitrovich, Gest, Gill, Jones, & Sanford DeRousie, 2009; Downer, Locasale-Crouch, Hambre, & Pianta, 2009; Sheridan, Edwards, Marvin, & Knoche, 2009; Zaslow, 2009).

The current study strived toward these same goals: that is, to examine processes and factors associated with the teachers and the experimental professional development that might enhance or impede the impact of the professional development on teacher outcomes. Specifically, these factors included teacher entry characteristics. For example, were teacher credentials related to mentoring that took place during the professional development? Were teacher credentials related to the outcomes and classroom characteristics; for example, the number of children in a class who are dual language learners and the number who have disabilities? Process variables are those associated with fidelity (e.g., whether in-class mentoring forms were appropriately completed and whether the specified in-class mentoring took place). Hours of mentoring in the professional development were also measured. Finally, the relationship between mentors and teachers was assessed (e.g., teachers' ratings of mentors and mentors rating of success with teachers).

Professional development content

Intentional teaching (culturally responsive practice; include each child; differentiate instruction; effective teaching strategies; bridging assessment, instruction, and curriculum; integrate intentional teaching with current curriculum model)

Process

LEARN model (learn, enact, assess, reflect, network)

Structure

Institutes—5 days across 9 months
Community meetings—six monthly face-to-face, small-group site meetings
In-classroom support—six monthly in-class modeling and mentoring sessions
Online mentoring—ongoing access to mentoring and support

Possible associated factors

Teacher entry characteristics (e.g., credential, quality, attitude, and beliefs)

Mentoring associated with fidelity

Amount of mentoring

Relationship between mentors and teachers

Outcomes for teachers

Gained usable knowledge on intentional teaching strategies

Transferred knowledge of intentional teaching into classroom practice (enacted knowledge)

Assessed and reflected to make instructional decisions (adaptive, reflective knowledge)

Learned intentional teaching strategies that are sustained beyond the time of active engagement in the professional development

Figure A.2.   Processes, factors, and teacher outcomes.

Our participants included 18 teachers from one public-school-based and two community-based Head Start programs within a 50-mile radius of a metropolitan city. Half of the 18 teachers were classroom lead teachers, three were teacher 2s, two were teacher assistants, and four were paraprofessionals. Lead teacher qualifications included at least 2 years of experience in an accredited early childhood school or center, a bachelor's degree in early childhood education preferred, but at least an associate's degree in the early childhood education field. Qualifications for the second teacher in the classes varied, with teacher 2 qualifications being similar to those of the lead teacher. Teacher assistant qualifications were a child development associate's degree and at least 2 years of experience in an accredited early childhood school or center. Paraprofessional qualifications were a high school diploma or GED. Five of the 18 participants were African American, nine were Caucasian, three were Hispanic, and one was African American/Caucasian. Fourteen indicated that they spoke English only, three spoke Spanish and English, and three spoke Arabic and English. In terms of education, three held a master's degree, seven held a bachelor's degree, one held an associate's degree, and seven held a high school diploma. Nine had more than 11 years of teaching experience, seven had 6–10 years, and two had 0–5 years.

The average classroom size was 18 children. All classes had dual language learners, with eight of the classrooms having 10 or more dual language learners, two having five to nine dual language learners, five having three or four dual language learners, and three having one to two dual language learners. Three classrooms had more than five languages spoken in class, seven had four or five, and eight had two or three languages spoken in class. Five classrooms had five children with individualized education programs (IEPs), two classrooms had three children with IEPs, six classrooms had two children with IEPs, three classrooms had one child with an IEP, and two classrooms did not have any children with IEPs.

Teachers' attitudes, beliefs, and efficacy were measured for all teachers on the TMAS, TMES, ECCOM, and CLASS, as described previously. Attitude and beliefs and motivation for professional development tended to be positive, means above the average accompanied by relatively small standard deviations and the lowest score on the range being above average. One scale was different, the multicultural efficacy scale. Efficacy is different from attitudes and beliefs in that teachers rate what they think are their skills related to a topic area, in this case multicultural practice. Overall, teachers in this study rated their multicultural efficacy as above average, but the standard deviation was relatively large and the range included a rating at the very bottom of the scale.

Coaching measures were collected on the following:

- *Mentors ratings of their success in coaching teachers in use of intentional teaching.* A four-point Likert-type scale with indictors of unsuccessful to successful was collected on 10 aspects of intentional teaching (e.g., including children's prior knowledge).

- *Cooperation between teacher and mentor so that mentor was prepared for in-class coaching.* This included documentation of the type and nature of in-class coaching that teachers requested (options related to the professional development project) and mentors' documentation of preparation for in-class mentoring. (See Figure 1.2, Implementation and Mentoring Form, in Chapter 1.) Basically, this is documentation of the information surrounding in-class mentoring.

- *Incidence of in-class coaching/feedback.* Documentation was collected that in-class coaching took place and that mentors gave teachers feedback on the coaching.

Figure A.3 depicts significant relationships between teacher and classroom characteristics, mentoring, and teacher outcomes. All correlations are significant at a minimum .05 level; solid lines are positive correlations, and dashed lines are negative correlations. Though we did not have enough participants in this sample to perform more advanced models of associations between variables in the study, the significant correlations depicted in the figure provide information for future research and for professional development providers. Awareness of possible variables affecting success of the professional development allows for thoughtful adjustments in implementation based on the group for which the professional development is provided. First, we address the relationships between teacher and classroom demographic characteristics that correlate significantly with mentoring variables or teacher outcomes. After each association between a demographic and mentoring variable, we address how the particular mentoring variable was related to teacher outcomes. Next, we address mentoring variables that correlated with teacher outcomes.

One teacher characteristic was associated with a mentoring variable. Teacher's number of years taught was negatively related to the mentor's rating of success with the teacher ($r = -.542$, $p = .020$). Teachers who taught more years had mentors who rated their mentoring as less successful. As noted previously, mentors rated their success with teachers using a 10-item Likert-type scale related to the implementation of the model. Therefore, mentors rated themselves as more successful with teachers who had less teaching experience. Given this association, we think it is important to evaluate carefully all possibilities when a mentor is not having success with a mentee. When doing the professional development itself, the number of years that teachers have taught and its meaning did not jump out as an area in need of careful examination. In using the

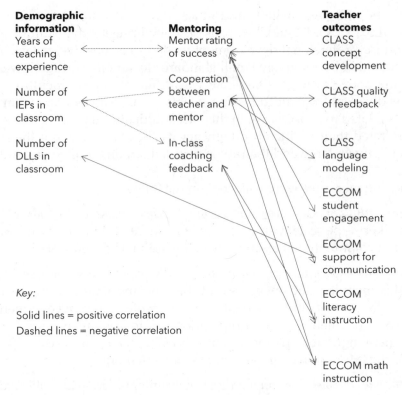

Figure A.3. Demographic and mentoring associated with the teacher outcomes (IEP, individualized education plan; DLL, dual language learner; CLASS, Classroom Assessment Scoring System; ECCOM, Early Childhood Classroom Observation Measure).

professional development model in the future, we will be cognizant of and examine this more carefully to understand its function.

One of the classroom-level characteristics, number of children with IEPs, was negatively related with two of the mentoring variables that assessed fidelity of implementation; that is, cooperation between teacher and mentor so that the mentor was prepared for in-class mentoring and incidence of in-class mentoring and feedback ($r = -.572$, $p = .016$ and $r = -.631$, $p = .007$, respectively). Recall from the presentation of demographic data that five classes had more than 1/4th of their students with IEPs, whereas another five classes had one or no children with IEPs (with variations in between). Teachers in one of the programs noted that often, children with IEPs were placed with certain teachers. The negative correlation of number of children with IEPs and program mentoring fidelity indicated that future work is needed to understand and be cognizant of the function of over- or underrepresentation of children with IEPs and associated context such as specialists in the classroom as they interact with professional development implementation.

An additional classroom demographic characteristic, number of dual language learners in the classroom, was not significantly related to the mentoring variables but related directly and positively to a teacher outcome that assessed the support for communication (ECCOM) provided by teachers ($r = .568$; $p = .027$). This positive association between the number of dual language learners and support for communication is interesting, given the integral role of supportive communication environments for children who are dual language learners. Recall also that there were posttest differences in supportive communication environments between those who received the professional development and the control participants.

Mentoring variables were associated with teacher outcomes. A positive association was found among mentors' rating of their success with their mentees and a number of teacher outcomes, specifically the CLASS measure of concept development ($r = .560$, $p = .030$) and ECCOM measures of student engagement ($r = .540$, $p = .038$), support for communication ($r = .550$, $p = .034$), and literacy instruction ($r = .630$, $p = .016$). All three of four of these teacher outcome measures were ones in which we found positive impact on those who received the professional development and the control participants. Refer to the previous experimental study.

The cooperation between the teacher and the mentor so that the mentor was prepared for in-class mentoring is a feature of the professional development model described in this appendix and in detail in Chapter 1. It provided a mechanism so that mentors received critical information to provide high quality mentoring. Cooperation between the teacher and the mentor so that the mentor was prepared for in-class mentoring was positively associated with two CLASS measures (quality of feedback, $r = .709$, $p = .003$, and language modeling, $r = .594$, $p = .020$) and ECCOM math instruction ($r = .533$, $p = .041$).

In-class mentoring and feedback were positively associated with two of the ECCOM measures (literacy instruction, $r = .538$, $p = .047$, and math instruction, $r = .747$, $p = .001$). When in-class mentoring and feedback were provided at higher levels, there was an association with higher teacher quality scores in literacy and math instruction (ECCOM) scores. As mentioned previously, literacy instruction was one of the significant areas of teacher improvement in the experimental study previously mentioned. These last two variables, cooperation between the teacher and the mentor and in-class mentoring and feedback, were collected as part of fidelity data, and their association with teacher outcomes is positive and clear. They provided an indicator of whether mentors actually provided the in-class mentoring and gave feedback after the in-class mentoring took place.

In summary, in this examination of variables related to positive outcomes, we found that teacher and classroom characteristics were associated with mentoring variables and, in one case, teacher outcomes. We found that mentoring variables were related to teacher outcomes.

FINDINGS ACROSS STUDIES

In this chapter, we present research that supports engaging early childhood teachers and assistant teachers in professional development based on principles of adult learning and focused on intentional teaching practices across the curriculum and throughout the school day. Our model focused on usable knowledge (Snow et al., 2005) and provided continuous, multifaceted professional development that moved beyond one-time workshops that lack the coherence and depth needed to support the learning of new content and instructional strategies that lead to positive children's outcomes (Darling-Hammond & Bransford, 2005; Diamond et al., 2013; Varol, Farran, Bilbrey, & Guess Hofer, 2012; Zaslow, Tout, Halle, & Starr, 2011). Over the course of 9 months, we engaged teachers and assistant teachers in the four facets of the professional development: LEARN institute days, in-classroom mentoring, community meetings, and online support. We provided opportunities for teachers and assistant teachers to meet in a large-group setting on LEARN institute days to focus on learning content and strategies to apply in their classrooms (Diamond et al.). In between the LEARN institute days, a mentor provided monthly in-class mentoring (Diamond et al.; Powell et al., 2010), facilitated monthly small-group, on-site community meetings (Buysse et al., 2010; Diamond et al.; Vescio et al., 2008), and provided online networking and support as needed (Mashburn et al., 2010; Pianta, Mashburn et al., 2008; Saltzberg & Polyson, 1995; Snyder et al., 2011).

We designed these experiences using the LEARN framework that supports learning new knowledge, enacting new strategies in the classroom, assessing their effectiveness, reflecting on next steps, and networking with peers and a mentor (Nasser et al., 2015; Snow et al., 2005). During the professional development, we engaged teachers and assistant teachers in learning and applying content and strategies focused on intentional teaching practices, including 1) responding to children's cultural diversity, 2) including all children, 3) using assessment to inform curriculum and instruction, and 4) implementing intentional teaching strategies within the context of mandated curriculum (Nasser et al.). Throughout the text, we elaborate on this professional development. In addition, the professional development areas mentioned previously included continuous emphasis on intentional teaching, evidence-based strategies, and play. These sections are also elaborated in the text.

Specifically, based on the definition of intentional teaching we developed in a previous study (Burns et al., 2012), we wanted to promote intentional, high-quality conversations with children in learning centers and small groups where adults and children jointly share responsibility. We also sought to enhance teachers' and assistant teachers' ability to provide evidence-based instructional strategies that promote children's learning within a positive classroom environment and rich curriculum (Burns et al.). Consistent with these goals, in this study, we examined teachers' individualized support of children's learning using reciprocal, codirected conversations and evidence-based instructional strategies. We believe that developing teachers' and assistant teachers' usable knowledge about and strategies for engaging and interacting with children would enhance their individualized support of learning for all children, which would ultimately result in positive outcomes for children. This expectation that children will benefit when teachers engage in high-quality professional development is consistent with evidence that suggests that high-quality professional development can lead to enhanced learning for children as well as teachers (Diamond et al., 2013).

Although our analyses did not detect any significant differences on the self-report data, we found significant differences on some subscales of the observational measures that indicate that a multifaceted approach to professional development can have an effect on teachers' intentional teaching practices, especially in terms of engaging children in learning, supporting their communication skills, encouraging instructional conversations, promoting their concept development, and implementing literacy instruction. These findings support and further elaborate on the three parts of our definition of intentional teaching that include teachers providing 1) instructional strategies within a positive classroom climate; 2) learning opportunities designed to meet the individual needs, interests, and prior knowledge of children in their instructional setting using rich curriculum content; and 3) opportunities for high-quantity as well as high-quality reciprocal, codirected conversation between teachers and children in learning centers or small groups with all children rather than a selected few (Burns et al., 2012).

These findings illustrate what teachers do who incorporate intentional teaching practices into their interactions with young children versus those who take a more didactic, teacher-centered approach to teaching or who provide little teacher input. The results also support the premise that continuous, multifaceted professional development can make a difference in teachers' intentional teaching practices.

As was evident from the results for subscales of the ECCOM (Stipek & Byler, 2004) and the CLASS (Pianta, La Paro et al., 2008), teachers who participated in professional development made efforts to engage all children in active, productive learning that promoted their understanding and developed skills and strategies. They engaged children individually in conversations and listened to and acknowledged what they were saying. They tended to ask questions, encourage elaboration, and provide opportunities for children to speak in front of others. In addition, they promoted listening to others and encouraged supportive conversational interactions with peers. They also supported children's participation in conversations focused on identified curricular topics and cognitive skills. They listened intently to children's thoughts and encouraged children to share questions, ideas, and elaborations related to specific topics of instruction. In addition, they focused attention on instructional strategies that promoted children's reasoning and creativity as well as on ways to help children make connections between what they are learning and the world around them.

IMPLICATIONS AND FUTURE DIRECTIONS

The results of these studies provide valuable insights into what teachers do when they implement intentional teaching practices with young children and the effect that continuous, multifaceted professional development can have on teachers' development of intentional teaching practices. Because of the current interest in intentional teaching (e.g., Bodrova & Leong, 2007; Burns et al., 2012; Copple & Bredekamp, 2009; De Marco, Zeisel, & Odom, 2015; Espinosa, 2010; Esso, Taylor, Pratt, & Roberts, 2012; Epstein, 2007; Jung & Conderman, 2013; Jung & Reifel, 2011; McIlwain, Burns, & White, 2016; Pianta, Belsky, Vandergrift, Houts, & Morrison, 2008; Pierce & Bruns, 2013; Sackes, 2014; Tepylo, Moss, & Stephenson, 2015), it is important to develop an evidence base that contributes to a collective understanding of the construct of intentional teaching (Burns et al., 2012) and how intentional teaching practices can be developed (Nasser et al., 2015).

Although many studies examine the effectiveness of professional development within specific domains, such as language and literacy (e.g., Diamond & Powell, 2011; Girolametto, Weitzman, & Greenberg, 2012; Landry, Anthony, Swank, & Monseque-Bailey, 2009; Mashburn et al., 2010), mathematics (e.g., Rudd, Lambert, Satterwhite, & Smith, 2009; Thornton, Crim, & Hawkins, 2009; Tirosh, Tsamir, Levenson, Tabach, & Barkai, 2014), or science (e.g., Furtado, 2010; Roehrig, Dubosarsky, Mason, Carlson, & Murphy, 2011), our study examined the effectiveness of professional development focused on intentional teaching practices that can be implemented across curricular areas. The results of our study suggest that teachers can develop and refine their intentional teaching practices when engaged in continuous, multifaceted professional development.

Our findings support the features of effective professional development designed for early childhood educators identified by Zaslow, Tout, Halle, Whittaker, and Lavelle (2010), including that there were specific goals focused on linking knowledge and practice and a process that included 1) educators' participation from the same school and classrooms, 2) a match between the content and the intensity and duration, 3) an emphasis on educators assessing the impact of their professional development, and 4) an alignment with the standards and the context of the organization.

CONCLUSION

It is important that teachers of young children have opportunities to engage in multi-faceted, high-quality professional development designed to enhance their teaching and, ultimately, children's learning. Recognizing the importance of developing a professional development model that engages teachers in meaningful ways and contributes to their professional growth, we built a yearlong professional development program that emphasized intentional teaching practices in a variety of learning contexts, including LEARN institute days, in-class mentoring, community meetings, and online support. It is evident that participating in such a model can affect aspects of teachers' instructional interactions with young children. On a practical level, the results of this study indicate that professional development can influence teaching practices when there is an emphasis on play and evidence-based practices that respond to children's cultural diversity and their strengths and needs, while using assessment to inform curriculum and instruction and implementing intentional teaching strategies within the context of mandated curriculum. At a minimum, professional development focused on intentional teaching can affect the ways teachers deliver 1) instructional strategies within a positive classroom climate; 2) learning opportunities designed to meet the individual needs, interests, and prior knowledge of children in their instructional setting using rich curriculum content; and 3) opportunities for high-quantity as well as high-quality reciprocal, codirected conversation between teachers and children in learning centers or small groups, with all children rather than a selected few (Burns et al., 2012).

References

CHAPTER 1

Aikens, N., Akers, L., & Atkins-Burnett, S. (2016). *Professional development tools to improve the quality of infant and toddler care: A review of the literature.* OPRE Report 2016-96. Washington, DC: Office of Planning, Research and Evaluation, Administration for Children and Families, U.S. Department of Health and Human Services.

Algozzine, B., Babb, J., Algozzine, K., Mraz, M., Kissel, B., Spano, S., & Foxworth, K. (2011). Classroom effects of an early childhood educator professional development partnership. *NHSA Dialog, 14,* 246–262. doi:10.1080/15240754.2011.613125

Allen, L., & Kelly, B. B. (2015). *Transforming the workforce for children birth through age 8: A unifying foundation.* Washington, DC: National Academies Press.

Artman-Meeker, K., Fettig, A., Barton, E. E., Penney, A., & Zeng, S. (2015). Applying an evidence-based framework to early childhood coaching literature. *Topics in Early Childhood Special Education, 35,* 183–196. doi:10.1177/0271121415595550

Avalos, B. (2011). Teacher professional development in *Teaching and Teacher Education* over ten years. *Teaching and Teacher Education, 27,* 10–20. doi:10.1016/j.tate.2010.08.007

Ayling, D., Owen, H., & Flagg, E. (2012). Thinking, researching and living in virtual professional development community of practice. In M. Brown, M. Hartnett, & T. Steward (Eds.), *Future challenges, sustainable futures: ascilite2012 proceedings* (pp. 67–74). Retrieved from http://www.ascilite.org/conferences/Wellington12/2012/images/custom/ayling%2c_diana_-_thinking.pdf

Bowman, B., Donovan, M. S., & Burns, M. S. (2000). *Eager to learn: Educating our preschoolers.* Washington, DC: National Academy Press.

Bransford, J. D., Brown, A. L., & Cocking, R. R. (2000). *How people learn: Brain, mind, experience, and school.* Washington, DC: National Academy Press.

Brouwer, P., Brekelmans, M., Nieuwenhuis, L., & Simons, R. J. (2012). Community development in the school workplace. *International Journal of Educational Management, 26*(4), 403–418. doi:10.1108/09513541211227809

Brown, J. R., Knoche, L. L., Edwards, C. P., & Sheridan, S. M. (2009). Professional development to support parent engagement: A case study of early childhood practitioners. *Early Education and Development, 20*(3), 482–506. doi: 10.1080/10409280902783475

Buchanan, M. L., Morgan, M., Cooney, M., & Gerharter, M. (2006). The University of Wyoming Early Childhood Summer Institute: A model for professional development that leads to changes in practice. *Journal of Early Childhood Teacher Education, 27,* 161–169. doi:10.1080/10901020600675125

Burns, M. S., Kidd, J. K., Nasser, I., Aier, D. J., & Stechuk, R. (2012). An interaction, a conversation, often in the context of play: Constructing intentional teaching in early childhood education. *NHSA Dialog, 15,* 272–285. doi:10.1080/15240754.2012.694496

Buysse, V., Winton, P. J., & Rous, B. (2009). Reaching consensus on a definition of professional development for the early childhood field. *Topics in Early Childhood Special Education, 28*(4), 235–243. doi:10.1177/0271121408328173

Castillo, L. (2014). *Nana in the city.* New York, NY: Houghton Mifflin Harcourt.

Darling-Hammond, L., & Bransford, J. (Eds.). (2005). *Preparing teachers for a changing world: What teachers should learn and be able to do.* San Francisco, CA: Jossey-Bass.

Diamond, K. E., Justice, L. M., Siegler, R. S., & Snyder, P. A. (2013). *Synthesis of IES research on early intervention and early childhood education.* (NCSER 2013-3001). Washington, DC: National Center for Special Education Research. Retrieved from https://ies.ed.gov/ncser/pubs/20133001/pdf/20133001.pdf

Diamond, K. E., & Powell, D. R. (2011). An iterative approach to the development of a professional development intervention for Head Start teachers. *Journal of Early Intervention, 33,* 75–93.

Donovan, M. S., Bransford, J. D., & Pellegrino, J. W. (1999). *How people learn: Bridging research and practice.* Washington, DC: National Academy Press.

Gupta, S. S., & Daniels, J. (2012). Coaching and professional development in early childhood classrooms: Current practices and recommendations for the future. *NHSA Dialog: A Research-to-Practice Journal for the Early Childhood Field, 15*(2), 206–220. doi:10.1080/15240754.2012.665509

Kidd, J. K., Sánchez, S. Y., & Thorp, E. K. (2008). Defining moments: Developing culturally responsive dispositions and teaching practices in early childhood preservice teachers. *Teaching and Teacher Education, 24*(2), 316–329. doi:10.1016.j.tate.2007.06.003

Knoche, L. L., Kuhn, M., & Eum, J. (2013). "More time. More showing. More helping. That's how it sticks": The perspectives of early childhood coaches. *Infants and Young Children, 26,* 349–365.

Landry, S. H., Anthony, J. L., Swank, P. R., & Monseque-Bailey, P. (2009). Effectiveness of comprehensive professional development for teachers of at-risk preschoolers. *Journal of Educational Psychology, 101*(2), 448–465. doi:10.1037/a0013842

Lloyd, C. H., & Modlin, E. L. (2012). *Coaching as a key component in teachers' professional development: Improving classroom practices in Head Start settings. OPRE Report 2012–14.* Washington, DC: Office of Planning, Research and Evaluation, Administration of Children and Families, U.S. Department of Health and Human Services.

Lonigan, C. J., Anthony, J. L., Bloomfield, B. G., Dyer, S. M., & Samwel, C. S. (1999). Effects of two shared-reading interventions on emergent literacy skills of at-risk preschoolers. *Journal of Early Intervention, 22,* 306–322.

Markussen-Brown, J., Juhl, C. B., Piasta, S. B., Bleses, D., Højen, A., & Justice, L. M. (2017). The effects of language and literacy-focused professional development on early educators and children: A best-evidence meta-analysis. *Early Childhood Research Quarterly, 38,* 97–115. doi:10.1016/j.ecresq.2016.07.002

Nasser, I., Kidd, J. K., Burns, M. S., & Campbell, T. (2015). Head Start classroom teachers' and assistant teachers' perceptions of professional development using a LEARN framework. *Professional Development in Education, 41,* 344–365. doi:10.1080/19415257.2013.833538

National Association for the Education of Young Children. (2011). *Early childhood education professional development: Training and technical assistance glossary.* Washington, DC: Author.

National Literacy Panel. (2008). *Developing early literacy: Report of the National Literacy Panel.* Washington, DC: National Institute for Literacy.

Neuman, S. B., & Cunningham, L. (2009). The impact of professional development and coaching on early language and literacy instructional practices. *American Educational Research Journal, 46*(2), 532–566. doi:10.3102/0002831208328088

Neuman, S. B., & Wright, T. S. (2010). Promoting language and literacy development for early childhood educators. *Elementary School Journal, 111*(1), 63–86.

Rudd, L. C., Lambert, M. C., Satterwhite, M., & Smith, C. H. (2009). Professional development + coaching = enhanced teaching: Increasing usage of math mediated language in preschool classrooms. *Early Childhood Education Journal, 37,* 63–69. doi:10.1007/s10643-009-0320-5

Sanford DeRousie, R. M., & Bierman, K. L. (2012). Examining the sustainability of an evidence-based preschool curriculum: The REDI program. *Early Childhood Research Quarterly, 27,* 55–65. doi:10.1016.ecresq.2011.07.003

Schachter, R. E. (2015). An analytic study of the professional development research in early childhood education. *Early Education and Development, 26,* 1057–1085. doi:10.1080/10409289.2015.1009335

Sheridan, S. M., Edwards, C. P., Marvin, C. A., & Knoche, L. L. (2009). Professional development in early childhood programs: Process issues and research needs. *Early Education and Development, 20*(3), 377–401. doi:10.1080/10409280802582795

Shernoff, E. S., Maríñez-Lora, A. M., Frazier, S. L., Jakobsons, L. J., Atkins, M. S., & Bonner, D. (2011). Teachers supporting teachers in urban schools: What iterative research designs can teach us. *School Psychology Review, 40,* 465–485.

Snow, C., Griffin, P., & Burns, M. S. (2005). *Knowledge to support the teaching of reading: Preparing teachers for a changing world.* San Francisco, CA: John Wiley & Sons.

Tooley, M., & Connally, K. (2016). *No panacea: Diagnosing what ails teacher professional development before reaching for remedies.* Washington, DC: New America.

Trivette, C. M., Rabb, M., & Dunst, C. J. (2012). Steps to successful professional development in Head Start. *NHSA Dialog: A Research-to-Practice Journal for the Early Childhood Field, 15*(1), 127–134. doi:10.1080/15240754.2011.637644

Varol, F., Farran, D. C., Bilbrey, C., Vorhaus, E. A., & Guess Hofer, K. (2012). Professional development for preschool teachers: Evidence for practice. *NHSA Dialog: A Research-to-Practice Journal for the Early Childhood Field, 15*(1), 122–126. doi:10.1080/15240754.2011.638742

Wasik, B. A., & Bond, M. A. (2001). Beyond the pages of a book: Interactive book reading and language development in preschool classrooms. *Journal of Educational Psychology, 93,* 243–250.

Wayne, A. J., Yoon, K. S., Zhu, P., Cronen, S., & Garet, M. S. (2008). Experimenting with teacher professional development: Motives and methods. *Educational Researcher, 37*(8), 469–479. doi:10.3102/0013189X08327154

Weber-Mayrer, M. M., Piasta, S. B., & Pelatti, C. Y. (2015). State-sponsored professional development for early childhood educators: Who participates and associated implications for future offerings. *Journal of Early Childhood Teacher Education, 36,* 41–60. doi:10.1080/10901027.2014.996927

Wenger, E. C., & Snyder, W. M. (2000). Communities of practice: The organizational frontier. *Harvard Business Review, 78*, 139–146.

What Works Clearinghouse. (2007). *Dialogic reading.* Washington, DC: Institute of Educational Sciences. Retrieved from https://ies.ed.gov/ncee/wwc/Docs/InterventionReports/WWC_Dialogic_Reading_020807.pdf

What Works Clearinghouse. (2009). *WWC quick review of the report "The impact of two professional development interventions of early reading instruction and achievement."* Washington, DC: Institute of Educational Sciences. Retrieved from https://ies.ed.gov/ncee/wwc/Docs/QuickReview/pdr_rev0309.pdf

Zaslow, M., Tout, K., Halle, T., & Starr, R. (2011). Professional development for early childhood educators: Reviewing and revising conceptualizations. *Handbook of Early Literacy Research, 3*, 425–434.

Zaslow, M., Tout, K., Halle, T., Whittaker, J. V., & Lavelle, B. (2010). *Toward the identification of features of effective professional development for early childhood educators: Literature review.* Washington, DC: Office of Planning, Evaluation and Policy Development, U.S. Department of Education. Retrieved from https://www2.ed.gov/rschstat/eval/professional-development/literature-review.pdf

Zucker, T. A., Cabell, S. Q., Justice, L. M., Pentimonti, J. M., & Kaderavek, J. N. (2013). The role of frequent, interactive prekindergarten shared reading in the longitudinal development of language and literacy skills. *Developmental Psychology, 49*, 1425–1439.

CHAPTER 2

Banks, J., Cochran-Smith, M., Moll, L., Richert, A., Zeichner, K., LePage, P.,... Duffy, H. (2005). Teaching diverse learners. In L. Darling-Hammond & J. Bransford (Eds.), *Preparing teachers for a changing world: What teachers should learn and be able to do* (pp. 232–274). San Francisco, CA: Jossey-Bass.

Beck, I. L., McKeown, M. G., & Kucan, L. (2013). *Bringing words to life: Robust vocabulary instruction* (2nd ed.). New York, NY: Guilford Press.

Bodrova, E., & Leong, D. J. 2007. *Tools of the mind: The Vygotskian approach to early childhood education.* (2nd ed.). Upper Saddle River, NJ: Pearson Education/Merrill.

Bowman, B., Donovan, M. S., & Burns, M. S. (2000). *Eager to learn: Educating our preschoolers.* Washington, DC: National Academy Press.

Bransford, J. D., Brown, A. L., & Cocking, R. R. (2000). *How people learn: Brain, mind, experience, and school.* Washington, DC: National Academy Press.

Burns, M. S., Johnson, R. T., & Assaf, M. M. (2012). *Preschool education in today's world: Teaching children with diverse backgrounds and abilities.* Baltimore, MD: Paul H. Brookes Publishing Co.

Burns, M. S., Kidd, J. K., Nasser, I., Aier, D. J., & Stechuk, R. (2012). An interaction, a conversation, often in the context of play: Constructing intentional teaching in early childhood education. *NHSA Dialog: A Research-to-Practice Journal for the Early Childhood Field, 15*, 272–285.

Copple, C., & Bredekamp, S. (2009). *Developmentally appropriate practice in early childhood programs serving children birth through age 8* (3rd ed.). Washington, DC: National Association for the Education of Young Children.

De Marco, A. C., Zeisel, S., & Odom, S. L. (2015). An evaluation of a program to increase physical activity for young children in child care. *Early Education and Development, 26*, 1–21.

Epstein, A. (2007). *The intentional teacher: Choosing the best strategies for young children's learning.* Washington, DC: National Association for the Education of Young Children.

Espinosa, L. (2010). *Getting it right for young children from diverse backgrounds: Applying research to improve practice.* Upper Saddle River, NJ: Pearson.

Esso, E. L., Taylor, J. M., Pratt, J. M., & Roberts, S. A. (2012) Illustrating the complexity of relationships in kindergarten and first grade. *Young Children, 67*(5), 24–33.

Gronlund, G., & Stewart, K. (2011). Intentionality in action: A strategy that benefits preschoolers and teachers, *Young Children, 66*(6), 28–33.

Helm, J. H., & Katz, L. G. (2010). *Young investigators: The project approach in the early years,* (2nd ed.). New York, NY: Teachers College Press.

Hohmann, M., Weikart, D. P., & Epstein, A. S. (2008). *Educating young children: Active learning practices for preschool and child care programs* (3rd ed.). Ypsilanti, MI: High Scope Press.

Jung, H. Y., & Reifel, S. (2011). Promoting children's communication: A kindergarten teacher's conception and practice of effective mathematics instruction. *Journal of Research in Childhood Education, 25*, 194–210.

Jung, M., & Conderman, G. (2013). Intentional mathematics teaching in early childhood classrooms. *Childhood Education, 89*, 173–177.

Katz, L. G., Chard, S. C., & Kogan, Y. (2014). *Engaging children's minds: The project approach* (3rd ed.). Santa Barbara, CA: Praeger.

Keats, E. J. (1964). *Whistle for Willie.* New York, NY: Penguin Putnam.

Kidd, J. K., Burns, M. S., La Croix, L., & Cossa, N. L. (2014). Prekindergarten and kindergarten teachers in high poverty schools speak about young children's authoring (and we need to listen). *Literacy and Social Responsibility, 7*(1), 50–71.

La Paro, K. M., Pianta, R. C., & Stuhlman, M. (2004). The classroom assessment scoring system: Findings from the prekindergarten year. *Elementary School Journal, 104,* 409–426.

Ladson-Billings, G. (1994). *The dreamkeepers.* San Francisco, CA: Jossey-Bass.

McIlwain, M. J., Burns, M. S., & White, C. S. (2016a). From research to evidence-based practice: An account of the scientific implementation of dialogic buddy reading. *Dialog, 18,* 47–71.

McIlwain, M. J., Burns, M. S., & White, C. S. (2016b). The implementation and study of dialogic buddy reading in a Head Start classroom. *Dialog, 18,* 85–90.

Nasser, I., Kidd, J. K., Burns, M. S., & Campbell, T. (2015). Head Start classroom teachers' and assistant teachers' perceptions of professional development using a LEARN framework. *Professional Development in Education, 41,* 344–365.

Paley, V. G. (1991). *The boy who would be a helicopter.* Cambridge, MA: Harvard University Press.

Pearson Early Learning Group. (2005). *Read together, talk together.* Upper Saddle River, NJ: Pearson.

Pianta, R. C., Belsky, J., Vandergrift, N., Houts, R., & Morrison, F. J. (2008). Classroom effects on children's achievement trajectories in elementary school. *American Educational Research Journal, 2,* 365–397.

Pianta, R. C., La Paro, K. M., & Hamre, B. K. (2008). *Classroom assessment scoring system.* Baltimore, MD: Paul H. Brookes Publishing Co.

Pierce, C. D., & Bruns, D. A. (2013). Aligning components of recognition and response and response to intervention to improve transition to primary school. *Early Childhood Education Journal, 41,* 347–354.

Sackes, M. (2014). How often do early childhood teachers teach science concepts? Determinants of the frequency of science teaching in kindergarten. *European Early Childhood Education Research Journal, 22,* 169–184.

Sackes, M., Trundle, K. C., Bell, R. L., & O'Connell, A. A. (2011). The influence of early science experience in kindergarten on children's immediate and later science achievement: Evidence from the early childhood longitudinal study. *Journal of Research in Science and Teaching, 48,* 217–235.

Sleeter, C. E. (2011). An agenda to strengthen culturally responsive pedagogy. *English Teaching: Practice and Critique, 10*(2), 7–23.

Soto, G. (1996a). *El Viejo y su puerta.* New York, NY: Putnam & Grosset.

Soto, G. (1996b). *The old man and his door.* New York, NY: Putnam & Grosset.

Stipek, D., & Byler, P. (2004). The early childhood classroom observation measure. *Early Childhood Research Quarterly, 19,* 375–397

Tepylo, D. H., Moss, J., & Stephenson C. (2015). A developmental look at a rigorous block play program. *Young Children, 70,* 18–25.

Whitehurst, G. J. (2008). *Dialogic reading: An effective way to read to preschoolers.* Retrieved from http://www.readingrockets.org/article/400

Wright, C., Diener, M. L., & Kemp, J. L. (2013). Storytelling dramas as a community building activity in an early childhood classroom. *Early Childhood Education Journal, 41,* 197–210.

CHAPTER 3

Anderson-McNamee, J. K., & Baily, S. J. (2010). The importance of play in early childhood development. *Montana State University Extension—Family and Human Development.* Retrieved from http://store.msuextension.org/publications/HomeHealthandFamily/MT201003HR.pdf

Bodrova, E., & Leong, D. J. (2003). The importance of being playful. *Educational Leadership, 60*(7), 50–53.

Bodrova, E., & Leong, D. J. (2012). Assessing and scaffolding: Make-believe play. *Young Children, 67*(1), 28–34.

Bodrova, E., & Leong, D. J. (2015). Vygotskian and post-Vygotskian views on children's play. *American Journal of Play, 7*(3), 371–388.

Bowman, B., Donovan, M. S., & Burns, M. S. (2000). *Eager to learn: Educating our preschoolers.* Washington, DC: National Academy Press.

Bredekamp, S., & Copple, C. (1997). *Developmentally appropriate practices in early childhood programs* (2nd ed.). Washington, DC: NAEYC.

Brown, M. H., & Freeman, N. K. (2001). We don't play that way at preschool: The moral and ethical dimensions of controlling children's play. In S. Reifel and M. H. Brown (Eds.), *Early education and care and reconceptualising play. Advances in early education and day care* (Vol. 2, pp. 259–274). Oxford, United Kingdom: Elsevier Science.

Burns, M. S., Johnson, R. T., & Assaf, M. M. (2012). *Preschool education in today's world: Teaching children with diverse backgrounds and abilities.* Baltimore, MD: Paul H. Brookes Publishing Co.

Burns, M. S., & Kidd, J. K. (2016). Play and early writing. In D. Couchenour & J. K. Chrisman (Eds.), *Encyclopedia of contemporary early childhood education* (pp. 1026–1028). Thousand Oaks, CA: SAGE. doi:10.4135/9781483340333.n305

Burns, M. S., Kidd, J. K., Nasser, I., Stechuk, R., & Aier, D. (2012). An interaction, a conversation, often in the context of play: Constructing intentional teaching in early childhood education. *NHSA Dialog: A Research to Practice Journal for the Early Childhood Field, 15*(3), 1–14.

Carle, E. & Martin, Jr., B. (1996). *Brown bear, brown bear, what do you see?* New York, NY: Henry Holt.

Carlson, F. M. (2011). Rough play: One of the most challenging behaviors. *Young Children, 66*(4), 18–25.

Davidson, F. W. (Producer). (2003). *Play: A Vygotskian approach with Ph.D.s Elena Bodrova and Deborah J. Leong. Early childhood education series* [video]. San Luis Obispo, CA: Davidson Films.

Diamond, A., Barnett, S., Thomas, J., & Munro, S. (2007). Preschool program improves cognitive control. *Science, 318,* 1387–1388.

Dickey, D., Castle, K., & Pryor, K. (2016). Reclaiming play at school. *Childhood Education, 92*(2), 111–117.

Dockett, S., & Fleer, M. (2002). *Play and pedagogy in early childhood: Bending the rules.* Melbourne, Australia: Harcourt.

Eliason, C., & Jenkins, L. (2016). *A practical guide to early childhood curriculum* (10th ed.). New York, NY: Pearson.

Elkind, D. (2007). *The hurried child: Growing up too fast too soon* (25th anniversary ed.). New York, NY: Da Capo Lifelong Learning.

Elkonin, D. B. (2005). The subject of our research: The developed form of play. *Journal of Russian and East European Psychology, 43*(1), 22–48. doi:10.1080/10610405.2005.11059242.

Epstein, A. S. (2003). How planning and reflection develop young children's thinking skills. *Young Children, 58*(5), 28–36.

Evans, J., & Pellegrini, A. D. (1997). Surplus energy theory: An enduring but inadequate justification for break time. *Educational Review, 49,* 229–236.

Gmitrova, V., & Gmitrov, J. (2003). The impact of teacher-directed and child-directed pretend play on cognitive competence in kindergarten children. *Early Childhood Education Journal, 30*(4), 241–246.

Hirsh-Pasek, K., Golinkoff, R. M., & Eyer, D. (2003). *Einstein never used flash cards: How children really learn— and why they need to play more and memorize less.* Emmaus, PA: Rodale Press.

Howe, N., & Bruno, A. (2010). Sibling pretend play in early and middle childhood: The role of creativity and maternal context. *Early Education and Development, 21*(6), 940–962. doi:10.1080/10409280903440638

Kagan, S. H., Scott-Little, C., & Frelow, V. S. (2009). Linking play to early learning and development guidelines: Possibility or problematic. *Zero to Three, 30*(1), 18–25.

Kernan, M. (2006). *The place of the outdoors in constructions of a "good" childhood: An interdisciplinary study of outdoor provision in early childhood education in urban settings* (Doctoral Thesis, University College, Dublin, Ireland). Unpublished.

Kernan, M. (2007). Play as a context for early learning and development: Background paper to the Framework for Early Learning. Commissioned by the National Council for Curriculum and Assessment (NCCA). Dublin: NCCA.

Koralek, D. G. (2004). *Spotlight on young children and play.* Washington, DC: National Association for the Education of Young Children.

Leong, D. L., & Bodrova, E. (2013). Chopsticks and counting chips: Do play and foundational skills need to compete for the teacher's attention in an early childhood classroom? *Young Children, 58*(3), 10–17. Retrieved from https://www.publichealthbaron.info/uploads/7/1/0/3/71038325/play_article_1.pdf

Miller, E., & Almon, J. (2009). *Crisis in the kindergarten: Why children need to play in school.* College Park, MD: Alliance for Childhood.

Myck-Wayne, J. (2010). In defense of play: Beginning the dialog about the power of play. *Young Exceptional Children, 13*(4), 14–23. doi:10.1177/1096250610376616

Parten, M. B. (1932). Social participation among preschool children. *Journal of Abnormal and Social Psychology, 27,* 243–269.

Pellegrini, A. D. (2005) *Recess: Its role in education and development.* Mahwah, NJ: Lawrence Erlbaum.

Perlmutter, J. C., & Burrell, L. (1995). Learning through "play" as well as "work" in the primary grades. *Young Children, 50*(5), 14–21.

Piaget, J. (1962). *Play, dreams, and imitation in childhood.* New York, NY: Norton.

Seitz, H. J. (2006). The plan: Building on children's interest. *Beyond the Journal: Young Children on the Web.* Retrieved from https://www.brandeis.edu/lemberg/employees/pdf/seitzbuilding.pdf

Sherman, S. (2014). Let's lighten up: Play and humor have important roles in learning. *Virginia Journal of Education,* 13–15.

Singer, D., Golinkoff, R. M., & Hirsh-Pasek, K. (2006). *Play learning: How play motivates and enhances children's cognitive and social-emotional growth.* New York, NY: Oxford University Press.

Stuber, G. M. (2007). Centering your classroom: Setting the stage for engaged learners. *Young Children, 62*(4), 58–59.

Sylva, K., Melhuish, E. C., Sammons, P., Siraj, I., & Taggart, B. (2004). The Effective Provision of Pre-School Education (EPPE) project: Findings from pre-school to end of key stage 1. London, United Kingdom: DfES/Institute of Education, University of London.

Vygotsky, L. (1978). *Mind in society: The development of higher psychological processes.* Cambridge, MA: Harvard University Press.

White, R. E. (2012). The power of play: A research summary on play and learning. *Minnesota Children's Muse,* 1–31.

Wood, E., & Attfield, J. (2005). *Play, learning and the early childhood curriculum* (2nd ed.). London, United Kingdom: Paul Chapman.

CHAPTER 4

Barton, E. E., & Smith, B. J. (2014). *Fact sheet of research on preschool inclusion.* Retrieved from http://www.pyramidplus.org/sites/default/files/Inclusion%20Fact%20Sheet%202014_0.pdf

Barton, E. E., & Smith, B. J. (2015). Advancing high-quality preschool inclusion: A discussion and recommendations for the field. *Topics in Early Childhood Special Education, 35*(2), 69–78.

Burns, M. S., Johnson, R. T., & Assaf, M. M. (2012). *Preschool education in today's world: Teaching children with diverse backgrounds and abilities.* Baltimore, MD: Paul H. Brookes Publishing Co.

Buysse, V., Goldman, B. D., & Skinner, M. L. (2002). Setting effects on friendship formation among young children with and without disabilities. *Exceptional Children, 68,* 503–517.

Campbell, P. H., Kennedy, A. A., & Milbourne, S. A. (2012). *CARA's kit for toddlers: Creating adaptations for routines and activities.* Baltimore, MD: Paul H. Brookes Publishing Co.

Carrington, S., Berthelsen, D., Nickerson, J., & Nicholson, J. M. (2016). Teachers' experiences of inclusion with children with developmental disabilities across the early years of school. *Developmental Disabilities, 26,* 139–154.

Cate, D., Diefendorf, M., McCullough, K., Peters, M. L., & Whaley, K. (Eds.). (2010). *Quality indicators of inclusive early childhood programs/practices: A compilation of selected resources.* Chapel Hill: University of North Carolina, FPG Child Development Institute, National Early Childhood Technical Assistance Center.

Catlett, C. (2009, July). *The right stuff: Resources to support your work.* Presented at the National Early Childhood Inclusion Institute, Chapel Hill, NC.

CONNECT: The Center to Mobilize Early Childhood Knowledge (Producer). (2013). *Foundations of inclusion birth to five* [video download]. Retrieved from http://community.fpg.unc.edu/connect-modules/resources/videos/foundations-of-inclusion-birth-to-five

Cross, A. F. (2004). Adaptations to support development and membership. *Early childhood center inclusion research series: Children with significant disabilities in inclusive community settings.* Bloomington: Indiana University, Indiana Institute on Disability and Community, Early Childhood Center. Retrieved from https://www.iidc.indiana.edu/styles/iidc/defiles/ecc/inclres-adaptations.pdf

Cross, A. F., Traub, E. K., Hutter-Pishgahi, L., & Shelton, G. (2004). Elements of successful inclusion for children with significant disabilities. *Topics in Early Childhood Special Education, 24,* 169–183.

Diamond, K. E., & Hong, S.-Y. (2010). Young children's decisions to include peers with physical disabilities in play. *Journal of Early Intervention, 32,* 163–177.

Diamond, K. E., & Huang, H. (2005). Preschoolers' ideas about disabilities. *Infants and Young Children, 18,* 37–46.

Dinnebeil, L. A., Boat, M., & Bae, Y. (2013). Integrating principles of universal design into the early childhood curriculum. *Dimensions of Early Childhood, 41,* 3–13.

Division for Early Childhood of the Council for Exceptional Children. (2014). *DEC recommended practices in early intervention/early childhood special education 2014.* Retrieved from http://www.dec-sped.org/recommendedpractices.

Division for Early Childhood of the Council for Exceptional Children, & National Association for the Education of Young Children. (2009). *Early childhood inclusion: A joint position statement of the Division for Early Childhood (DEC) and the National Association for the Education of Young Children (NAEYC).* Chapel Hill: University of North Carolina, FPG Child Development Institute.

English, K., Goldstein, H., Kaczmarek, L., & Shafer, K. (1996). "Buddy skills" for preschoolers. *Teaching Exceptional Children, 28,* 62–66.

Fuchs, D., Fuchs, L., & Burish, P. (2000). Peer-assisted learning strategies: An evidence-based practice to promote reading achievement. *Learning Disabilities Research and Practice, 15,* 85–91.

Grisham-Brown, J., Pretti-Frontczak, K., Hawkins, S. R., & Winchell, B. N. (2009). Addressing early learning standards for all children within blended preschool classrooms. *Topics in Early Childhood Special Education, 29,* 131–142.

Guo, Y., Sawyer, B. E., Justice, L. M., & Kaderavek, J. N. (2013). Quality of the literacy environment in inclusive early childhood education classroom. *Journal of Early Intervention, 35,* 40–60.

Guralnick, M. J., & Bruder, M. B. (2016). Early childhood inclusion in the United States: Goals, current status, and future directions. *Infants and Young Children, 29,* 166–177. doi:10.1097/IYC.0000000000000071

Head Start Center for Inclusion. (n.d.). *Creating and using social stories.* Retrieved from http://headstartinclusion.org/social_stories

Hebbeler, K., & Spiker, D. (2016). Supporting young children with disabilities. *The Future of Children, 26,* 185–205. Retrieved from https://futureofchildren.princeton.edu/sites/futureofchildren/files/resource-links/starting_early_26_2_full_journal.pdf

Hollingsworth, H. L., & Buysse, V. (2009). Establishing friendships in early childhood inclusive settings: What roles do parents and teachers play? *Journal of Early Intervention, 31,* 287–307.

Hsieh, W. H., & Hsieh, C. M. (2012). Urban early childhood teachers' attitudes towards inclusive education. *Early Child Development and Care, 182,* 1167–1184.

Individuals with Disabilities Education Improvement Act (IDEA) of 2004, PL 108-446, 20 U.S.C. §§ 1400 *et seq.*

Jolivette, K., Stichter, J. P., Sibilsky, S., Scott, T. M., & Ridgley, R. (2002). Naturally occurring opportunities for preschool children with or without disabilities to make choices. *Education and Treatment of Children, 25,* 396–415.

Katz, L. G., & Chard, S. (2000). *Engaging children's minds: The project approach.* Norwood, NJ: Ablex.

Leatherman, J. M., & Niemeyer, J. A. (2005). Teachers' attitudes toward inclusion: Factors influencing classroom practice. *Journal of Early Childhood Teacher Educators, 26,* 23–36.

Lee, F. L. M., Yeung, A. S., Tracey, D., & Barker, K. (2015). Inclusion of children with special needs in early childhood education: What teacher characteristics matter? *Topics in Early Childhood Special Education, 35,* 79–88.

Milbourne, S. A., & Campbell, P. H. (2012). *CARA's kit: Creating adaptations for routines and activities.* Philadelphia, PA: Child and Family Studies Research Programs, Thomas Jefferson University.

Milbourne, S. A. (2009, July). *Promoting young children's participation by creating adaptations and routines.* Presented at the National Early Childhood Inclusion Institute, Chapel Hill, NC.

Mitchell, L. C., & Hedge, A. V. (2007). Beliefs and practices on in-service preschool teachers in inclusive settings: Implications for personnel preparation. *Journal of Early Childhood Teacher Education, 28,* 353–366. doi:10.1080/10901020701686617

Muccio, L. S., & Kidd, J. K. (2018). "I'm the one with the child with a disability": Head Start teachers' perspectives on inclusive education. *Journal of School Connections, 6,* 36–70.

Muccio, L. S., Kidd, J. K., White, C. S., & Burns, M. S. (2014). Head Start instructional professionals' inclusion perceptions and practices. *Topics in Early Childhood Special Education, 34,* 40–48.

National Professional Development Center on Inclusion. (2009). *Research synthesis points on early childhood inclusion.* Chapel Hill: University of North Carolina, FPG Child Development Institute, Author. Retrieved from http://npdci.fpg.unc.edu/sites/npdci.fpg.unc.edu/files/resources/NPDCI-ResearchSynthesisPoints-10-2009_0.pdf

National Professional Development Center on Inclusion. (2011). *Research synthesis points on practices that support inclusion.* Chapel Hill: University of North Carolina, FPG Child Development Institute, Author. Retrieved from http://npdci.fpg.unc.edu/sites/npdci.fpg.unc.edu/files/resources/NPDCI-ResearchSynthesisPointsInclusivePractices-2011_0.pdf

Nguyen, T., & Hughes, M. (2012). The perspectives of professionals and parents on inclusion in Head Start programs. *Journal of Special Education Apprenticeship, 1,* 1–27. Retrieved from http://josea.info/archives/vol1no2/article-04-FT.pdf

Odom, S. L., Buysse, V., & Soukakou, E. (2011). Inclusion for young children with disabilities: A quarter century of research. *Journal of Early Intervention, 33,* 344–356.

Odom, S. L., DeKlyen, M., & Jenkins, J. R. (1984). Integrating handicapped and nonhandicapped preschool children: Developmental impact on the nonhandicapped children. *Exceptional Children, 51,* 41–48.

Odom, S. L., Vitztum, J., Wolery, R., Lieber, J., Sandall, S., Hanson, M. J.,… Horn, E. (2004). Preschool inclusion in the United States: A review of research from an ecological systems perspective. *Journal of Research in Special Education Needs, 4,* 17–49.

Rafferty, Y., Boettcher, C., & Griffin, K. W. (2001). Benefits and risks of reverse inclusion for preschoolers with and without disabilities: Parents' perspectives. *Journal of Early Intervention, 24,* 266–286. doi:10.1177/105381510102400403

Rakap, S., Cig, O., & Parlak-Rakap, A. (2015). Preparing preschool teacher candidates for inclusion: Impact of two special education courses in their perspectives. *Journal of Research in Special Education Needs, 68,* 1–12.

Sandall, S. R. (2003). Play modifications for children with disabilities. *Young Children, 58*(3), 54–57.

Soukakou, E. P., Winton, P. J., West, T. A., Sideris, J. H., & Rucker, L. M. (2014). Measuring the quality of inclusive practices: Findings from the inclusive classroom profile pilot. *Journal of Early Intervention, 36,* 223–240.

Stanton-Chapman, T. L., & Brown, T. S. (2015). A strategy to increase the social interactions of 3-year-old children with disabilities in an inclusive classroom. *Topics in Early Childhood Special Education, 35,* 4–14.

Stanton-Chapman, T. L., Denning, C. B., & Jamison, K. R. (2012). Communication skill building in young children with and without disabilities in a preschool classroom. *Journal of Special Education, 46,* 78–93.

Strain, P. S., & Bovey, E. H. (2011). Randomized, controlled trial of the LEAP model of early intervention for young children with autism spectrum disorders. *Early Childhood Special Education, 31,* 133–154.

Tomlinson, C. A. (2000). Differentiation of instruction in the elementary grades. ERIC Digest. Retrieved from https://files.eric.ed.gov/fulltext/ED443572.pdf

Warren, S. R., Martinez, R. S., & Sortino, L. A. (2016). Exploring quality indicators of a successful full-inclusion preschool program. *Journal of Research in Childhood Education, 30,* 540–553.

Yang, C.-H., & Rusli, E. (2012). Teacher training in using effective strategies for preschool children with disabilities in inclusive classrooms. *Journal of College Teaching and Learning, 9,* 53–64.

CHAPTER 5

Banks, J. A. (2004). Teaching for social justice, diversity, and citizenship in a global world. *Educational Forum, 68,* 296–305. doi:10.1080/00131720408984645

Bonds-Raacke, J. (2008). Cinderella and Sleeping Beauty: Developing a course on Disney and fairytale movies. *Journal of Instructional Psychology, 35*(3), 232–240.

Bransford, J. D., Brown, A. L., & Cocking, R. R. (2000). *How people learn: Brain, mind, experience, and school.* Washington, DC: National Academy Press.

Bromley, K. D. (1998). *Language art: Exploring connections.* Needham Heights, MA: Allyn & Bacon.

Bui, Y. N., & Fagan, Y. M. (2013). The effects of an integrated reading comprehension strategy: A culturally responsive teaching approach for fifth-grade students' reading comprehension. *Preventing School Failure, 57*(2), 59–69. doi:10.1080/1045988X.2012.664581

Cartledge, G., & Kourea, L. (2008). Culturally responsive classrooms for culturally diverse students with and at risk for disabilities. *Exceptional Children, 74,* 351–371.

Chen, D. W., Nimmo, J., & Fraser, H. (2009). Becoming a culturally responsive early childhood educator: A tool to support reflection by teachers embarking on the anti-bias journey. *Multicultural Perspectives, 11,* 101–106. doi:10.1080/15210960903028784

de Melendez, W. R., & Ostertag, V. (1997). *Teaching young children in multicultural classrooms: Issues, concepts, and strategies.* New York, NY: Delmar.

Esposito, J., & Swain, A. N. (2009, spring). Pathways to social justice: Urban teachers' uses of culturally relevant pedagogy as a conduit for teaching for social justice. *Perspectives on Urban Education,* 38–48.

Ford, D. Y. (2010). Culturally responsive classrooms: Affirming culturally different gifted students. *Multicultural Issues, 33,* 50–53.

Ford, D. Y., & Kea, C. D. (2009). Creating culturally responsive instruction: For students' and teachers' sakes. *Focus on Exceptional Children, 41*(9), 1–16.

Garcia, E., Arias, M. B., Murri, N. J. H., & Serna, C. (2010). Developing responsive teachers: A challenge for a demographic reality. *Journal of Teacher Education, 61,* 132–142.

Gay, G. (1995). Bringing multicultural theory and practice. *Multicultural Education, 3,* 4–9.

Gay, G. (2002). Preparing for culturally responsive teaching. *Journal of Teacher Education, 53,* 106–116.

Griswold, W. (2012). *Cultures and societies in a changing world.* Thousand Oaks, CA: Pine Forge Press.

Haley, M., & Austin, T. (2014). *Content-based second language teaching and learning: An interactive approach* (2nd ed.). Upper Saddle River, NJ: Pearson Education.

Kalyanpur, M. (2003). A challenge to professionals: Developing cultural reciprocity with culturally diverse families. *Focal Point: A National Bulletin on Family Support and Children's Mental Health, 17*(1), 1–5.

Kidd, J., Burns, M. S., Nasser, I., Assaf, M., & Muccio, L. (2009, April). Sustaining teachers' effective pedagogy (STEP): A model for professional development with Head Start teachers. Presented at the annual meeting of the American Educational Research Association, San Diego, CA.

Kidd, J. K., Sanchez, S. Y., & Thorp, E. K. (2008). Defining moments: Developing culturally responsive dispositions and teaching practices in early childhood preservice teachers. *Teaching and Teacher Education, 24,* 316–329. doi:10.1016/j.tate.2007.06.003

Killen, M., & Wainryb, C. (2000). Independence and interdependence in diverse cultural contexts. *New Directions for Child and Adolescent Development, 2000*(87), 5–21.

Lin, M., Lake, V., & Rice, D. (2008). Teaching anti-bias curriculum in teacher education programs: What and how. *Teacher Education Quarterly, 35*(2), 187–200.

Maude, S. P., Hodges, L. N., Brotherson, M. J., Hughes-Belding, K., Peck, N., Weigel, C., & Sharp, L. (2009). Critical reflections on working with diverse families: Culturally responsive professional development strategies for early childhood and early childhood special educators. *Multiple Voices for Ethnically Diverse Exceptional Learners, 12,* 38–53.

Montgomery, W. (2001). Creating culturally responsive, inclusive classrooms. *Teaching Exceptional Children, 33*(4), 4–9.

Phuntsog, N. (2001). Culturally responsive teaching: What do selected United States elementary school teachers think? *Intercultural Education, 12,* 51–64. doi:10.1080/14675980120033966

Schrodt, K., Fain, J. G., & Hasty, M. (2015). Exploring culturally relevant texts with kindergarteners and their families. *Reading Teacher, 68,* 589–598. doi:10.1002/trtr.1363

Seefeldt, C., Castle, S., & Falconer, R. (2014). *Social studies for the preschool/primary child* (9th ed.). Upper Saddle River, NJ: Pearson Education.

Sherman, S. (2014). Let's lighten up: Play and humor have important roles in learning. *Virginia Journal of Education,* 13–15.

Sirin, R. S., Ryce, P., & Mir, M. (2009). How teachers' values affect their evaluation of children of immigrants: Findings from Islamic and public schools. *Early Childhood Research Quarterly, 24,* 463–473.

Sleeter, C. E. (2011). An agenda to strengthen culturally responsive pedagogy. *English Teaching: Practice and Critique, 10*(2), 7–23.

Souto-Manning, M. (2013). *Multicultural teaching in the early childhood classroom: Approaches, strategies and tools, preschool–2nd grade.* New York, NY: Teachers College Press.

Souto-Manning, S., & Mitchell, C. H. (2010). The role of action research in fostering culturally responsive practices in a preschool classroom. *Early Childhood Education, 37,* 269–277. doi:10.1007/s10643-009-0345-9

U.S. Department of Health and Human Services, Administration for Children and Families, Office of Head Start. (2015). *Head Start early learning outcomes framework: Ages birth to five.* Washington, DC: Author. Retrieved from https://eclkc.ohs.acf.hhs.gov/sites/default/files/pdf/elof-ohs-framework.pdf

Yang, S. L., Hsiao, Y. J., & Hsiao, H. C. (2014). Culturally responsive teaching with new Taiwanese children: Interviews with class teachers in elementary schools. *Asia Pacific Journal of Education, 34,* 288–304. doi:10.1080/02188791.2013.853647

Zhao, Y. (2010). Preparing globally competent teachers: A new imperative for teacher education. *Journal of Teacher Education, 61,* 422–431.

CHAPTER 6

Abedi, J. (2008). Classification system for English language learners: Issues and recommendations. *Educational Measurement: Issues and Practice, 27*(3), 17–31.

Antoniou, P., & James, M. (2014). Exploring formative assessment in primary school classrooms: Developing a framework of actions and strategies. *Educational Assessment, Evaluation and Accountability, 26,* 153–176. doi:10.1007s11092-013-9188-4

Bassok, D., Latham, S., & Rorem, A. (2016). Is kindergarten the new first grade? *AERA Open, 2*(1), 1–31.

Black, P., & Wiliam, D. (2010). Inside the black box: Raising standards through classroom assessment. *Phi Delta Kappan, 92*(1), 81–90. doi:10.1177/ 003172171009200119

Brassard, M. R., & Boehm, A. E. (2007). *Preschool assessment: Principles and practices.* New York, NY: Guilford Press.

Bricker, D., Capt, B., & Pretti-Frontczak, K. (2002). *Assessment, evaluation, and programming system for infants and children (AEPS®): Test* (2nd ed.). Baltimore, MD: Paul H. Brookes Publishing Co.

Bricker, D., Pretti-Frontczak, K., Johnson, J., & Straka, E. (2002). *Assessment, evaluation, and programming system for infants and children (AEPS®): Administration guide* (2nd ed.). Baltimore, MD: Paul H. Brookes Publishing Co.

Child Care Bureau. (n.d.). *A guide to good start, grow smart in child care.* Retrieved from files.eric.ed.gov/fulltext/ED499401.pdf

Cimpian, J. R., Thompson, K. D., & Makowski, M. B. (2017). Evaluating English learner reclassification policy effects across districts. *American Evaluation Research Journal, 54,* 255–278. doi:10.3102/0002831216635796

Council of Chief State School Officers (CCSSO) & National Governors Association (NGA). (2010). *Common core state standards for English language arts & literacy in history/social studies, science, and technical subjects.* Retrieved from http://www.corestandards.org/wp-content/uploads/ELA_Standards1.pdf

DeLuca, C., & Klinger, D. A. (2010). Assessment literacy development: Identifying gaps in teacher candidates' learning. *Assessment in Education: Principles, Policy and Practice, 17,* 419–438.

Division for Early Childhood of the Council for Exceptional Children. (2007). *Promoting positive outcomes for children with disabilities: Recommendations for curriculum, assessment, and program evaluation.* Missoula, MT: Author.

Earl, L. M. (2003). *Assessment as learning: Using classroom assessment to maximize student learning.* Thousand Oaks, CA: Corwin Press.

Enciso, P. E. (2001). Taking our seats: The consequences of positioning in reading assessments. *Theory into Practice, 40,* 166–174.

Espinosa, L. (2010). Assessment of young English language learners. In E. Garcia & E. Frede (Eds.), *Young English language learners: Current research and emerging directions for practice and policy* (pp.119–142). New York, NY: Teachers College Press.

Every Student Succeeds Act of 2015, PL 114-95, 20 U.S.C. §§ 6301 *et seq.*

FairTest. (2008, January). *A victory: Head start reauthorization drops flawed testing.* Retrieved from https://www.fairtest.org/victory-head-start-reauthorization-drops-flawed-te

Field, A., & Hole, G. (2003). *How to design and report experiments.* London, United Kingdom: SAGE.

Gilliam, W. S., & Frede, E. (2015). Accountability and program evaluation in early education. In R. C. Pianta, W. S. Barnett, S. M. Sheridan, & L. M. Justice (Eds.), *Handbook of early childhood education* (pp. 73–91). New York, NY: Guilford.

Goldstein, J., & Flake, J. K. (2016). Towards a framework for the validation of early childhood assessment systems. *Education Assessment Research and Accountability, 27,* 273–294. doi:10.1007/s11092-015-9231-8

Gullo, D. F., & Hughes, K. (2011). Reclaiming kindergarten: Part I. Questions about theory and practice. *Early Childhood Education Journal, 38,* 323–328. doi:10.1007/s10643-010-0429-6

Head Start Performance Standards, 81 Fed. Reg. 61,294 (2016).

Im, H. (2017). Kindergarten standardized testing and reading achievements in the U.S.: Evidence from the early childhood longitudinal study. *Studies in Educational Evaluation, 55,* 9–18.

Improving Head Start for School Readiness Act of 2007, PL 110-134, 42 U.S.C. §§ 9801 *et seq.*

Jenkins, S., & Page, R. (2004). *What do you do with a tail like this?* New York, NY: Houghton Mifflin.

Kaufman, A. S. (1978). The importance of basic concepts in the individual assessment of preschool children. *Journal of School Psychology, 16*, 207–211.

Kirova, A., & Hennig, K. (2013). Culturally responsive assessment practices: Examples from an intercultural multilingual early learning program for newcomer children. *Power and Education, 5*, 106–119.

Lakin, J. M. (2014). Test directions as a critical component of test design: Best practices and the impact of examinee characteristics. *Educational Assessment, 19*(1), 17–34. doi:10.1080/10627197.2014.869448

Lightfoot, C., Cole, M., & Cole. S. (2013). *The development of children* (7th ed.). New York, NY: Worth.

Linder, T. W. (2008). *Transdisciplinary play-based assessment* (2nd ed.). Baltimore, MD: Paul H. Brookes Publishing Co.

Massachusetts Department of Elementary and Secondary Education. (2016). *Guidance on identification, assessment, placement, and reclassification of English learners*. Malden, MA: Author.

Maxwell, K. L., & Clifford, R. M. (2004). School readiness assessment. *Young Children, 59*(1), 42–46.

McGoey, K. E., McCobin, A., & Lindsey, G. (2016). Early childhood assessment for diverse learners. In S. L. Graves & J. J. Blake (Eds.), *Psychoeducational assessment and intervention for ethnic minority children: Evidence-based approaches* (pp. 115–131). Washington, DC: American Psychological Association.

Meisels, S. J., & Atkins-Burnett, S. (2004). The Head Start national reporting system. *Young Children, 59*(1), 64–66.

Miller, E., & Almon, J. (2009). *Crisis in the kindergarten: Why children need to play in school*. Takoma Park, MD: Alliance for Childhood. Retrieved from ERIC Database [ERIC Document 504839].

National Association for the Education of Young Children, & National Association of Early Childhood Specialists in State Departments of Education. (2003). *Early childhood curriculum, assessment, and program evaluation: Building an effective, accountable system in programs for children birth through age 8*. Washington, DC: National Association for the Education of Young Children.

National Research Council. (2001). *Classroom assessment and the national science education standards*. Washington, DC: National Academy Press.

Newborg, J. (2005). *Battelle developmental inventory* (2nd ed.). Rolling Meadows, IL: Riverside.

Notari-Syverson, A., Losardo, A., & Lim, Y. S. (2003). Assessment of young children from culturally diverse backgrounds: A journey in progress. *Assessment for Effective Intervention, 29*, 39–51.

Ochoa, S. H., Powell, M. P., & Robles-Piiia, R. (1996). School psychologists' assessment practices with bilingual and limited-English-proficient students. *Journal of Psychoeducational Assessment, 14*, 250–275.

Office of Superintendent of Public Instruction, State of Washington. (2008). *A guide to assessment in early childhood: Infancy to age eight*. Retrieved from http://www.k12.wa.us/EarlyLearning/GuideAssess.aspx

Office of Superintendent of Public Instruction, State of Washington. (2015). *Identifying English language learners: Definitions and procedures*. Retrieved from http://www.k12.wa.us/MigrantBilingual/pubdocs/TBIPGuidelinesIdentification.pdf

Roach, A. T., Wixson, C., & Talapatra, D. (2010). Aligning an early childhood assessment to state kindergarten content standards: Application of a nationally recognized alignment framework. *Educational Measurement: Issues and Practice, 29*, 25–37.

Schon, J., Shaftel, J., & Markham, P. (2008). Contemporary issues in the assessment of culturally and linguistically diverse learners. *Journal of Applied School Psychology, 24*, 163–189.

Shepard, L. A., Kagan, S. L., & Wurtz, E. (Eds.). (1998). *Principles and recommendations for early childhood assessments*. Washington, DC: National Education Goals Panel.

Squires, J., & Bricker, D. (2009). *Ages & stages questionnaires* (3rd ed.). Baltimore, MD: Paul H. Brookes Publishing Co.

Teaching Strategies. (2010). *GOLD*. Washington, DC: Teaching Strategies.

Winter, P. C., Kopriva, R. J., Chen, C., & Emick, J. E. (2006). Exploring individual and item factors that affect assessment validity for diverse learners: Results from a large-scale cognitive lab. *Learning and Individual Differences, 16*, 267–276, doi:10.1016/j.lindif.2007.01.001

Victoria, Australia, Department of Education and Early Childhood Development. (2012). *Strength-based approach: A guide to writing transition learning and development statements*. Retrieved from http://www.education.vic.gov.au/documents/childhood/professionals/learning/strengthbappr.pdf

CHAPTER 7

Banerjee, R. A., & Luckner, J. L. (2013). Assessment practices and training needs of early childhood professionals. *Journal of Early Childhood Teacher Education, 34*, 231–248. doi:10.1080/10901027.2013.816808

Bardige, B. S., & Segal, M. M. (2005). *Building literacy with love: A guide for teachers and caregivers of children from birth through age 5*. Washington, DC: Zero to Three.

Birbili, M., & Tzioga, K. (2014). Involving parents in children's assessment: Lessons from the Greek context. *Early Years, 34*(2), 161–174.

Boardman, M. (2007). "I know how much this child has learned. I have proof!" Employing digital technologies for documentation processes in kindergarten. *Australian Journal of Early Childhood, 32*, 59–66.

Bransford, J. D., Brown, A. L., & Cocking, R. R. (2000). *How people learn: Brain, mind, experience, and school*. Washington, DC: National Academy Press.

DeLuca, C., & Hughes, S. (2014). Assessment in early primary education: An empirical study of five school contexts. *Journal of Research in Childhood Education, 28*, 441–460.

Division for Early Childhood of the Council for Exceptional Children. (2007). *Promoting positive outcomes for children with disabilities: Recommendations for curriculum, assessment, and program evaluation*. Retrieved from https://www.naeyc.org/sites/default/files/globally-shared/downloads/PDFs/resources/position-statements/PrmtgPositiveOutcomes.pdf

Feldman, E. N. (2010). Benchmarks curricular planning and assessment framework: Utilizing standards without introducing standardization. *Early Childhood Education Journal, 38*, 233–242. doi:10.1007/s10643-010-0398-9

Fisher, D., & Frey, N. (2010). *Enhancing RTI: How to ensure success with effective classroom instruction and intervention*. Alexandria, VA: ASCD.

Gibbons, (1982). *The post office book: Mail and how it moves*. New York, NY: Scholastic.

Grisham-Brown, J., Hallam, R., & Brookshire, R. (2006). Using authentic assessment to evidence children's progress toward early learning standards. *Early Childhood Education Journal, 34*(1), 45–51. doi:10.1007/s10643-006-0106-y

Gropper, N., Hinitz, B. F., Sprung, B., & Froschl, M. (2011). Helping young boys be successful learners in today's early childhood classrooms. *Young Children, 66*(1), 34–41.

Gullo, D. F., & Hughes, K. (2011). Reclaiming kindergarten: Part I. Questions about theory and practice. *Early Childhood Education Journal, 38*, 323–328. doi:1007/s10643-010-0429-6

Isenberg, J. P., & Jalongo, M. R. (2001). *Creative expression and play in early childhood* (3rd ed.). Upper Saddle River, NJ: Prentice Hall.

Kidd, J. K. (2011). Unlearning colorblindness and learning from families. In A. M. Lazar & P. Ruggiano Schmidt (Eds.), *We can teach and we can learn: Achievement in culturally responsive literacy classrooms* (pp. 218–234). New York, NY: Teachers College Press.

Kidd, J. K., Pasnak, R., Gadzichowski, K. M., Gallington, D. A., McKnight, P. E., Boyer, C. E., & Carlson, A. (2014). Instructing first grade children on patterning improves reading and mathematics. *Early Education and Development, 25*(1), 134–151. doi:10.1080/10409289.2013.794448

Kidd, J. K., Sánchez, S. Y., & Thorp, E. K. (2008). Defining moments: Developing culturally responsive dispositions and teaching practices in early childhood preservice teachers. *Teaching and Teacher Education, 24*(2), 316–329. doi:10.1016.j.tate.2007.06.003

Kostelnik, M. J., Soderman, A. K., Whiren, A. P., & Rupiper, M. L. (2015). *Developmentally appropriate curriculum: Best practices in early childhood education* (6th ed.). New York, NY: Pearson.

Linder, T. W. (2008). *Transdisciplinary play-based assessment* (2nd ed.). Baltimore, MD: Paul H. Brookes Publishing Co.

Martinsen, H., Nærland, T., & Vereijken, B. (2010). Observation-based descriptions of social status in preschool. *Early Child Development and Care, 180*, 1231–1241. doi:10.1080/03004430902943975

McGarvey, L. M. (2012). What is a pattern? Criteria used by teachers and young children. *Mathematical Thinking and Learning, 14*, 310–337.

National Association for the Education of Young Children. (2009, July). *NAEYC standards for early childhood professional preparation* (Position Statement 2009). Retrieved from https://www.naeyc.org/sites/default/files/globally-shared/downloads/PDFs/resources/position-statements/2009%20Professional%20Prep%20stdsRevised%204_12.pdf

National Association for the Education of Young Children, & National Association of Early Childhood Specialists in State Departments of Education. (2003). *Early childhood curriculum, assessment, and program evaluation: Building an effective, accountable system in programs for children birth through age 8*. Retrieved from https://www.naeyc.org/sites/default/files/globally-shared/downloads/PDFs/resources/position-statements/pscape.pdf

National Council of Teachers of Mathematics (Ed.). (2000). *Principles and standards for school mathematics*. Reston, VA: Author.

Papic, M. M., Mulligan, J. T., & Mitchelmore, M. C. (2011). Assessing the development of preschoolers' mathematical patterning. *Journal for Research in Mathematics Education, 42*(3), 237–268.

Pyle, A., & DeLuca, C. (2013). Assessment in the kindergarten classroom: An empirical study of teachers' assessment approaches. *Early Childhood Education Journal, 41*, 373–380. doi:10.1007/s10643-012-0573-2

Raffi. (1987). *Down by the bay*. New York, NY: Crown.

Read, K., Gardner, P., & Mahler, B. C. (1993). *Early childhood programs: Human relationships and learning*. Fort Worth, TX: Harcourt Brace Jovanovich.

Shepard, L. A. (2000). The role of assessment in a learning culture. *Educational Researcher, 29*(7), 4–14.

Snow, C. E., & Van Hemel, S. B. (2008). *Early childhood assessment: Why, what, and how? Report of the Committee on Developmental Outcomes and Assessments for Young Children*. Washington, DC: National Academies Press.

Thaler, M. (1994). *Never mail an elephant*. Mahwah, NJ: Troll Communications.

Virginia Department of Education. (2009). *Mathematics standards of learning for Virginia public schools: Kindergarten.* Retrieved from http://doe.virginia.gov/testing/sol/standards_docs/mathematics/2009/stds_mathk.pdf

Wohlwend, K. E. (2009). Mediated discourse analysis: Researching young children's non-verbal interactions as social practice. *Journal of Early Childhood Research, 7,* 228–243.

Wortham, S. C. (2008). *Assessment in early childhood education* (5th ed.). Upper Saddle River, NJ: Pearson.

CONCLUSION

Burns, M. S., Kidd, J. K., Nasser, I., Aier, D. J., & Stechuk, R. (2012). An interaction, a conversation, often in the context of play: Constructing intentional teaching in early childhood education. *NHSA Dialog: A Research-to-Practice Journal for the Early Childhood Field, 15,* 272–285.

Nasser, I., Kidd, J. K., Burns, M. S., & Campbell, T. (2015). Head Start classroom teachers' and assistant teachers' perceptions of professional development using a LEARN framework. *Professional Development in Education, 41,* 344–365. doi:10.1080/19415257.2013.833538

Snow, C., Griffin, P., & Burns, M. S. (2005). *Knowledge to support the teaching of reading: Preparing teachers for a changing world.* San Francisco, CA: John Wiley & Sons.

APPENDIX

Bodrova, E., & Leong, D. J. (2007). *Tools of the mind: The Vygotskian approach to early childhood education.* (2nd ed.). Upper Saddle River, NJ: Pearson Education/Merrill.

Bowman, B., Donovan, M. S., & Burns, M. S. (2001). *Eager to learn: Educating our preschoolers.* Washington, DC: National Academy Press.

Bransford, J. D., Brown, A. L., & Cocking, R. R. (2000). *How people learn: Brain, mind, experience, and school.* Washington, DC: National Academy Press.

Burns, M. S., Kidd, J. K., Nasser, I., Aier, D. J., & Stechuk, R. (2012). An interaction, a conversation, often in the context of play: Constructing intentional teaching in early childhood education. *NHSA Dialog, 15,* 272–285.

Buysse, V., Castro, D. C., & Peisner-Feinber, E. (2010). Effects of a professional development program on classroom practices and outcomes for Latino dual language learners. *Early Childhood Research Quarterly, 25,* 194–206.

Copple, C., & Bredekamp, S. (2009). *Developmentally appropriate practice in early childhood programs serving children birth through age 8* (3rd ed.). Washington, DC: National Association for the Education of Young Children.

Darling-Hammond, L., & Bransford, J. (Eds.). (2005). *Preparing teachers for a changing world: What teachers should learn and be able to do.* San Francisco, CA: Jossey-Bass.

De Marco, A. C., Zeisel, S., & Odom, S. L. (2015). An evaluation of a program to increase physical activity for young children in child care. *Early Education and Development, 26,* 1–21.

Diamond, K. E., Justice, L. M., Siegler, R. S., & Snyder, P. A. (2013). *Synthesis of IES research on early intervention and early childhood education.* (NCSER 2013-3001). Washington, DC: National Center for Special Education Research. Retrieved from https://ies.ed.gov/ncser/pubs/20133001/pdf/20133001.pdf

Diamond, K. E., & Powell, D. R. (2011). An iterative approach to the development of a professional development intervention for Head Start teachers. *Journal of Early Intervention, 33,* 75–93.

Domitrovich, C. E., Gest, S. D., Gill, S., Jones, J., & Sanford DeRousie, R. (2009). Implementation quality: Lessons learned in the context of the Head Start REDI trial. *Early Childhood Research Quarterly, 25,* 284–298.

Downer, J. T., Locasale-Crouch, J., Hambre, B., & Pianta, R. (2009). Teacher characteristics associated with responsiveness and exposure to consultation and online professional development resources. *Early Education and Development, 20,* 431–455. doi: 10.1080/10409280802688626

Epstein, A. S. (2007). *The intentional teacher: Choosing the best strategies for young children's learning.* Washington, DC: National Association for the Education of Young Children.

Espinosa, L. (2010). *Getting it right for young children from diverse backgrounds: Applying research to improve practice.* Upper Saddle River, NJ: Pearson.

Esso, E. L., Taylor, J. M., Pratt, J. M., & Roberts, S. A. (2012). Illustrating the complexity of relationships in kindergarten and first grade. *Young Children, 67*(5), 24–33.

Furtado, L. (2010). Kindergarten teachers' perceptions of an inquiry-based science teaching and learning professional development intervention. *New Horizons in Education, 58*(2), 104–120.

Girolametto, L., Weitzman, E., & Greenberg, J. (2012). Facilitating emergent literacy: Efficacy of a model that partners speech-language pathologists and educators. *American Journal of Speech-Language Pathology, 21*(1), 47–63.

Griffin, J. A. (2009). Professional development and preschool intervention research: I would rather have a talking frog. *Early Education and Development, 20*, 373–376.

Guyton, E. M., & Wesche, M. V. (2005). The multicultural efficacy scale: Development, item selection, and reliability. *Multicultural Perspectives, 7*(4), 21–29.

Hauser-Cram, P., Sirin, S. R., & Stipek, D. (2003). When teachers' and parents' values differ: Teachers' ratings of academic competence in children from low-income families. *Journal of Educational Psychology, 95*(4), 813–820.

Jung, H. Y., & Reifel, S. (2011). Promoting children's communication: A kindergarten teacher's conception and practice of effective mathematics instruction. *Journal of Research in Childhood Education, 25*, 194–210.

Jung, M., & Conderman, G. (2013). Intentional mathematics teaching in early childhood classrooms. *Childhood Education, 89*, 173–177.

Landry, S. H., Anthony, J. L., Swank, P. R., & Monseque-Bailey, P. (2009). Effectiveness of comprehensive professional development for teachers of at-risk preschoolers. *Journal of Educational Psychology, 101*(2), 448–465.

La Paro, K., Pianta, R., & Stuhlman, M. (2004). The classroom assessment scoring system: Findings from the prekindergarten year. *Elementary School Journal, 104*(5), 409–426.

Mashburn, A. J., Downer, J. T., Hamre, B. K., Justice, L. M., & Pianta, R. C. (2010). Consultation for teachers and children's language and literacy development during pre-kindergarten. *Applied Developmental Science, 14*(4), 179–196.

McGraw-Hill Education. (2010). *DLM early childhood express*. New York, NY: Author.

McIlwain, M. J., Burns, M. S., & White, C. S. (2016). The implementation and study of dialogic buddy reading in a Head Start classroom. *Dialog, 18*, 85–90.

Nasser, I., Kidd, J. K., Burns, M. S., & Campbell, T. (2015). Head Start classroom teachers' and assistant teachers' perceptions of professional development using a LEARN framework. *Professional Development in Education, 41*, 344–365.

Pianta, R. C., Belsky, J., Vandergrift, N., Houts, R., & Morrison, F. J. (2008). Classroom effects on children's achievement trajectories in elementary school. *American Educational Research Journal, 2*, 365–397.

Pianta, R. C., La Paro, K. M., & Hamre, B. K. (2008). *Classroom assessment scoring system: Manual pre-K*. Baltimore, MD: Paul H. Brookes Publishing Co.

Pianta, R. C., Mashburn, A. J., Downer, J. T., Hamre, B. K., & Justice, L. (2008). Effects of web-mediated professional development resources on teacher–child interactions in pre-kindergarten classrooms. *Early Childhood Research Quarterly, 23*, 431–451.

Pierce, C. D., & Bruns, D. A. (2013). Aligning components of recognition and response and response to intervention to improve transition to primary school. *Early Childhood Education Journal, 41*, 347–354.

Ponterotito, J. G., Baluch, S., Greig, T., & Rivera, L. (1998). Development and initial score validation of the teacher multicultural attitude survey. *Educational and Psychological Measurement, 58*, 1002–1016.

Powell, D. R., Diamond, K. E., Burchinal, M. R., & Koehler, M. J. (2010). Effects of an early literacy professional development intervention on Head Start teachers and children. *Journal of Educational Psychology, 102*, 299–312.

Roehrig, G. H., Dubosarsky, M., Mason, A., Carlson, S., & Murphy, B. (2011). We look more, listen more, notice more: Impact of sustained professional development on Head Start teachers' inquiry-based and culturally-relevant science teaching practices. *Journal of Science Education and Technology, 20*(5), 566–578.

Rudd, L. C., Lambert, M. C., Satterwhite, M., & Smith, C. H. (2009). Professional development + coaching = enhanced teaching: Increasing usage of math mediated language in preschool classrooms. *Early Childhood Education Journal, 37*, 63–69.

Sackes, M. (2014). How often do early childhood teachers teach science concepts? Determinants of the frequency of science teaching in kindergarten. *European Early Childhood Education Research Journal, 22*, 169–184.

Saltzberg, S., & Polyson, S. (1995). Distributed learning on the World Wide Web. *Syllabus, 9*(1), 9–12.

Sheridan, S. M., Edwards, C. P., Marvin, C. A., & Knoche, L. L. (2009). Professional development in early childhood programs: Process issues and research needs. *Early Education and Development, 20*(3), 377–401.

Snow, C., Griffin, P., & Burns, M. S. (2005). *Knowledge to support the teaching of reading: Preparing teachers for a changing world*. San Francisco, CA: John Wiley & Sons.

Snyder, P., Hemmeter, M. L., & McLaughlin, T. (2011). Professional development in early childhood intervention: Where we stand on the silver anniversary of PL 99–457. *Journal of Early Intervention, 33*(4), 357–370.

Stipek, D., & Byler, P. (2004). The early childhood classroom observation measure. *Early Childhood Research Quarterly, 19*, 375–397.

Tepylo, D. H., Moss, J., & Stephenson C. (2015). A developmental look at a rigorous block play program. *Young Children, 70*, 18–25.

Thompson, J. E., & Twibell, K. K. (2010). Teaching hearts and minds in early childhood classrooms: Curriculum for social and emotional development. In O. A. Barbarin & B. H. Wasik (Eds.), *Handbook of child development and early education* (pp. 199–222). New York, NY: Guilford Press.

Thornton, J. S., Crim, C. L., & Hawkins, J. (2009). The impact of an ongoing professional development program on prekindergarten teachers' mathematics practices. *Journal of Early Childhood Teacher Education, 30*(2), 150–161.

Tirosh, P., Tsamir, D., Levenson, E., Tabach, M., & Barkai, R. (2014). Developing preschool teachers' knowledge of students' number conceptions. *Journal of Mathematics Teacher Education, 17,* 61–83.

Varol, F., Farran, D. C., Bilbrey, C., Vorhaus, E. A., & Guess Hofer, K. (2012). Professional development for preschool teachers: Evidence for practice. *NHSA Dialog: A Research-to-Practice Journal for the Early Childhood Field, 15,* 122–126.

Vescio, V., Ross, D., & Adams, A. (2008). A review of research on the impact of professional learning communities on teaching practice and student learning. *Teaching and Teacher Education, 24,* 80–91.

Wenger, E. C., & Snyder, W. M. (2000). Communities of practice: The organizational frontier. *Harvard Business Review, 78,* 139–146.

Zaslow, M. J. (2009). Strengthening the conceptualization of early childhood professional development initiatives and evaluations. *Early Education and Development, 20,* 527–536.

Zaslow, M., Tout, K., Halle, T., & Starr, R. (2011). Professional development for early childhood educators: Reviewing and revising conceptualizations. *Handbook of Early Literacy Research, 3,* 425–434.

Zaslow, M., Tout, K., Halle, T., Whittaker, J. V., & Lavelle, B. (2010). Toward the identification of features of effective professional development for early childhood educators: Literature review. Retrieved from https://www2.ed.gov/rschstat/eval/professional-development/literature-review.pdf

Index

Page numbers followed by *f*, *t*, and *h* indicate figures, tables, and handouts, respectively.